The Basic Writer's Book

Second Edition

ANNE AGEE
Anne Arundel Community College

GARY KLINE

Eric P. Hibbison, *Consulting Editor*

PRENTICE-HALL, INC.   *Englewood Cliffs, New Jersey 07632*

Library of Congress Cataloging-in-Publication Data

AGEE, ANNE.
  The basic writer's book.

  Includes index.
  1. English language—Rhetoric. I. Kline, Gary.
II. Title.
PE1408.A42 1985   808'.042   84-22291
ISBN 0-13-066176-7

Editorial/production supervision and
  interior design: Chrys Chrzanowski
Cover design: Joe Curcio
Manufacturing buyer: Harry P. Baisley

Printed in the United States of America

10 9 8 7 6 5 4 3 2

0-13-066176-7   01

Prentice-Hall International, Inc., *London*
Prentice-Hall of Australia Pty. Limited, *Sydney*
Editora Prentice-Hall do Brasil, Ltda., *Rio de Janeiro*
Prentice-Hall Canada Inc., *Toronto*
Prentice-Hall Hispanoamericana, S.A., *Mexico*
Prentice-Hall of India Private Limited, *New Delhi*
Prentice-Hall of Japan, Inc., *Tokyo*
Prentice-Hall of Southeast Asia Pte. Ltd., *Singapore*
Whitehall Books Limited, *Wellington, New Zealand*

Contents

PART TWO   BASIC PARAGRAPH PATTERNS   145

7   Basic Paragraph Structure   147

8   Basic Paragraph Strategies   174

PART THREE   THE WRITING PROCESS   199

9 Exploring   201

10 Focusing, Organizing, and Drafting   225

SPECIAL STUDY: A CLOSER LOOK AT VERBS   354

Preface

We believe now, as strongly as we did when we wrote the first edition of *The Basic Writer's Book*, that writing is important to our students both for its practical value in the working world and as a tool for the logical and imaginative thinking so necessary for independent human beings.

In preparing this second edition, therefore, we have stayed with the principles that guided our earlier work:

We have tried to familiarize students with the various grammatical, syntactic, lexical, and rhetorical options available to a writer in any situation and to increase students' ability to discriminate among these options.

We have emphasized rhetorical considerations of audience, purpose, and style as the operative standards for effective writing.

We have kept grammatical terminology to a minimum and have focused on those aspects of grammar and mechanics which contribute most significantly to effective writing.

We have used sentence-combining extensively because it allows students to concentrate on effective presentation of ideas.

Thanks to many helpful comments from teachers and students who have worked with the first edition of *The Basic Writer's Book*, we have also made some changes that we hope will make the book even more useful:

We have emphasized the writing process, explaining it in more detail, adding new techniques for the various stages of composing, and showing the process through case studies.

We have substantially revised the exercises, adding new subject matter and varying the types of student activity called for.

We have added new writing practices, all of which include a rhetorical context.

We have added more examples of various paragraphing strategies.

We have expanded the discussion of essay writing.

Besides revising the content of *The Basic Writer's Book*, we have also made some organizational changes to increase the flexibility of the text.

Part One concentrates on sentences, developing fluency with modification, subordination, and coordination.

Part Two provides a structure for paragraphing and some suggestions for expanding the principles of paragraphing to longer pieces of writing.

Part Three focuses on the writing process from exploring a subject and audience to revising and editing a draft.

The Special Study of Verbs gives an in-depth treatment of one of the most important aspects of written language.

This arrangement of material allows classes to begin with any part of the book depending on the needs of the students and the design of the course. Courses emphasizing sentence structure may begin with Part One and include all the material on verbs. Courses emphasizing paragraph writing may begin with Part Two or Part Three and use Part One and the study of verbs as review material or as independent work for some students.

ACKNOWLEDGMENTS

We are especially grateful to our students who have shown us the strengths and weaknesses of *The Basic Writer's Book*; to our reviewers Rebecca Argall, Memphis State University; Eric P. Hibbison; and Maureen A. Pohs, University of Texas at El Paso, who have read our manuscripts so carefully and have made such thoughtful suggestions for improvement; to our colleagues, families, and friends, who have given us their generous support and encouragement over the years.

We hope this new edition of *The Basic Writer's Book* will bring many students to share the challenge and the pleasure we feel as writers.

Anne Agee
Gary Kline

Guide to Revising and Editing

mm	Misplaced modifier; put this modifier next to the word it describes (pp. 324–25)
org	Improve the organization of paragraph (pp. 227–35)
//	Use parallel structure (pp. 264–66)
passive	Change this sentence from passive to active (pp. 327–29)
pl	Consult dictionary for correct plural
pn	Make pronoun agree with the word it replaces (pp. 315–17)
quote	Put quotation marks here
ref	Make it clear what word this pronoun refers to (pp. 314–15)
rep	You repeated yourself unnecessarily here (p. 282)
run-on	Punctuate correctly between sentences (pp. 335–36)
semi-colon	Use a semi-colon here (pp. 333–34)
shift	Keep the verb tense and point of view consistent (pp. 326–27)
sp	Check this word in the dictionary and then add it to your spelling notebook (pp. 297–99)
sub	Subordinate this idea (pp. 74–75)
sup	You need more support for your T.S. (pp. 156–61)
tense	Choose appropriate time for the verb (pp. 357–74)
trans	Use a transition (pp. 261–64)
TS	Improve topic sentence (pp. 150–56)
unity	Stay with the main idea (pp. 245–46)
var	Use more variety in your sentence patterns (pp. 136–40)
wordy	Say this in fewer words (pp. 281–86)

Checklist for Revising and Editing

1. Does the paragraph have a topic sentence that clearly states the subject and the controlling idea?

2. Is the topic sentence appropriate to the audience and purpose?

3. Does every supporting sentence relate directly to the subject and controlling idea?

4. Are there enough supporting details to make the point convincingly? Are the details factual and concrete?

5. Are the supporting details arranged in a logical order?

6. Is the strategy of development suited to the subject, audience, and purpose?

7. Are there transitions or other signals to show connections between ideas?

8. Is there a concluding sentence which restates the main idea?

9. Are less important details in subordinate parts of the sentence? Are more important details emphasized by the sentence structure?

10. Is there some variety in sentence patterns?

11. Is each word as precise as possible? Is the language suited to the audience and purpose?

12. Have any doubtful words been checked in the dictionary for spelling and/or meaning?

13. Has every sentence been checked for structure problems that could confuse a reader?

14. Does the punctuation help to focus the reader's attention on important ideas? Is every punctuation mark there for a definite purpose?

15. Has someone else looked at the first draft of this paper?

Part One

Basic Sentence Patterns

Ever since you sat in kindergarten and practiced *The man ran* you've been using sentences to communicate ideas in writing. After writing sentences for so long, you know a lot about them. This book will be building on that knowledge to help you become a more skillful writer.

Being a good writer means knowing how to rework sentences to make them as effective as possible. A good writer can take the first draft of a sentence and expand or tighten it, make its parts more precise, shape and reshape it until it does exactly what is necessary for the situation.

This section of the book will give you practice in working with the basic structure of sentences and in choosing alternative ways of expressing ideas.

The British statesman, orator, and writer, Winston Churchill, claimed that an outstanding part of his education was learning to understand the organization of sentences: "I got into my bones the essential structure of the ordinary English sentence—which is a noble thing." To grow as a writer is to appreciate this nobility.

1

1

Basic Sentence Structure

If you have ever taken piano or guitar lessons, or lived in the same house with someone who has, you know that beginning musicians spend a lot of time practicing patterns of notes known as scales and chords. Because every composition they may play or create is built on these patterns, students play them over and over again until their hands and ears have "memorized" the relationships among these sets of sounds.

Until these patterns become almost automatic, every new piece of music must be learned one note at a time. But once the musician has mastered these forms, he or she can recognize them easily in a new piece and can even create variations that will add interest to the music or allow the music to be adapted for special circumstances.

In fact, almost every profession—from marine biologist to shortstop—involves certain patterns of thought and action that beginners must absorb before they can advance in that field.

As a writer, you also need to become very familiar with the basic patterns of your trade, sentences. All your written and spoken compositions are built from these basic sets of relationships among words. Once you have mastered the patterns of the sentence, you can control the shape and direction of your writing more easily.

To exercise that control, you have to become consciously aware of information about sentences that you have absorbed unconsciously over the years.

Also, since you and your classmates and your teacher will be discussing the effect of various sentences, it is important that you all be able to use the same terms for the parts of the sentence. This first part of the book will review some basic information about sentences.

The first step in controlling sentences is to recognize what is and what is not a sentence.

EXERCISE A

Look at the word groups below. Which ones do you recognize as sentences? Put a check next to each group of words that you think is a sentence. Then copy at the bottom of the list all of those word groups which you and your teacher agree are sentences.

_____ 1. A spinach salad

_____ 2. Has made a spinach salad

_____ 3. The chef making a spinach salad

_____ 4. The chef made a spinach salad

_____ 5. The chef who made a spinach salad

_____ 6. The mechanic

_____ 7. To replace the radiator

_____ 8. The mechanic to replace the radiator

_____ 9. The mechanic will replace the radiator

_____ 10. If the mechanic will replace the radiator

_____ 11. Parked illegally

_____ 12. Beside the door

_____ 13. The officer listed the suspect's previous arrests

_____ 14. The papers that littered his desk

_____ 15. We are leaving for Orlando in the morning

_____ 16. Since Cheyenne is the capital of Wyoming

_____ 17. Originally built as a stable

_____ 18. She reached the summit first

_____ 19. The muscular, blond soldier laughing

_____ 20. After apologizing for ten minutes

_____ 21. David's voice enthralls the audience

_____ 22. Through a maze of corridors

_____ **23.** To avoid unfavorable publicity

_____ **24.** Although the market for small computers is growing

_____ **25.** You will find clean towels in the closet

_____

_____

_____

_____

_____

_____

_____

What do the word groups you just copied have in common that makes you know they are sentences? Each one communicates a complete idea by presenting:

1. a subject–verb unit
2. with its action placed in past, present, or future time,
3. not introduced by a subordination signal.

SUBJECTS

Every group of words that is a sentence names the person or thing that is being talked about. In other words, every sentence has a SUBJECT. In "The man ran," *man* is what the writer wants to talk about in the sentence. *Man* is the SUBJECT.

EXERCISE B

Go back and circle the SUBJECTS in the sentences you just copied. (Notice that SUBJECTS can be either nouns like "the chef" or "David," or pronouns like "she." Both kinds of words can tell a reader who or what is the center of attention in a sentence.)

If you look again at the word groups in Exercise A, you will see that numbers 2, 7, 11, 12, 17, 20, 22, and 23 do not tell you who or what is being talked about. In number 20, for example, you don't know who is doing the apologizing. These word groups, therefore, are not sentences because they leave out one essential part of the idea, the subject.

EXERCISE C

Who or what is the center of attention in these sentences?

1. Napoleon won the battle of Austerlitz.
2. Ms. Barclay hired a new sales representative.
3. New car sales are down again this month.
4. Franklin Delano Roosevelt was elected President in 1932.
5. Few comedians made it as big as the Marx Brothers.
6. Skiing can be expensive.
7. Television is one of the most profound developments of this century.
8. Robins seldom fly that far south.
9. Agnes, Linda, and Kathy write historical novels under the name Elspeth Carp.
10. Neutrons allow us to probe the hidden structure of matter.

All of the sentences in Exercise C, above, follow the typical pattern of English sentences: the subject comes first. Sometimes, however, you may want to put the subject at the end of the sentence to call special attention to it. (*Clinging to the rock were several bright orange starfish.*) Or you may introduce the subject by using the "Here is. . . ./Here are. . . ." or "There is. . . ./There are. . . ." patterns. (*Here are the revised tax forms.*) In general, however, your reader expects to find the subject at the beginning of the sentence.

EXERCISE D

Identify the subjects of the sentences below, and then rewrite each one so that the subject comes first. For each pair, put a star next to the version you like better.

1. On the rock coiled a hideous serpent.

   _____

2. Here are the specimens for the test.

   _____

3. Coming up fast on the outside was Pocomoke Pride.

   _____

4. Wildly raged the wind!

   _____

5. There lay everything needed for happiness.

   _____

EXERCISE E

Add a logical subject to each of the following sentences.

1. There are _____ near my house.

2. _____ waited.

3. _____ drew up a contract for them.

4. Facing the hunters was _____.

5. _____ locked up the building at 5 o'clock.

6. _____ were stacked on the desk.

7. Around the patio grew _____.

8. Here is the _____.

9. _____ make me nervous.

10. _____ filled the room.

VERBS

Besides establishing the subject, every sentence also tells you what the subject is doing and places that action in past, present, or future time. The VERB in a sentence shows a subject involved in past, present, or future action. Sometimes a verb may have more than one part—an action word and a time indicator—like these verbs:

will find	(*find* shows the action; *will* shows future)
were talking	(*talking* shows the action; *were* shows past)
have swum	(*swum* shows the action; *have* shows repeated past)

If you look again at the word groups in Exercise A, you will see that numbers 1, 3, 6, 8, 17, and 19 either show no action or do not show action in a time frame. (*-ing* verbs and *to* _____ verbs do not show time, and, therefore, they can't function alone as the verb in a sentence.) Number 6, for example, doesn't show what action the mechanic is engaged in. Number 19 uses a verb form—*laughing*—that doesn't show time. These word groups are not sentences, then, because they don't show a verb in past, present, or future time.

EXERCISE F

Go back and underline the verbs in the sentences you copied for Exercise A. Mark each verb as past, present, or future action. Notice the position of the verb in these sentences—right after the subject.

EXERCISE G

What words in the sentences below show the action that the subject is involved in? What time frame—past, present, or future—is indicated for each verb? Which sentences do not follow the usual subject–verb pattern?

1. Mindy answered politely.
2. Will Mrs. Tallchief go with you?
3. Toyota has cornered the small car market this year.
4. Dr. Assad comes highly recommended.
5. The congregation stood up.
6. Henry David Thoreau published *Walden* in 1854.
7. I will take my vacation next week.
8. Martin Luther commands more attention than other Reformation figures.
9. When did the coach begin the passing drill?
10. Turn off the lights.
11. Ted counted and sorted the tickets.
12. Everyone will need five copies of the memo.
13. His father said "No!"
14. Can you ship the order by Tuesday?
15. Notify your supervisor before leaving the area.

EXERCISE H

By adding a verb, show what each of these subjects is doing.

1. We _____.
2. The citizens of the state of Oregon _____.
3. Charles and Don _____.
4. The new landlord _____.
5. Her grandmother _____.
6. Everyone _____.
7. Michele _____.
8. A delivery truck _____.
9. The supervisor _____.
10. Several cats _____.

Although most verbs clearly show some action, one special set of verbs—the forms of the verb *to be*—merely indicate the existence of some condition. These *to be* verbs are worth memorizing because they appear very often, and you need to recognize them right away as verbs. The box below shows the forms of the verb *to be*.

TO BE VERBS

am   is   are
was   were
will be
has been   have been   had been   will have been

EXERCISE I

Identify the verbs in the sentences below. Remember that the *to be* forms function as verbs.

1. New cars are very expensive.
2. Used cars cost a lot, too.
3. Ohio is "the mother of presidents."
4. Many presidents of the United States have come from Ohio.
5. By 10 o'clock, I was exhausted.
6. Sam and I had loaded three cords of wood.
7. The Dow-Jones average has risen ten points this week.
8. Some investors were encouraged by this rise.
9. Will you be available for a conference on Thursday?
10. Thomas Edison's inventions changed American industry.

(Verbs are probably the most important tools of language. They can help you to show meaning in a variety of ways. There is a detailed discussion of verbs on pages 356–86. You may want to increase your skill with verbs by studying and practicing that additional material.)

SUBORDINATION SIGNALS

The basic pattern of meaning your readers expect to find in a sentence is SUBJECT–VERB. However, not every subject–verb group is a sentence. For instance, look at this word group from Exercise A: "If the mechanic will replace the radiator." There is a subject, *mechanic,* and a verb, *will replace.* But the signal word, *if,* tells you this idea is incomplete. *If* is one of a whole group of SUBORDINATION SIGNALS. Writers use these signals to show that a given group of words is not a complete idea.

"The chef who made a spinach salad" also uses a subordination signal, *who.* The box below shows some of the most important subordination signals.

SUBORDINATION SIGNALS

After	Since	When
Although	So that	Which
As if	That	While
Because	Though	Who
Before	Unless	Whom
If	Until	Whose

Subordination Signals are explained in detail in Chapter 4.

EXERCISE J

Remove the subordination signals from the following groups of words in order to make them sentences.

1. After Mr. Torres placed the order. . . .

   _____

2. Unless you can demonstrate your results scientifically. . . .

   _____

3. The new car that is on the lot. . . .

   _____

4. Those students who live within one mile of the school. . . .

   _____

5. When the Brooklyn Bridge was completed in 1883. . . .

   _____

SUMMARY

A sentence expresses a complete thought by presenting

| a SUBJECT and a VERB that shows past, present, or future time | which are not introduced by a SUBORDINATION SIGNAL. |

EXERCISE K

Rewrite each of the word groups below so that it is a sentence. Make each word group a complete thought by adding a subject, supplying a verb that shows time, adding a subject–verb unit, or removing a subordination signal. Circle the unsubordinated subject–verb group in each of your sentences.

EXAMPLE:
"Parked illegally" is not a sentence. But these are:
Dan parked illegally.
Parked illegally, Dan got a ticket.

1. Beside the door. . . .

_____

2. The papers that littered his desk. . . .

_____

3. Since Cheyenne is the capital of Wyoming. . . .

_____

4. Originally built as a stable. . . .

_____

5. The muscular, blond soldier laughing. . . .

_____

PUNCTUATING COMPLETE SENTENCES

Most sentences begin with a capital letter and end with a period, a question mark, or an exclamation point. In writing, you use punctuation at the ends of sentences to signal your reader that a new idea is coming.

The punctuation in the set of sentences below, for instance, clearly indicates that there are three main ideas.

Can the Wildcats clinch the pennant by July? If their pitching improves and their bats stay hot, they have a good chance. All their fans, hoping the Cats can pull it off, will certainly be rooting for them!

A group of words that is punctuated as a sentence but is not a sentence is called a FRAGMENT. A FRAGMENT expresses only a piece of an idea, not a complete thought. (For instance, all of the word groups in Exercise K were fragments until you rewrote them so that they had all the necessary elements of a sentence.)

Sometimes, you may use sentence fragments in casual conversation when you are sure that your audience understands the whole idea. But most writing situations demand that you express each idea completely. A sentence fragment in writing may prevent your reader from seeing the whole idea that you are trying to express. This series of fragments, for instance, would probably leave a reader somewhat confused.

Can the Wildcats clinch the pennant? By July if their pitching improves and their bats stay hot. They have a good chance. All their fans hoping the Cats can pull it off. Will certainly be rooting for them!

EXERCISE L

In the following paragraph, the capitalization and punctuation that mark the beginning and end of each sentence have been left out. Read the paragraph carefully and supply the necessary signals to show where each sentence begins and ends. All the commas and other punctuation marks are correct. Don't change them. Underline the basic subject–verb unit in each of your sentences. (This paragraph was originally written as ten sentences.)

America's early settlers built their houses to suit their location they had to build for the American climate with American materials they couldn't always have the kind of house that they were used to in New England, for example, the colonists built longhouses of thatch and bent trees they couldn't build English-style houses until tools arrived from England in the Southwest, there was no lumber available therefore, the Spaniards made shelters from desert clay in the Southeast, the French raised the first floors of their houses off the ground as a protection from dampness they also built large open porches to take advantage of any cool breezes throughout the country, the colonists adapted their houses to American conditions.

EXERCISE M

In the paragraph below, some fragments have been punctuated as sentences. Rewrite this paragraph making sure that all the sentences present a complete idea with a subject–verb unit. Underline each unsubordinated subject–verb unit in the rewritten paragraph.

A baby's first year. An expensive year for his parents. New parents may spend up to $5,000 on a child during that first twelve months. Medical costs, of course, to eat up a large chunk of the budget. New parents, besides paying the doctor's fee, also the cost of a hospital room, nursery care, laboratory work. And medicines. In addition, the new mother and father must paying for clothing and furniture. As well as food for their child. Finally, parents must allow for extra costs such as babysitting, impulsive toy-buying, and special pictures of the new addition to the family. While parents may look forward to lots of fun with a new baby. They should not being surprised if their budget gets tighter.

WRITING PRACTICE

You have just acquired a pen pal of your own age in another country. You want to introduce yourself and the way you live by describing your favorite way to spend a Saturday.

Think about the things you like to do on Saturdays. Make a list of some of your favorite activities. Then write a five- or six-sentence description of your favorite way to spend a Saturday.

Check your writing to make sure that each sentence gives your reader the basic subject–verb information needed to understand your ideas. Be sure that correct punctuation separates one sentence from the next.

2

Adding to the Basic Sentence

The subject–verb unit, as you saw in Chapter 1, presents the basic information needed to communicate an idea in writing. But writing would be a slow and frustrating process if you wrote only in simple subject–verb sentences, and the communication would probably not be very effective.

Making sure that your reader has the basic subject/verb information is only the first step in writing an effective sentence. Once you are sure that you have shown who or what is the center of attention and what action is involved, you need to fine-tune the sentence so it presents your idea to your reader as accurately as possible. You can make changes in the basic sentence so that it describes the subject and the action more precisely.

MAKING THE VERB EFFECTIVE

Choosing the Verb Form

One way to ensure clear communication of an idea is to make the verb do all it can for you. Besides describing the main action of a sentence, a verb tells your reader the time of the action—in the past, in the present, or in the future.

For instance, look at these four sentences:

The cell divided.
The cell is dividing.
The cell will divide.
The cell has divided.

Each sentence has the same subject and the same basic verb, but each sentence says something slightly different about when the cell division took place.

In the first sentence, the division was completed at some time in the past. In the second, the division is going on now, in the present. In the third, the division has not yet occurred. In the fourth, the division has just been completed. Each verb form places the action in a different time frame. In your writing, be sure you choose the verb that gives the time frame you have in mind.

(A full discussion on using verbs to show time relationships is presented on pages 356–79. You may use that additional material to sharpen your skill in controlling verbs.)

Besides placing action in time, the form of a verb can also help your readers interpret the meaning of the action. The right helping verb can show such shades of meaning as certainty, uncertainty, or obligation, as illustrated below:

The cell can divide.	(*emphasizes ability*)
The cell did divide.	(*emphasizes certainty*)
The cell may divide.	(*emphasizes possibility*)
The cell should divide.	(*emphasizes expectation*)

Each of these sentences expresses a slightly different understanding of the action of dividing.

The following helping verbs commonly add slightly different meanings to the action of a verb:

can, could	(*shows ability, power, or skill to act*)
do, does, did	(*shows intensity or certainty of action*)
may, might	(*shows possibility or potential for action*)
must	(*shows obligation to act*)
shall, should	(*shows expectation of action, obligation to act*)
will, would	(*shows likelihood of action, willingness to act*)

EXERCISE A

Identify the verb in each sentence below. Then rewrite each sentence, changing the time or understanding of the verb. Be prepared to explain the difference in meaning between the original sentence and your sentence.

EXAMPLE:

The computer failed.

The computer may have failed.

The first sentence shows a definite failure sometime in the past. The second sentence shows the possibility of a failure in the past.

1. I did stop.

_____

2. You may go.

_____

3. Paul and Virginia ski.

_____

4. The fire will crackle.

_____

5. Lori weeps.

_____

6. The knight has triumphed.

_____

7. Twelve candidates ran.

_____

8. The violinist performed.

_____

9. Jeff will be promoted.

_____

10. The blizzard has ended.

_____

Describing the Action of the Verb

In addition to choosing the appropriate time and interpretation, you can also control the effect of the verb by using ADVERBS to show the conditions of the action. Adverbs are words or groups of words that show when, where, why, how, or to what degree some action is done.

For example, can you see how adverbs are used in the sentences below to describe the action of the verb more precisely?

> Terri visits _frequently_. (_When_ does Terri visit?)
> _Quickly_, the truck stopped. (_How_ did the truck stop?)
> Ed went _to the store_. (_Where_ did Ed go?)
> I had _completely_ forgotten. (_To what degree_ had I forgotten?)
> Daniel whistled _for joy_. (_Why_ did Daniel whistle?)

Notice that _frequently, quickly,_ and _completely_ all end in _-ly_. The _-ly_ ending is a good clue that a word is being used as an adverb. Not all adverbs, however, are single words. You can also use groups of words to show the circumstances of an action.

These words often introduce modifying phrases:

about	beside	of
above	between	on
across	beyond	over
after	by	since
against	despite	through
along	down	throughout
among	during	to
around	except	toward
as	for	under
at	from	until
because of	in	up
before	inside	upon
behind	in spite of	with
below	into	within
beneath	near	without
	next to	

EXERCISE B

Identify in the sentences below the words that show when, where, why, how, or to what degree the action of the sentence occurred.

1. Max barely finished.
2. The victim has partially recovered.
3. Elephants never forget.
4. The children lined up next to the bus.
5. In my spare time, I will study.
6. The guard saluted immediately.
7. The mayor served at the soup kitchen.
8. Quietly, the cantor began.
9. Sam nodded to show his consent.
10. Because of her impatience, the negotiations stalled.

EXERCISE C

By adding adverbs to the following sentences, show something about the conditions under which the actions occurred.

EXAMPLE:
Clem left. (when?)
Clem left on Sunday.

1. The fans shouted. (why?)

    _____

2. The fans shouted. (how?)

    _____

3. The bird soared. (where?)

    _____

4. The city was evacuated. (to what degree?)

    _____

5. The garden bloomed. (when?)

    _____

6. The soldiers marched. (why?)

    _____

7. The stock market rose. (to what degree?)

    _____

8. Catherine the Great ruled. (where and when?)

    _____

9. Tanya complained. (when and how?)

    _____

10. The books were shelved. (how and where?)

    _____

(The forms and uses of ADVERBS are presented in more detail on pages 322–26. You may use that additional material to sharpen your skill at describing verbs.)

Completing the Verb

A sentence like

The captain requested.

probably raises a question in the mind of a reader: *What* was requested? You could supply that information with another sentence:

A transfer was requested.

But probably you would automatically combine these two sentences to produce

The captain requested a transfer.

When you use a word or phrase (group of words) to complete the action of a verb, you are using an OBJECT COMPLEMENT. An object complement allows you to show the goal or result or conclusion of the action begun in the verb.

For instance, can you see the complement or completer of the action in each of these sentences?

Jean found the money. (What did Jean find?)
The tree crushed Rosita's car. (What did the tree crush?)
Tanzania closed its border. (What did Tanzania close?)

EXERCISE D

In the sentences below identify the words that show the goal, result, or conclusion of the verb's action. (*Note:* not all verbs can take an object.)

1. Congress passed the law.
2. Arteries carry blood away from the heart.
3. A dictionary defines words.
4. The painting hung in the gallery.
5. Wilt has joined the team.
6. Nancy had her first child in October.
7. Can we count on your support?
8. Joyce rose from her chair.
9. The waves tossed the ship.
10. Chester opened the package.

EXERCISE E

Combine each of the following pairs of sentences to produce one sentence in which an object complement shows the goal or result of the action of the verb.

EXAMPLE:

Mrs. Burton planted.

Zinnias were planted.

Mrs. Burton planted zinnias.

1. Kelly will deliver.
   The pizza will be delivered.

   _____

2. Our congregation built.
   A temple was built.

   _____

3. The agent has sold.
   The house has been sold.

   _____

4. Alice is singing.
   A ballad is being sung.

   _____

5. Writing requires.
   Practice is required.

   _____

   _____

EXERCISE F

Combine each set of sentences below into one sentence in which the action of the verb is described by an adverb and/or completed by an object.

EXAMPLE:

Matt scored.

The winning goal was scored.

It was scored with a well-placed kick.

It was scored in the last few seconds of the game.

With a well-placed kick, Matt scored the winning goal in the last few seconds of the game.

1. The star cooled.
   The cooling happened slowly.
   The cooling happened over millions of years.

   _____

   _____

2. Edgar Allan Poe perfected.
   The short story was perfected.
   His perfecting took place in the nineteenth century.

   _____

   _____

3. Houston rises.
   The rising happens unexpectedly.
   It rises from the flat Texas prairie.

   _____

   _____

4. Sam played.
   The song was played.
   He played it for her.
   It was played again.

   _____

   _____

5. The clerk entered.
   The record was entered.
   It was entered on the terminal.
   It was entered quickly.

   _____

   _____

6. The police officer arrested.
   A burglar was arrested.
   She was arrested yesterday.
   She was arrested after a long search.

   _____

   _____

7. The peas were grown.
   Mr. Thornton grew them.
   They grew in his garden.
   They grew last spring.

   _____

   _____

8. Bread for the World hired.
   Dr. Ramírez was hired.
   The hiring was done last year.
   She was hired as a regional coordinator.

   _____

   _____

9. The librarian opened.
   The fines book was opened.
   It was opened to the last page.
   He opened it wearily.

   _____

   _____

10. I followed.
    The ice cream truck was followed.
    I followed it with my eyes.
    I followed it wistfully.
    It was followed down the street.

    _____

    _____

EXERCISE G

Describe the action more precisely in each of the following sentences by adding an object complement and/or an adverb. (Some verbs are complete in themselves and do not take complements.) Then write a second version of the sentence with a slightly different meaning by changing the verb form and making any other changes needed to go along with the new verb's meaning.

EXAMPLE:

The motor will start.

A. *The motor will start easily.*

B. *The motor has never started easily.*

1. Martha runs.

   A. _____

   _____

   B. _____

   _____

2. The director has signalled.

   A. _____

   _____

   B. _____

   _____

3. The president called.

   A. _____

   _____

   B. _____

   _____

4. Reggie lifted.

   A. _____

   _____

   B. _____

   _____

5. You can read.

   A. _____

   _____

   B. _____

   _____

SUMMARY: MAKING THE VERB EFFECTIVE

1. Choose the verb form that shows most accurately the time and meaning you intend.
2. Choose adverbs to show the exact conditions of time, place, manner, and degree of action that you intend.
3. Clarify the action of the verb by using an object complement to show its goal or result.

MAKING THE SUBJECT EFFECTIVE

Just as you can modify the verb to make a sentence more effective, you can also make changes in the subject of a sentence to make it communicate more effectively.

Choosing the Subject

For one thing, you can often choose one of several ideas as the central focus of a sentence. For instance, look at the sentences combined below:

> The Health Board prohibits.⎱ *The Health Board*
> Swimming is prohibited. ⎰ *prohibits swimming.*

This version of the sentence makes the Health Board the subject or center of attention. But suppose you wanted to focus your reader's attention on what was prohibited. Then you could choose to make swimming the subject of the sentence:

> Swimming is prohibited by the Health Board.

Most sentences have more than one potential focus, as the example below shows.

> A lawyer presented.
> The defendant's case was presented.

> **A.** *A lawyer presented the defendant's case.*
> **B.** *The defendant's case was presented by a lawyer.*

By making *lawyer* the subject, version A puts the emphasis on *who* did the presenting. By making *case* the subject, version B gives more importance to *what* got presented. Which version you chose to write would depend on which idea was more important in a particular writing situation. You can exercise control over a sentence by deciding which idea you want your reader to focus on and making that idea the subject.

EXERCISE H

Practice controlling the focus of a sentence by combining each of the following pairs of sentences in two different ways, each version emphasizing a different idea.

> EXAMPLE:
> Margie finished.
> The report was finished.
> (focus on Margie)   A. *Margie finished the report.*
> (focus on the report) B. *The report was finished by Margie.*

1. Every sentence presents.
   A subject is presented.

   (focus on sentence)   **A.** _____

   (focus on subject)   **B.** _____

2. Steve swam.
   A splendid race was swum.

   (focus on Steve)   **A.** _____

   (focus on race)   **B.** _____

3. Jacob has studied.
   The Talmud has been studied.

   (focus on Jacob)   **A.** _____

   (focus on Talmud)   **B.** _____

4. Aliens are invading.
   The earth is being invaded.

   (focus on aliens)   **A.** _____

   (focus on earth)   **B.** _____

5. Wallie pitched.
   A no-hitter was pitched.

   (focus on Wallie)   **A.** _____

   (focus on no-hitter)   **B.** _____

6. The students had rented.
   An old house had been rented.

   (focus on students)   **A.** _____

   (focus on house)   **B.** _____

7. General Sherman spared.
   The city was spared.

   (focus on Sherman)   **A.** _____

   (focus on the city)   **B.** _____

8. The group played.
   Scott Joplin's music was played.

   (focus on group)   **A.** _____

   (focus on music)   **B.** _____

9. Volvos keep.
   A high resale value is kept.

   (focus on Volvos)   **A.** _____

   (focus on value)   **B.** _____

10. The statistics show.
    A decline is shown.

(focus on statistics) **A.** _____

(focus on decline) **B.** _____

When your sentences emphasize the *doer* of an action, like

Mrs. Burton planted zinnias

you are writing ACTIVE sentences. Most sentences are active because most of the time you and your readers are most interested in the *doer*.

When your sentences emphasize the *receiver* of an action, like

Zinnias were planted by Mrs. Burton

you are writing PASSIVE sentences.

Passive sentences use a special verb form. Do you see the difference between *planted* and *were planted*? Pages 329–31 of this book discuss the use of passive verbs. You may refer to that discussion in deciding whether or not to write a passive sentence.

Describing the Subject

Having chosen which idea you want to focus on as the subject of the sentence, you can then add descriptive detail that will help your reader understand more precisely the idea presented in the subject.

A sentence like

The tenor was lazy

emphasizes one quality of the singer, his laziness.

A sentence like

That book is green

emphasizes one quality of the book, its color.

Notice how the verbs in these descriptive sentences relate the subject to one particular quality. *Tenor* is linked to *lazy*. *Book* is linked to *green*. The word being described is the subject of the sentence; the quality used to describe it is the complement.

These descriptive sentences use the *to be* verbs mentioned in Chapter 1 (am, is, are, was, were, will be, has been, have been, had been, will have been) as *linking verbs*.

In the last section, you may have noticed that the *to be* verbs also functioned as *part* of the verb in passive sentences. But when these words function as linking verbs, they stand alone as the main verb. The linking verbs work almost like an equals sign (=) between the subject and the complement.

I am busy.	I = busy
Amelia was angry.	Amelia = angry
His coats were plaid.	coats = plaid

In addition to the *to be* verbs, these verbs may sometimes function as linking verbs: *appear, become, feel, grow, look, prove, remain, seem, smell, sound, taste,* and *turn.*

When these verbs function as linking verbs, they identify some particular quality with the subject. For example,

I feel sad.	I = sad
The music sounds mysterious.	music = mysterious
Jan seemed enthusiastic.	Jan = enthusiastic

A complement after a linking verb may also be a noun that identifies the subject. For example,

Milton was the runner-up.	Milton = runner-up
Mrs. Kain became a principal in 1978.	Mrs. Kain = principal

A complement used with a linking verb is called a SUBJECT COMPLEMENT since it refers back to and describes the subject of the sentence.

EXERCISE I

Which words in the following sentences complete the action of a verb? Which completing words refer back to and describe the subject? (Not all these sentences have complements.)

EXAMPLES:

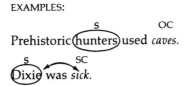

1. June ate the strawberry preserves.
2. The fire destroyed one wing of the museum.

3. Paul is everybody's buddy.
4. The books were collected in boxes.
5. The skiers grew weary.
6. Computers will be installed next week.
7. The *Delta Queen* still cruises the Mississippi.
8. Jane Austen remains my favorite author.
9. You should dust your hands with flour.
10. Nefertiti was the queen of Egypt.
11. The flea found a comfortable home on the Great Dane.
12. The woods are beautiful at this time of year.
13. Cowboys were the work force of the Old West.
14. Sharon ran the New York Marathon.
15. That statement is nonsense.
16. Vesuvius covered Pompeii with ashes.
17. Conrad caught the early train to Philadelphia.
18. Hanukkah is also called "The Festival of Lights."
19. Venice became the dominant sea power in the West.
20. Langen will begin his campaign next month.

EXERCISE J

Emphasize one quality of each subject below by adding a linking verb and a subject complement.

EXAMPLE:

The flowers

The flowers were fragrant.

1. Spiders

    _____

2. Albert Einstein

    _____

3. My car

    _____

4. Their house

    _____

5. The union leaders

_____

6. Several books

_____

7. The box

_____

8. Your garden

_____

9. Leonard's foot

_____

10. Inez

_____

(Linking verbs are presented in more detail on pages 379–80. Refer to that section of the book if you need more information or practice with this sentence pattern.)

The linking verb sentence is a useful tool if the main point of your sentence is to describe some quality of the subject. Most of the time, however, you are trying to show the subject involved in some action. Then, the qualities of the subject are important, but they are not the main point of the sentence.

For instance, suppose you had this base sentence:

The tenor sang his part badly.

You might want to influence the reader's attitude toward the tenor by explaining something about him. Perhaps the tenor was nervous, in which case the reader might sympathize. Or perhaps he was lazy, in which case the reader might criticize.

You could add a linking verb sentence to describe the tenor.

The tenor sang his part badly.
The tenor was nervous.

Or you could combine the two sentences to produce

The _nervous_ tenor sang his part badly.

The first option puts more emphasis on the nervousness of the tenor, but it also delays establishing the connection between his being nervous and his singing badly.

Suppose you want to add some information about the kind of part the tenor had to sing.

The tenor sang the part badly. ＼
The tenor was nervous.   ＞
The part was difficult.

The nervous tenor sang the difficult part badly.

Here, the combined version is much more efficient at conveying the necessary information.

When you use words or phrases to give more precise information about some person or thing in a sentence, you are using ADJECTIVES. *Nervous* and *difficult* in the sentence above are both adjectives.

Adjectives usually answer the questions *which one?* or *what kind?* For example:

He was wearing a *red* shirt.   (what kind of shirt?)
The girl *with the blue eyes* smiled.   (which girl?)

Notice that the normal position for a single-word adjective is right in front of the word it describes. If the adjective is a group of words, a phrase, it comes right after the word it describes.

The *youngest* tenor *in the company* sang the part of *the hero's friend.*
The girl *near the door* flirted with the *young* tenor.

The words shown in the box on page 17 can be used to introduce adjective modifiers as well as adverb modifiers.

EXERCISE K

Identify in the sentences below the words that show which one of something or what kind of something is being discussed. Remember that adjectives can be single words or groups of words.

1. The hot lights caused the woman's cheap make-up to run.
2. A faded painting fills the wall of the abandoned chapel.
3. Mr. Nakasara has been a loyal employee for thirty years.
4. The crippled farm boy became a wealthy man.
5. The white-winged flying machine stood on its launch rails.
6. The man in the gray suit disappeared before our eyes.
7. The harried secretary looked forward to a vacation with her husband.
8. The snow-covered trees with their tiny lights made a dazzling display.
9. For an intimate dinner in an informal atmosphere, we recommend the Café Carlyle.

10. The Chicago Historical Society holds an outstanding collection of President Lincoln's belongings.

EXERCISE L

Combine each of the following sets of sentences so that description and action are shown in one sentence.

EXAMPLE:

The waves rolled toward the beach.

They were lazy.

The beach was deserted.

The lazy waves rolled toward the deserted beach.

1. The aqueduct carries water to the city.
   The aqueduct is Roman.
   The aqueduct is ancient.

   _____

   _____

2. The pilot tested the plane.
   The plane was experimental.
   The plane was solar-powered.

   _____

   _____

3. We gathered the pine cones in baskets.
   The baskets were old-fashioned.
   The pine cones were huge.

   _____

   _____

4. The gardener leaned on the rake.
   The gardener was tired.
   The rake was sturdy.

   _____

   _____

5. The dolphins brought the sailor to land.
   The dolphins were watchful.
   The sailor was drowning.

   _____

   _____

6. Making champagne takes care.
    The champagne is great.
    The care is great.

    _____

7. The students clustered around the desk.
    The students were anxious.
    The desk was the teacher's.

    _____

8. The driver eased the car onto the freeway.
    The driver was the general's.
    The freeway was crowded.

    _____

9. The painting hung crookedly on the wall.
    The painting was glorious.
    The painting was by da Vinci.
    The wall was crumbling.
    The wall was in an apartment.

    _____

10. The supervisor watched the crew.
    The supervisor was stern.
    The supervisor was suspicious.
    The crew was inexperienced.
    The crew was from the prison.

    _____

    _____

    _____

EXERCISE M

In the following sentences, show some specific identifying detail about the subject or another noun by adding an adjective.

1. The manager stood by the door. (what kind of manager?)

    _____

2. Thomas Jefferson designed the house. (which house?)

   _____

3. The team boarded the plane. (which team?)

   _____

4. Hats are coming back in style this year. (what kind of hats?)

   _____

5. With a shout, Millie crossed the line. (what kind of shout?)

   _____

6. The room was filled with the scent. (which room? what kind of scent?)

   _____

7. The tapping came from the window. (what kind of tapping?)

   _____

8. We gave him a gift. (what kind of gift?)

   _____

9. The chef arranged the food on a tray. (which chef? what kind of food?)

   _____

10. The role was played by an actor. (which role? which actor?)

    _____

    _____

(The forms and uses of adjectives are presented in more detail on pages 320–22. If you want to polish your skill with adjectives, refer to that section of the book.)

EXERCISE N

Make the sentences below more precise by adding an adjective to one or more of the nouns.

EXAMPLE:
The dog ran into the alley.
The _lame_ dog ran into the alley _behind the garage._

1. Margaret fired her marketing director.

   _____

   _____

2. The monster opened its mouth.

   _____

   _____

3. The runners sprinted for the tape.

_____

_____

4. The chrysanthemums will flower after the frost.

_____

_____

5. Juanita has made copies of the memo.

_____

_____

6. The Postal Service issues stamps.

_____

_____

7. The governor held her press conference.

_____

_____

8. The school superintendent cut the budget.

_____

_____

9. The man put his apron on the table.

_____

_____

10. Chuck is the winner.

_____

_____

SUMMARY: MAKING THE SUBJECT EFFECTIVE

1. Choose as the subject the idea you want your reader to focus on.
2. Use a linking verb sentence to emphasize some quality of the subject.
3. Choose adjectives to describe the subject precisely.

USING SENTENCE MODIFIERS EFFECTIVELY

Placement of Modifiers

When you use modifiers (that is, adjectives or adverbs), you have to place them carefully so that it is absolutely clear what they are describing. Misplaced modifiers can confuse your reader.

For instance, if you wrote this note to a friend, your friend might not be able to figure out your meaning:

> The teacher said on Thursday there would be a
> test.

Did the teacher make the announcement on Thursday, or is the test going to be on Thursday? This information could make a big difference in your friend's plans for the weekend.

If you meant that the teacher made the announcement on Thursday, you should have said:

> On Thursday, the teacher said there would be a
> test.

If you meant that the test would be on Thursday, you should have said:

> The teacher said there would be a test on Thurs-
> day.

In general, a modifier should be as close as possible to the word it describes.

EXERCISE O

Rewrite each of the following sentences to include the modifier given in parentheses. Be sure that the modifier is placed where it will be clearly understood. Be prepared to explain which word the modifier describes.

EXAMPLE:
The man petted the monkey.
(in the red sweater)

The man in the red sweater petted the monkey.

The man petted the monkey in the red sweater.

1. Jamie scrambled the eggs.
   (ten-year-old)

   _____

2. Chandra promised she would study with me.
   (that afternoon)

   _____

3. The boy rode a fine gelding.
   (with a thick, shining mane)

   _____

4. Mary Beth played a game of hockey.
   (mean)

   _____

5. Mr. Gonzales said that he never smoked.
   (during an interview with the doctor)

   _____

6. Wendell asked the governor for a pardon.
   (notorious)

   _____

7. Mama Cantelloni uses the finest ingredients for her pizza.
   (only)

   _____

8. The tour guide sold pieces of wood as souvenirs.
   (strange and twisted)

   _____

9. The missing ship was found.
   (with the new sonar equipment)

   _____

10. The Cloverdale Cardinals won every game this season.
    (almost)

    _____

11. The newscaster announced a truce.
    (in Chicago)

    _____

12. Ms. Henderson asked the clerk to check the order.
    (at once)

    _____

13. My uncle has said he would write a novel.
    (for ten years)

    _____

14. A movie will be shown on how to repair engines.
    (in the Laudner Auditorium)

    _____

15. The children left the restaurant.
    (with chocolate on their faces)

    _____

16. The queen gave Snow White a poisoned apple.
    (beautiful but evil)

    _____

17. The whole class fainted at the sight of the finished statue.
    (nearly)

    _____

18. General Benjamin rode a horse.
    (in full battle gear)

    _____

19. I watched the gull hover.
    (on outspread wings)

    _____

20. Francis gave his money to the old man.
    (generous)

    _____

Avoiding Too Many Modifiers

While you don't want all your sentences to be bare skeletons like "The man ran," you also don't want to write sentences that are overloaded with detail:

> The man in the brown silk shirt with a red, rumpled handkerchief in the left breast pocket ran wildly out of the burning bank on the corner looking frantically in all directions for someone to help him.

A sentence like the one above has so much added to the basic sentence that a reader is likely to lose the underlying meaning and become confused. In writing sentences, you have to be careful to choose just the right amount of detail, enough to make sure your reader understands your idea clearly, but not so much that he or she gets lost.

Look again at the overloaded sentence above. Could some of the details be left out? If it's important to distinguish this man from some other man in the scene, then you would want some detail about what the man was wearing. But it's unlikely that there were two men with brown silk shirts, so you probably don't need to give the extra detail about the handkerchief and which pocket it was in. In fact, if you are trying to create an atmosphere of panic, so much detail about the man's clothes may even distract the reader from that central idea.

It might be effective to break this long sentence into two sentences, both of which emphasize the man's panic:

> *The man in the brown silk shirt ran wildly out of the burning bank. He looked frantically for someone to help him.*

(*In all directions* can be eliminated since *frantically* suggests that anyway.)

EXERCISE P

In each of the following sets of sentences, you are given more detail than will work well in one sentence. Select enough detail to compose one good sentence or divide the details into two sentences that will work well together. Be prepared to explain why you chose certain details.

EXAMPLE:

The girl loaded her grocery cart.

The girl was pudgy.

The girl had blonde hair.

The girl wore green shorts.

The shorts were tight.

She loaded the cart dreamily.

She loaded it with cakes and pies.

She loaded it with bags of chips and pretzels.

She loaded the cart with cans of diet soda.

The soda was passion-fruit flavored.

The cart was chrome.

The chrome gleamed.

> *The pudgy girl in tight green shorts dreamily loaded her cart. The gleaming chrome was filled with cakes, pies, bags of pretzels and chips, and cans of passion-fruit-flavored diet soda.*

> *or*

> *Dreamily, the pudgy blonde loaded her cart with bags of chips and pretzels, cakes, pies, and cans of passion-fruit-flavored diet soda.*

1. Our neighbor struggled to start the Ford.
   He is eighty years old.
   He is cranky.
   His struggle was unsuccessful.
   He struggled determinedly.
   The struggle lasted for an hour.
   He struggled in his back yard.

The Ford was red.
It was rusted.
It was built in 1940.

_____

_____

_____

2. The heroine fell into the pit.
    She was blonde.
    She was athletic.
    The pit was filled with vipers.
    The pit was filled with mummies.
    The vipers were writhing.
    The vipers were coiled.
    They were hissing.
    The mummies were decayed.
    They were crumbling.
    They were disgusting.
    She fell with a scream.

_____

_____

_____

3. The art is a form of self-defense.
    The art is of karate.
    The art is ancient.
    The art is respected.
    The form is disciplined.
    Karate was developed in the Orient.
    It was developed many centuries ago.
    It was developed by monks.
    The monks were Chinese.
    The monks were peaceful.
    The self-defense involves no weapons.

_____

_____

_____

4. The kitten chased the ball.
    The kitten was gray.
    The kitten was no bigger than Bob's hand.
    She chased the ball all over the room.
    The room was sunny.
    She chased the ball ferociously.
    She chased it like a panther.

She chased it for most of the morning.
The ball was huge.
It was black and white.
It had a slow leak.

_____

_____

_____

5. The bus pulled into the station.
It did this with a jerk.
It was exactly four hours late.
The bus was dust-covered.
The bus was filled with band members.
The bus was filled with instruments.
The band belonged to Garfield High School.
The station was in Pittsburgh.
The station was dark.
The station was empty.
The band members were tired.
The band members were hungry.

_____

_____

_____

EXERCISE Q

Combine each set of sentences below into one sentence that describes the subject and the action precisely. In constructing your sentences, remember the techniques of emphasis that have been presented in this chapter: choice of subject, time or tone of verb, arrangement of sentence parts. Write two versions of each sentence, each one emphasizing a different aspect of the idea being presented. Feel free to change the verb form to suit your emphasis. Be prepared to discuss the difference in emphasis.

1. Our neighbors occupy a land mass.
Our neighbors are to the north.
Our neighbors are in Canada.
The land mass is vast.
It is over 3,000 miles wide.

A. _____

_____

B. _____

_____

2. Use will ruin.
   The use is of gas.
   The gas is leaded.
   Valves and plugs will be ruined.
   The use is continued.
   The ruin will affect many cars.
   The cars are modern.
   The ruin will be soon.

   A. _____

   _____

   B. _____

   _____

3. The legislature will tackle.
   The legislature is in our state.
   The tackling will be during the session.
   The session is upcoming.
   Issues will be tackled.
   The issues are complex.
   Issues like taxation are involved.

   A. _____

   _____

   B. _____

   _____

4. China dominated.
   The world was dominated.
   China was rich.
   China was powerful.
   This was during the T'ang dynasty.
   The T'ang dynasty lasted from A.D. 618 to 907.

   A. _____

   _____

   B. _____

   _____

5. Every order will be processed.
   The orders are for this album.
   The album contains country and western hits.
   The hits are by Willie.

The processing will be immediate.
The processing will be by our staff.

A. _____

_____

B. _____

_____

6. A manager needs integrity.
   The manager is in business.
   The manager is successful.
   The need is undoubted.
   The need is in all aspects.
   The aspects are of her job.

   A. _____

   _____

   B. _____

   _____

7. Archaeologists have discovered pyramids.
   Their discovery was at El Mirador.
   El Mirador is in Guatemala.
   The pyramids are ancient.

   A. _____

   _____

   B. _____

   _____

8. Growth is linked to developments.
   The developments are varied.
   Developments such as ragtime, dress designs, and Ziegfeld's Follies are involved.
   The growth is of dance.
   The dance is modern.

   A. _____

   _____

   B. _____

   _____

9. The residents supported.
   The shelter was supported.
   The residents were of the area.
   The area was near Star Street.
   The shelter was new.

The shelter was for men.
The men were homeless.
The support was wholehearted.

A. _____

_____

B. _____

_____

10. Bugs Bunny exemplifies a part.
The part is of the personality.
The personality is American.
Bugs is clever.
Bugs is gutsy.
Bugs is irreverent.

A. _____

_____

B. _____

_____

EXERCISE R

Make each of the following basic sentences more effective by adding
COMPLEMENTS, ADVERBS, or ADJECTIVES. Change the form of the verb if necessary to suit the purpose of your sentence.

1. The story recreates an age.

_____

_____

2. Mark closed.

_____

_____

3. The room seems.

_____

_____

4. Education is expensive.

_____

_____

5. The fly landed.

    _____

    _____

6. The leader strode.

    _____

    _____

7. Sales should increase.

    _____

    _____

8. The boat lurched.

    _____

    _____

9. The instructor shouted.

    _____

    _____

10. Our adventure began.

    _____

    _____

WRITING PRACTICE

1.   You promised to meet your (parent, spouse, friend, boss) at the airport. However, due to unforeseen circumstances, you won't be able to go. A friend has agreed to meet the plane, but doesn't know the person he is supposed to pick up. Give your friend a five- or six-sentence description of the person arriving on the plane.

   Before writing, close your eyes and try to visualize the person you are describing. Jot down some of the person's important physical characteristics. Decide on a logical order for arranging your description.

   When you write, try to use adjectives, adverbs, and complements to help your friend see the arriving passenger just as you see him or her.

   After you have written a draft, check to make sure that all your sentences are complete and correctly punctuated.

2.   The friend who agreed to meet the plane doesn't remember exactly how to get to the airport. Write out directions for him.

   Before writing, review the route to the airport in your mind, making notes about important landmarks and directions. Make sure your instructions are arranged in an easy-to-follow order.

When you write, try to use adjectives, adverbs, and complements to help your friend see the route to the airport clearly.

After you have written a draft, check your writing to make sure that all your sentences are complete and correctly punctuated.

3

Coordination

So far you have concentrated on presenting one idea completely and precisely. However, you can make a sentence do even more than this. You can use the form of a sentence to show the relationship between two or more ideas. One of the basic relationships that you can set up between ideas is CO-ORDINATION.

When you *coordinate* ideas, you say that one idea is just as important as, or has equal rank with, another idea. (*Co-* means *with, on the same level;* co-captains of a team, for instance, have *equal* importance.) The seven words in the box below can be used to show a coordinate relationship between ideas.

COORDINATION SIGNALS

Remembering the two words BOY FANS may help you remember the seven coordinating words.

{
But
Or
Yet
For
And
Nor
So
}

COORDINATING SUBJECTS WITH *AND*

The subject of the sentence, as you remember from Chapter 1, tells a reader who or what is the focus of attention in the sentence. If you want your sentence to focus on two subjects equally, you coordinate them:

Maryland must take the lead in cleaning up the Chesapeake Bay.
Virginia must take the lead in cleaning up the Chesapeake Bay.

> *Maryland and Virginia must take the lead in cleaning up the Chesapeake Bay.*

By using *and* to coordinate the two subjects, the combined sentence emphasizes that both states must act.

EXERCISE A

Using the example above as a model, combine each of the following pairs of sentences to produce a sentence that gives two subjects equal emphasis.

1. Soap operas show a lot about our problems.
   Situation comedies show a lot about our problems.

   _____

   _____

2. Gladys rode down from Spokane.
   Towanda rode down from Spokane.

   _____

   _____

3. Revving his motor gave Chuck a thrill.
   Making his tires smoke gave Chuck a thrill.

   _____

   _____

4. Katharine Hepburn became one of the great stars of American films.
   Spencer Tracy became one of the great stars of American films.

   _____

   _____

5. Koala bears live only in Australia.
    Wombats live only in Australia.

_____

_____

Look at another example:

George recommends the IBM
    computer.

Sheila recommends the IBM
    computer.

*George and Sheila recommend the
IBM computer.*

This sentence emphasizes that both of the people favor the IBM, but notice how the verb changes from *recommends* to *recommend* when you add to the subject. When you coordinate two subjects with *and*, you have to use a plural verb form. Most of the time, this is no problem since most plural verbs look just the same as singular verbs. The only exceptions are the verbs that describe action taking place in the present time. When these verbs have a subject, *he, she,* or *it,* they end in *-s.* When their subject is a *they,* these verbs don't end in *-s.* For example:

Cyril dances. (He *dances.*)
Cyril and Marvella dance. (They *dance.*)
Better supervision *is* necessary. (It *is.*)
Better supervision and broad reorganization *are* necessary. (They *are.*)
Hazel *misses* her father. (She *misses.*)
Hazel and her brother *miss* their father. (They *miss.*)

(There is a more detailed discussion of present tense verb forms on pages 359–61. Refer to that section if you need more explanation or examples.)

EXERCISE B

Combine each pair of sentences below to produce one sentence with two subjects coordinated by *and.* Be sure to use the appropriate verb form.

1. Elm grows well in this area.
    Birch grows well in this area.

_____

2. The Chevy needs a tune-up.
    The Ford needs a tune-up.

_____

3. Cats are people's best friends.
   Dogs are people's best friends.

   _____

4. The Tartars fled the Russian winter.
   The Huns fled the Russian winter.

   _____

5. Newton discovered the calculus.
   Leibnitz discovered the calculus. (*Both*)

   _____

6. Brass was common in early coins.
   Iron was common in early coins.

   _____

7. Kildeer live in the back meadow.
   Quail live in the back meadow.

   _____

8. The winner looks exhausted.
   The loser looks exhausted.

   _____

9. The humpback whale is an endangered species.
   The American bald eagle is an endangered species.

   _____

10. The new refrigerator has been installed.
    The new stove has been installed.

    _____

COORDINATING SUBJECTS WITH *OR*

Another way of coordinating subjects is to use *or*. When you use *or* (or *nor*), you are asking your reader to consider each subject separately. *Or* is used to suggest a choice between two alternatives, each of which deserves the same attention from your reader. In coordinating, you may pair *either* with *or* (and *neither* with *nor*) as the example below shows.

> Maryland needs to take the lead in cleaning up the Chesapeake Bay.
> Virginia needs to take the lead in cleaning up the Chesapeake Bay.

> *Either Maryland or Virginia needs to take the lead in cleaning up the Chesapeake Bay.*

Because the two subjects are coordinated with *or*, this sentence suggests that only one of the two states must act, not both. Notice how this differs from a sentence that joins the subjects by *and*. In this sentence, the verb stays singular because each subject is considered separately.

EXERCISE C

Using the example above as a model, combine each of the following pairs of sentences into one sentence whose subjects are coordinated by *or* or *either . . . or* or by *nor* or *neither . . . nor*.

1. Pearl uses the rehearsal studio every morning.
   Rose uses the rehearsal studio every morning.

   _____

2. France will lead Europe in the twenty-first century.
   Germany will lead Europe in the twenty-first century.

   _____

3. Overeating causes weight gain.
   Lack of exercise causes weight gain.

   _____

4. The Orioles will be leading the league in September.
   The Yankees will be leading the league in September.

   _____

5. Jogging will help keep you in shape.
   Swimming will help keep you in shape.

   _____

As long as the subjects being coordinated by *or* are both singular or both plural, you should have no problem with the verb form. What happens, though, when you coordinate a plural subject and a singular subject with *or*? Look at the example below.

The prime minister always greets the guests.	*The prime minister or the cabinet officers always greet the guests.*
The cabinet officers always greet the guests.	*The cabinet officers or the prime minister always greets the guests.*

In these examples, although there are two subjects, each subject is considered separately. Notice how this separation affects the verb form. In the sample on page 49, you had two singular subjects and you used a singular verb—*needs*. In the sample above, however, one subject is singular and one subject is plural. How do you decide whether the verb should be singular or plural? You solve this problem by making the verb agree with the subject closer to it.

Thus, if you say "the prime minister or the cabinet officers," you use the plural verb *greet* because *officers* is plural. If you say "the cabinet officers or the prime minister," you use the singular verb *greets* because *prime minister* is singular. Putting the plural subject closer to the verb usually makes a sentence sound more natural.

EXERCISE D

Combine each of the following pairs of sentences to produce one sentence whose subjects are coordinated by *or* or *nor*. Be sure to make the verb agree with the subject closer to it.

1. My younger sister is not allowed to go.
   My younger brothers are not allowed to go. (*Neither . . . nor*)

   _____

2. Insurance payments are due on the fifteenth.
   The rent is due on the fifteenth.

   _____

3. The tires have to be replaced every year.
   The battery has to be replaced every year.

   _____

4. The instructor always demonstrates the procedure.
   Her assistants always demonstrate the procedure.

   _____

5. The president approves the budget.
   The members of the board approve the budget.

   _____

EXERCISE E

Combine each of the following sentences two different ways. The first time use *and* to coordinate the subjects. The second time use *or* or *nor*. (When using *or*, you may use *either* with it. When using *nor*, you may use *neither* with it.) Be sure to select the appropriate verb form for each combination. Be prepared to discuss the difference in meaning between the two versions.

EXAMPLE:
Sunnyfield has been restored.
Hancock's Manor has been restored.
A. *Both Sunnyfield and Hancock's Manor have been restored.*
B. *Neither Sunnyfield nor Hancock's Manor has been restored.*

1. New York is America's most exciting city.
   Los Angeles is America's most exciting city.

   A. _____

   _____

   B. _____

   _____

2. The canaries want attention all the time.
   The parrot wants attention all the time.

   A. _____

   _____

   B. _____

   _____

3. English is often a child's worst subject in elementary school.
   Arithmetic is often a child's worst subject in elementary school.

   A. _____

   _____

   B. _____

   _____

4. Batman rescues the world from disaster once a week.
   Superman rescues the world from disaster once a week.

   A. _____

   _____

   B. _____

   _____

5. A light-rail system will solve that transportation problem.
   Express buses will solve that transportation problem.

   A. _____

   _____

   B. _____

   _____

6. Forty cases of frozen food are delivered every week.
   A truckload of canned goods is delivered every week.

   A. _____

   _____

B. _____

_____

7. The workers have not backed down on the contract.
   Management has not backed down on the contract.

   A. _____

   _____

   B. _____

   _____

8. A ferret makes a good pet.
   An otter makes a good pet.

   A. _____

   _____

   B. _____

   _____

9. Camping saves vacationers money.
   Special park passes save vacationers money.

   A. _____

   _____

   B. _____

   _____

10. Adam dislikes soap operas.
    His best friend dislikes soap operas.

    A. _____

    _____

    B. _____

    _____

EXPLAINING NOUNS

In each of the coordinating patterns you have tried so far, you have been coordinating two different subjects. There is one special kind of coordination, however, that coordinates two different versions of the same subject, as the sentence below shows:

My daughter is a good dancer.
She has had many years of training.

My daughter, a good dancer, has had many years of training.

In the combined version, the noun *dancer* explains something about the noun *daughter*. The EXPLAINING NOUN pattern coordinates one noun with another. The explaining noun restates the first noun in some way. Instead of using a coordination signal, the explaining noun is set off by commas and always follows immediately after the noun it explains. Here are more examples of the explaining noun pattern of coordination.

Disney World is a children's paradise.

It is also an excellent example of modern urban planning.

explaining noun

Disney World, a children's paradise, is also an excellent example of modern urban planning.

Bessie Smith was one of the greatest blues singers of all time.

Bessie Smith was a victim of segregated hospitals.

explaining noun

Bessie Smith, one of the greatest blues singers of all time, was a victim of segregated hospitals.

EXERCISE F

Identify the explaining nouns in each of the following sentences. Notice the position of each explaining noun and the punctuation used with this pattern of coordination.

1. Zircon, a mineral, usually forms pyramid-shaped crystals.
2. Ahmed, a straight-A student, offered to tutor Jackie.
3. Palmer, a Cy Young Award winner, has pitched in four World Series games.
4. Celeste, my favorite librarian, has been transferred to the Takoma branch.
5. Junipero Serra, a Spanish friar, founded California's first mission.
6. Dr. Kahlid, probably the most dedicated member of the staff, sat with the child all night.
7. Pacific Trust, a family-owned business, has never missed a dividend payment.
8. The frost, a disaster for the whole state, ruined our crop.
9. The general, a secretive man, did not explain his absence.
10. Narbeth Island, a gorgeous place in summer, was bleak in the winter.

EXERCISE G

Using the examples above as models, combine each pair of sentences below to produce a sentence in which one noun is explained by a coordinate noun. Remember to put commas around the explaining noun.

1. This apple is a winesap.
    It is my grandfather's favorite.

    _____

    _____

2. The white-haired man was a famous physicist.
    He was revered around the world.

    _____

    _____

3. The Hopi are a private people.
    They do not allow tourists to photograph their villages.

    _____

    _____

4. The woman was apparently the child's mother.
    She watched fondly as he recited his lines.

    _____

    _____

5. The mechanic was a grease-stained woman in her twenties.
    She raised the hood of the smoking car.

    _____

    _____

6. Thomas More was a scholar as well as a statesman.
    He served as Chancellor of England under Henry VIII.

    _____

    _____

7. Swimming is a demanding sport.
    It is dominated by the Americans and the Germans.

    _____

    _____

8. Richard Conway is the director of the program.
    He will become a vice-president next year.

    _____

    _____

9. Savannah is a living museum.
   Savannah began its restoration in the 1940s.

   _____

   _____

10. The Bar G is a working ranch.
    It is also a game sanctuary.

    _____

    _____

COORDINATING VERBS

Coordination also allows you to involve the subject of the sentence in several actions, each of which gets equal emphasis. You can do this by joining two verbs in a sentence with a coordinating word. For instance:

> Gene will cook the dinner.
> Gene will not wash the dishes.
> *Gene will cook the dinner but will not wash the dishes.*
> Last year, Hope went to Central America.
> Last year, Hope worked with the refugee families there.
> *Last year, Hope went to Central America and worked with the refugee families there.*

In case there are more than two verbs to be coordinated, commas should be used to separate each verb from the others.

> The little ones laughed, shouted, and jumped for joy.
> Parker struck a match, lit the two fuses, and ran for cover.

When you coordinate a series of actions, you also need to consider the order in which you will present the actions in the sentence. Be sure to choose the most logical sequence for the events. Move in a time order from first to last, or from least important to most important action. The model in the exercise below shows the actions arranged in a logical time sequence.

EXERCISE H

Using the coordination signal given, combine each of the following sets of sentences to show the same subject performing two or more coordinated actions.

EXAMPLE:

Everyone on the tour picnics in the shadow of the Pyramids.

Everyone on the tour gets up early.

Everyone on the tour boats down the Nile. (*and*)

Everyone on the tour gets up early, boats down the Nile, and picnics in the shadow of the Pyramids.

1. The striped bass rose.
    The striped bass swallowed the bait. (*and*)

    _____

2. The hurricane did not take any lives.
    The hurricane did not damage any property. (*nor*)

    _____

3. At the park, the kids can shriek on the roller coaster.
    At the park, the kids can scream in the haunted house. (*or*)

    _____

4. Every morning, someone spills food on the floor.
    Every morning, someone breaks a dish. (*or*)

    _____

5. Worker bees attend the queen.
    Worker bees gather pollen.
    Worker bees feed the newborn. (*and*)

    _____

    _____

6. Jefferson wrote the Declaration of Independence.
    Jefferson founded the University of Virginia.
    Jefferson served as President. (*and*)

    _____

    _____

7. Carmine bought a new car.
    Carmine had a sun-roof put in.
    Carmine lowered the front end. (*and*)

    _____

    _____

8. Russ lunged across the rocks.
    Russ saw Mary's foot slip.
    Russ could not catch her. (*but*)

    _____

    _____

9.   The gourmet sniffed at his wine.
     He savored its bouquet.
     He drank it in one gulp. (*and*)

_____

_____

10. Roger would beg from strangers.
     He would borrow from friends. (*or*)
     He would never steal from anyone. (*but*)

_____

_____

COORDINATING COMPLEMENTS

Sometimes an action may have several effects, or an idea may be completed in several ways. Coordination lets you give equal emphasis to each of the ways in which an action or idea may be completed. Remember to arrange the complements in some sensible order and to use the punctuation needed to help the reader see the series. For example:

The Orioles won the game, the series, and the pennant. (order of importance)

This tour visits Universal Studios, Disneyland, and Sea World. (time order)

The explaining noun pattern of coordination can also be used with complements:

Tom gently hugged the boy, a frightened six-year-old.

EXERCISE I

Combine each of the following sets of sentences to produce one sentence showing several aspects of the subject or completions of the action. Or use the explaining noun pattern to restate the complement.

EXAMPLE:
Franklin D. Roosevelt was Assistant Secretary of the Navy.
Franklin D. Roosevelt was President of the United States.
Franklin D. Roosevelt was Governor of New York.
Coordinate Series: *Franklin D. Roosevelt was Governor of New York, Assistant Secretary of the Navy, and President of the United States.*

Explaining Noun: Franklin D. Roosevelt, once Governor of New York, was Assistant Secretary of the Navy and then President of the United States.

1. Paulo filed three folders of correspondence.
    Paulo filed the minutes of the board meeting. (*and*)

    _____

2. The Great Plains are flat.
    The Great Plains are arid. (*and*)

    _____

3. Bruce can coordinate the reception.
    The reception will be a 2-hour extravaganza.

    _____

4. The press secretary did not confirm the rumor.
    The press secretary did not deny the rumor. (*neither . . . nor*)

    _____

5. The coach did not need outfielders.
    The coach needed infielders. (*but*)

    _____

6. Mike likes driving cabs.
    Cab driving is a job with flexible hours.

    _____

    _____

7. For the exam, Charlene reviewed the first seven chapters of the text.
    For the exam, Charlene reviewed her lab notes.
    For the exam, Charlene reviewed the teacher's lectures. (*and*)

    _____

    _____

8. I do not enjoy skiing.
    I do not enjoy snowmobiling.
    I do not enjoy ice skating. (*or*)

    _____

    _____

9. Should we pay the rent?
    Should we pay the gas and electric bill?
    Should we pay the telephone bill? (*or*)

    _____

    _____

10. Admiral Ward was firm.
    She was pleasant. (*but*)

She was strict.
She was reasonable. (*but*)

_____

_____

COORDINATING MODIFIERS

Sometimes, in order to communicate your idea clearly to the reader, you need more than one modifier. These modifiers can be arranged several ways.

Adjectives: Before Noun

You remember from Chapter 2 that most single-word adjectives are placed right before the word they describe, as in:

Our *new* sales manager clinched a *big* deal today.

Adjectives: After Noun

Sometimes it is more effective, especially with coordinated modifiers, to put them *after* the word being described, as in:

The redwoods, *ancient and majestic,* reach toward
the sky.

This kind of placement puts even more emphasis on the coordinated adjectives. (Remember, if you use this placement, you should set off the modifiers with commas.)

Adverbs

Adverbs, or words that describe the action of the verb, can be placed in any of several positions in the sentence.
For instance, these two sentences:

The nurse assessed the patient's progress sympathetically.
The nurse assessed the patient's progress professionally.

could become:

Professionally but sympathetically, *the nurse assessed the patient's progress.*

or

The nurse <u>professionally but sympathetically</u> assessed the patient's progress.

or

The nurse assessed the patient's progress <u>professionally but sympathetically.</u>

The placement depends on the amount of emphasis you want to give to the coordinated adverbs and on your sense of the rhythm of the sentence.

Sometimes no coordinating word is used between two adverbs or two adjectives, producing sentences like these:

<u>Professionally, sympathetically,</u> the nurse assessed the patient's progress.

or

The <u>fiery, listing</u> ship was finally abandoned.

Notice that in these examples a comma takes the place of a coordinating word.

Modifiers should always be chosen very carefully to point out to your reader something especially vivid or unusual; when you decide to coordinate your modifiers, you should choose with even greater care. Don't just string together vague or colorless modifiers.

EXERCISE J

Combine each of the following sets of sentences to produce one sentence that presents an idea more clearly by using several modifiers. As in the exercises above, remember to punctuate with commas in a series of more than two items.

EXAMPLE:

The officer strode to the pickup swiftly.

The officer strode to the pickup decisively.

The officer strode to the pickup swiftly and decisively.

or

Swiftly and decisively, the officer strode to the pickup.

1. The final rehearsal always goes spectacularly.
    The final rehearsal always goes disastrously. (*or*)

2. Jane went in fast for the dunk shot.
    Jane went in high for the dunk shot. (*and*)

3. The marriage service should be conducted joyously.
   The marriage service should be conducted reverently. (*but*)

   _____

4. Sherman's Trans Am moved into the straightaway smoothly.
   Sherman's Trans Am moved into the straightaway effortlessly. (*and*)

   _____

5. Her face was wrinkled.
   Her face was cheerful. (*but*)
   The old woman's face reflected a lifetime of hard work.

   _____

   _____

6. The porridge was not too hot.
   The porridge was not too cold. (*neither . . . nor*)
   The porridge tasted just right to Goldilocks.

   _____

   _____

7. Phyllis attacked the equation.
   Her attack was slow.*
   Her attack was methodical.* (*but*)

   _____

   _____

8. The Bayeux Tapestry shows the Battle of Hastings.
   The showing is vivid.*
   The showing is accurate.* (*and*)

   _____

   _____

9. Suddenly the bear was not cute.
   Suddenly the bear was not comic. (*neither . . . nor*)
   The bear snarled at us.

   _____

   _____

10. The poppy was bright.
    The poppy was fragile. (*and*)
    The poppy bobbed in the sunlight.

    _____

    _____

* Use adverb form.

EXERCISE K

Expand the following sentences by coordinating one of the parts: subject, verb, complement, or modifier. You may use the explaining noun pattern of coordination where appropriate. Give two different expansions for each sentence. Be prepared to explain the differences between your versions.

EXAMPLE:

The children ate popcorn before the show.

A.   *The children and their parents ate popcorn before the show.*

B.   *The children ate popcorn before the show, a cartoon feature.*

1.   The shortstop missed the grounder.

   A. _____

   _____

   B. _____

2.   The assistant manager is handling this month's sale.

   A. _____

   _____

   B. _____

3.   Louis Joliet bravely explored the uncharted Mississippi River.

   A. _____

   _____

   B. _____

4.   Ice cream is America's favorite food.

   A. _____

   _____

   B. _____

5.   Exotic herbs are found in South America.

   A. _____

   _____

B. _____

_____

6. A used car should be inspected thoroughly.

    A. _____

    _____

    B. _____

    _____

7. The Indian women made exquisite jewelry.

    A. _____

    _____

    B. _____

    _____

8. The narrow road wound its way through the jungle.

    A. _____

    _____

    B. _____

    _____

9. The menu this week will feature eggs.

    A. _____

    _____

    B. _____

    _____

10. First National Bank offered a free toaster with every new account.

    A. _____

    _____

    B. _____

    _____

COORDINATING SENTENCES

Comma, Coordination Signal

In Chapter 1, you saw that most sentences begin with a capital letter and end with a period so that a reader will be able to tell where one idea ends and the next one begins. Sometimes, however, two sentences are so closely related that you want your reader to consider them together, as part of the same idea. In that case, you can choose to coordinate those two sentences by replacing the period and the capital letter with a coordination signal. For example:

> Harry wanted a pizza.
> Everyone else wanted Mexican food.

To show the link between these two sentences more clearly, you might write them like this:

> *Harry wanted a pizza, but everyone else wanted Mexican food.*

This version uses one of the coordination signals that you are already familiar with to join two sentences. Writing the sentence this way gives equal emphasis to each idea. Notice that a comma must be used before the coordination signal between two sentences.

Here are some other possibilities for coordinating those two ideas:

> *Harry wanted a pizza, and everyone else wanted Mexican food.*
> *Harry wanted a pizza, so everyone else wanted Mexican food.*
> *Harry wanted a pizza, for everyone else wanted Mexican food.*

The different coordination words suggest different relationships between the two ideas. *But* emphasizes the contrast between Harry's wishes and everyone else's. *And* just presents the fact that there were two alternatives. *So* suggests that everyone else choose Mexican food simply to be different from Harry. *For* implies that Harry just wanted to be different from everyone else.

All of the coordinating words put equal emphasis on each idea, but each coordinating word suggests a slightly different relationship between the two ideas.

EXERCISE L

Show the connection between each of the following pairs of sentences by using a comma and one of the seven coordinating words (**but**, **or**, **yet**, **for**, **and**, **nor**, **so**). Try two different combinations for each pair, and be prepared to explain any difference in meaning between the two versions.

EXAMPLE:

Alex didn't have the money to take Kate out.
He told her he was busy.

A. *Alex didn't have the money to take Kate out, but he told her he was busy.*
B. *Alex didn't have the money to take Kate out, so he told her he was busy.*

Discussion: In the first sentence, the *but* emphasizes the *contrast* between the truth and Alex's version of reality. In the second, the *so* emphasizes that the lie was an *effect* of Alex's lack of money.

For the first five sentence pairs, use the coordination signals shown in parentheses. For the last five, choose signals you think are appropriate.

1. Emmett stopped smoking.
   Emmett got lower insurance rates. (*and, so*)

   A. _____

   _____

   B. _____

   _____

2. Clarissa could buy herself a new motorcycle.
   Clarissa could save some money for a trip to Vegas. (*and, or*)

   A. _____

   _____

   B. _____

   _____

3. Mark Antony could not keep power in Rome.
   Cleopatra remained his mistress. (*for, yet*)

   A. _____

   _____

   B. _____

   _____

4. Cats are independent and intelligent.
   Some people prefer dogs. (*yet, so*)

   A. _____

   _____

   B. _____

   _____

5. Mimi grew up watching "I Love Lucy."
   Now she is addicted to reruns of "Laverne and Shirley." (*so, but*)

   A. _____

   _____

   B. _____

   _____

6. We can hire an attorney to sue them.
   We can demonstrate in front of their headquarters.

   A. _____

   _____

   B. _____

   _____

7. Grandpa disapproved of the marriage.
   Grandma approved of it.

   A. _____

   _____

   B. _____

   _____

8. The Plains Indians needed the buffalo for food.
   Europeans killed whole herds for sport.

   A. _____

   _____

   B. _____

   _____

9. Brant always looks fashionable.
   He spends a fortune on clothes.

   A. _____

   _____

   B. _____

   _____

10. Virgil did not give an excuse for missing practice.
    Virgil did not explain why he was late for the game.

    A. _____

    _____

    B. _____

    _____

Semicolon, Linking Adverb

In coordinating sentences, you have another option besides a comma and one of the coordination signals. You can also use a semicolon (;), as in the sentence below:

Agatha Christie specializes in the classic British murder story; Ross Macdonald gives murder a contemporary American setting.

A semicolon emphasizes the closeness between the two ideas but does not specify the kind of relationship. Therefore, along with the semicolon, you may want to use a linking adverb, which will show your reader the specific relationship you intend between the two ideas.
For instance:

> Television news is superficial; <u>as a result,</u> I read
> the newspapers to stay informed.

Notice that the linking adverb needs a semicolon before it and a comma after it. The most frequently used linking adverbs are shown in the box below.

LINKING ADVERBS

as a result	nevertheless
consequently	on the other hand
furthermore	otherwise
however	then
in addition	therefore
meanwhile	thus
moreover	

EXERCISE M

Use a semicolon to combine the sentences below and indicate the closeness between them. Then use a linking adverb to bring out the *specific* relationship you want the reader to see. Be prepared to discuss any difference in meaning between the two versions. Signals are suggested for the first five pairs.

EXAMPLE:

Alex didn't have the money to take Kate out.

He told her he was busy.

A. *Alex didn't have the money to take Kate out; he told her he was busy.*

B. *Alex didn't have the money to take Kate out; therefore, he told her he was busy.*

Discussion: In both combined sentences, the second idea shows the *result* of Alex's lack of money, but in the first combination the reader has to guess at the connection. In the second, it is spelled out. The *extra help* given the reader is the difference.

1. Gordon has always rooted for the Raiders.
His best friend, Smitty, is a long-time fan of the Steelers. (; – *on the other hand*)

A. _____

_____

B. _____

_____

2. Ant society is often compared to human society.
The similarities are very slight. (; – *however*)

A. _____

_____

B. _____

_____

3. France once controlled the entire Mississippi Valley.
Many cities along the river have French names. (; – *as a result*)

A. _____

_____

B. _____

_____

4. Maria got a promotion.
She moved into a bigger apartment. (; – *therefore*)

A. _____

_____

B. _____

_____

5. David will have to borrow some money from Phil.
David might have to stay home this weekend. (; – *otherwise*)

A. _____

_____

B. _____

_____

6. Japan borrowed its writing system from China.
   It added characters of its own.

   A. _____

   _____

   B. _____

   _____

7. Radial tires provide better handling for your car.
   They deliver twice the mileage of traditional tires.

   A. _____

   _____

   B. _____

   _____

8. Trees cool and clean the air.
   Many cities are using them for urban renewal.

   A. _____

   _____

   B. _____

   _____

9. Eunice works for Union Trust.
   She banks with First National.

   A. _____

   _____

   B. _____

   _____

10. The receptionist was rude and sarcastic.
    She was the boss's favorite employee.

    A. _____

    _____

    B. _____

    _____

EXERCISE N

Add a coordinate sentence to each of the following sentences. Try to use different combining patterns rather then relying on just one. Be sure to choose the coordination signal or linking adverb that most clearly expresses the relationship you want to show between the two ideas. Remember the punctuation that goes with each pattern.

EXAMPLES:

Mt. Etna erupts about every twenty years.

Mt. Etna erupts about every twenty years, yet people still live on the slopes.

No one knows what to do with nuclear waste.

No one knows what to do with nuclear waste; nevertheless, the government is going ahead with reactor development.

1. The Senate hearing dragged on.

_____

_____

2. I came in a distant third.

_____

_____

3. Kevin's apartment has a fine view of Central Park.

_____

_____

4. Pledges to the building fund came in very quickly.

_____

_____

5. Hindus believe in reincarnation.

_____

_____

6. We do not think this is the best route for the new Interstate Highway.

_____

_____

7. All the children wanted to meet Big Bird.

_____

_____

8. A professional woman's clothes should express her own style.

_____

_____

9. Soccer is less violent than football.

_____

_____

10.   CK's Restaurant specializes in seafood.

_____

_____

EDITING PRACTICE

Read the following paragraphs carefully, checking for errors in using the writing techniques presented thus far. Make sure there are no sentence fragments. Make sure that singular subjects have singular verbs and plural subjects have plural verbs. Make sure that coordinate word groups have the necessary punctuation.

Underline any errors you find and then recopy the paragraph, correcting those errors.

1.   Forensic scientists experts in police evidence provides valuable clues in a murder by studying the corpse carefully. First, they may confirm the victim's identity. Scientists can check teeth against dental records or matching the corpse's fingerprints with those in a military police or government file. These experts also establishes the cause of death. By examining the body for wounds scars bites and other marks in addition they analyze the body organs for poisons or drugs. They can sometimes to identify the murder weapon by matching it to a wound scar or bruise on the body. Finally forensic scientists links a suspect to a crime through hair samples blood samples or toothmarks found on the body frequently. Although the work of these men and women are often tedious. Their findings can be dramatic in helping to solve a murder.

2.   The Kolodny—Gonzales match at Wimbledon presenting a classic match-up of energetic newcomer and crafty veteran. Vladimir Kolodny the Russian ace bounces onto the court like a lion coiled to spring on the other hand Jamie Gonzales the thirty-year-old Texan strolls onto the court with the controlled confidence of a lion tamer. Kolodny's strength is his lightning speed his serves seems to almost hit the opposite court. Before the ball has left his hand and he can move up for a net shot incredibly fast. Many of his opponents feels tired. Just watching him warm up before the game. Gonzales, however, bringing some powerful weapons of his own to this match. For one thing, he can place the ball with amazing accuracy and he has a knack for putting the ball where his opponent isn't. He have also mastered the fake-out. His entire body will seem poised to serve the ball to the left side of the court then he slams it down the right side. Grinning disconcertingly the whole time. Some people thinks the strong speedy Russian can upset the four-time Wimbledon champion this year but no one is willing to bet too heavily on it.

WRITING PRACTICE

1.   The college newspaper has asked you to share your expertise with your fellow students. Choose something that you know how to do well (line up a date for Saturday? buy a used car? make it through Bio lab?). Then list the steps you would go through to ensure success in this process. When you write, try to use the techniques of coordination to give each step in the process equal attention. You may choose to treat this subject humorously rather than seriously.

After you have composed a draft, check to make sure your sentences are complete and correctly punctuated.

2.   As a staff writer for *The Scholastic Weekly*, a current events newspaper for elementary school children, your job is to rewrite major news stories so that the children can understand them. Choose a national or international event now in the news and, in five to ten sentences, summarize it for your young readers.

To find the details of the story, you may want to check recent newspaper or magazine articles about this event. In writing the story, try to use the techniques of coordination so that every part of the story gets its proper share of attention and the relationships between events in the story are clear.

After you have composed a draft, check to be sure that all your sentences are complete and correctly punctuated.

4

Subordination

With coordination, you can show that two ideas in a sentence are equally important, as in this sentence:

BASE SENTENCE

Johann Gutenberg lived in Mainz, Germany, *and*

BASE SENTENCE

he perfected movable type.

This sentence tells a reader that where Gutenberg lived and what he did are equally important pieces of information.

Suppose, however, that you are writing about German contributions to Western civilization, and, therefore, you want to emphasize Gutenberg's residence. Then you might combine the ideas this way:

BASE SENTENCE

Johann Gutenberg lived in Mainz, Germany, *when*

SUBORDINATE WORD GROUP

he perfected movable type.

This sentence uses the technique of SUBORDINATION to suggest that what Gutenberg did is less important than where he lived.

Like coordination, subordination shows a relationship between ideas, but it is a relationship of inequality rather than equality. Subordination keeps a reader's attention focused on one idea more than on another. The base sentence, the unsubordinated part of the sentence, contains the main idea. The subordinate word group contains the related, but less important, idea.

For example:

SUBORDINATE WORD GROUP	BASE SENTENCE

When Gutenberg lived in Mainz, he perfected movable type.

Here the base sentence is "he perfected movable type." The place of residence is subordinated.

When you subordinate an idea, you put it in some form that is less than a complete sentence. To be considered a base sentence, a group of words must express a complete idea: it must present a subject and a verb that shows time, and they must not be introduced by a subordination signal. If any one of these requirements is lacking, you do not have a base sentence. You have, instead, a subordinate word group. Subordinate word groups usually define or describe some part of the base sentence, functioning as adjectives or adverbs.

You can make a sentence into a subordinate word group by:

1. **Putting a subordination signal in front of the subject–verb unit (adverb)**
2. **Replacing part of the base sentence with a subordination signal (adjective)**
3. **Changing the verb to a non-time form (verbal)**

USING ADVERB SUBORDINATION SIGNALS

Adverb subordination signals turn sentences into subordinate word groups telling when, where, how, or why the action occurs. Such word groups clarify the action in the base sentence.

These word groups can be introduced by any of the subordination signals in the box below.

ADVERB SUBORDINATION SIGNALS

When	Where	Why	How
after	where	because	although
as soon as	wherever	if	as
before		in case that	as if
once		in order that	as though
until		inasmuch as	even though
when		provided that	less than
whenever		since	more than
while		so that	so long as
		unless	than
		whereas	though

(Some of the signals may fit in more than one category.)

You can use any of these subordination signals simply by putting them in front of a subject–verb unit. That subject–verb unit is then automatically subordinated.

The use of different subordination signals may suggest different relationships between the same two ideas, as the sentences below illustrate.

The chef had been trained in Paris.

He demanded an exceptionally high salary.

Because the chef had been trained in Paris, he demanded an exceptionally high salary. (training caused the demand)

After the chef had been trained in Paris, he demanded an exceptionally high salary. (demand came after training)

Although the chef had been trained in Paris, he demanded an exceptionally high salary. (training does not justify demand)

Subordinate word groups follow different patterns of punctuation depending on where you place them in the sentence. When you begin a sentence with a subordinate word group, you need to mark the end of it with a comma. The comma tells your reader to get ready for the main idea.

INTRODUCING

After he developed the first Indian alphabet, Sequoyah
was revered by the Cherokee.

If the subordinate word group comes in the middle of the base sentence,
you need to set it off with commas on both sides so that your reader will not
be confused about which ideas belong in the base sentence.

INTERRUPTING

Sequoyah, *after he developed the first Indian alphabet,*
was revered by the Cherokee.

If you put the subordinate word group after the base sentence, you
usually don't need to use any punctuation to separate the two parts. The subordination signal itself tells your reader that the base sentence is finished.

Sequoyah was revered by the Cherokee *after he*

FOLLOWING

developed the first Indian alphabet.

EXERCISE A

Identify the base sentence and the subordinate word group in each of
the following sentences. Notice the punctuation used in each case.

1. Would you please settle your account immediately so that we can
   avoid legal action against you?
2. Even though he was in constant pain, Kennedy refused to slow
   down.
3. Amelia, once she learned to talk, was never quiet.
4. That engine is easy to fix if you have the proper tools.
5. Ed never learned to ski because he was too afraid of falling.
6. When she heard the news, his wife screamed.
7. Sun Yat-sen was forced out of China when his attempt at revolution failed.
8. Because she was depressed, Chris ate a whole bag of chocolate
   chip cookies.
9. Rice, although he had hit forty home runs that year, lost the MVP
   balloting.
10. Anne would never be satisfied until she could read Greek.

EXERCISE B

Combine each of the following pairs of sentences so that one idea in each sentence is subordinated. Give two versions of each sentence. Identify the base sentence and the subordinate word group in each sentence and be prepared to explain the difference in meaning between your two versions.

EXAMPLE:

Cory danced by the edge of the sea. (*while*)

She could hear music from under the waves. (*because*)

A.   *While Cory danced by the edge of the sea, she could hear music from under the waves.*

B.   *Cory danced by the edge of the sea because she could hear music from under the waves.*

Sample explanation: In the first sentence, she hears the music at the same time she is dancing. In the second, the music causes her dancing.

1.   Spring begins. (*as soon as*)
     The dogwood unfurls its simple flowers. (*when*)

     A.   _____

     B.   _____

     Explanation _____

     _____

2.   The serpent slithered across the quilt. (*as*)
     Sherlock Holmes struck at it with his stick. (*when*)

     A.   _____

     B.   _____

     Explanation _____

     _____

3.   John likes intelligent women. (*although, because*)
     John detests Valerie.

     A.   _____

     B.   _____

     Explanation _____

     _____

4.   Misery loves company. (*even though*)
     Being miserable is usually lonely. (*since*)

     A.   _____

B. _____

Explanation _____

_____

5. The sun touched the horizon. (*after*)
   The flamingos rose from the river. (*while*)

   A. _____

   B. _____

   Explanation _____

   _____

6. Gottlieb Daimler ushered in the automotive age with his invention of the gasoline engine.
   The public considered his invention dangerous.

   A. _____

   B. _____

   Explanation _____

   _____

7. The Senate voted to increase food aid to Africa.
   Thousands of Africans were dying of starvation.

   A. _____

   B. _____

   Explanation _____

   _____

8. Cable TV service was introduced.
   More people stayed home and watched television.

   A. _____

   B. _____

   Explanation _____

   _____

9. The tenors got louder.
   The basses got softer.

   A. _____

   B. _____

   Explanation _____

   _____

10. Oklahoma was opened to white settlers in 1889.
     Oklahoma was officially considered Indian Territory.

     A. _____

     B. _____

     Explanation _____

     _____

USING ADJECTIVE SUBORDINATION SIGNALS

The adjective subordination signals—who, whose, whom, which, and that—can turn a sentence into a subordinate word group by replacing some part of the base sentence. For example, look at this combination:

Lynn writes sensitive poetry.
Lynn has just published her second book.
A. Lynn, *who writes sensitive poetry,* has just published her second book.
B. Lynn, *who has just published her second book,* writes sensitive poetry.

Sentence A emphasizes the book publication by keeping it in the base sentence. Sentence B emphasizes the kind of poetry Lynn writes by putting that in the base sentence.

Here is another example:

Everyone calls the lion the King of Beasts.
The lion is an impressive creature.
The lion, which everyone calls the King of Beasts, is an impressive creature.

Which idea gets more emphasis in the sentence above, the fact that the lion is the King of Beasts or the fact that he is impressive?

Subordinate word groups introduced by who, whose, whom, which, and that describe some noun in the base sentence. In other words, these subordinate word groups function as adjectives.

When you use this subordination technique, there are several points to keep in mind.

1.   These subordinate word groups are always placed right after the words they are referring to so the reader will have no difficulty seeing the connection. In the sentences above, for instance, *who* comes immediately after *Lynn* because *who* really stands for *Lynn; which* comes immediately after *lion* because *which* stands for *lion.*

2.   *Who* and *whom* are used for people. Sometimes, sentiment may make a writer use *who* when referring to a pet or some object he or she thinks of as having a personality (ships, the earth, the sea, countries, and so on), but normally *that* and *which* are used for animals and objects.

3.   *Whose* is a special case. It can replace only a possessive in the base sentence. Here is an example of its use:

> Helen was the daughter of Zeus.
> ~~Helen~~'s beauty caused the Trojan War. *whose*
> *Helen, <u>whose beauty caused the Trojan War,</u> was the daughter of Zeus.*

Because *Helen's* is a possessive word, it needs to be replaced with the possessive subordination signal, *whose*. Here is another example:

> *Whose*
> ~~Gary~~'s car was stolen Tuesday.
> Gary broke his leg running for the bus Wednesday.
> *Gary, <u>whose car was stolen Tuesday,</u> broke his leg running for the bus Wednesday.*

4.   *Whom* is also a special case. It is used to replace an object in the base sentence, as the combination below shows.

> *whom.*
> The principal suspended ~~Zeke~~.
> Zeke returned with his attorney.
> *Zeke, <u>whom the principal suspended,</u> returned with his attorney.*

Because *Zeke* is the object of the verb *suspended*, you need to use the object form of the subordination signal to replace it. Here is another example of the use of *whom*, this time in a modifier phrase.

> *whom*
> We had dealt with Mr. ~~McCarthy~~ before.
> We bought our car from Mr. McCarthy.
> *We bought our car from Mr. McCarthy, <u>with whom we had dealt before.</u>*

5.   When the *who, which, whom,* or *whose* group interrupts the flow of the sentence to give the reader some extra information, it is placed between commas, as in the examples. (Cases where commas are not needed will be discussed later in this chapter.)

EXERCISE C

Underline the subordinate word group once and the base sentence twice in each sentence below. Draw an arrow to the word in the base sentence modified by each subordinate word group. Notice the punctuation pattern in each of these sentences.

1. The manufacturer, who is very reliable, sent me a refund immediately.
2. The shrimp salad, which I usually order, was not available.
3. The contest, which I entered on the spur of the moment, paid off handsomely.
4. The soldiers, who wore Revolutionary War uniforms, led the parade to the State House.
5. Jill, whose face was angelic, threw the first pie.
6. Sheriff Wayne, whom Martin had shot, swore revenge.
7. Waikiki, which was once a sparsely settled jungle peninsula, now hosts a million visitors a year.
8. Elizabeth Cochrane, whose pen name was Nellie Bly, opened the door to journalism for women.
9. Jonathan Swift was one of the most powerful satirists who ever lived.
10. Birds communicate with songs that send messages of warning or seduction to other members of their species.

EXERCISE D

Combine each pair of sentences below using first the *whom* signal and then the *who* signal as shown in parentheses.

EXAMPLE:

I mourn for the soldiers. (*whom*)

The soldiers died in Vietnam. (*who*)

A. *The soldiers for whom I mourn died in Vietnam.*

B. *I mourn for the soldiers who died in Vietnam.*

1. Liam had never before dated the girl. (*whom*)
   The girl asked Liam to the movies. (*who*)

   A. _____

   B. _____

2. Bernie translated the passage for the professor. (*whom*)
   The professor was a stickler for accuracy. (*who*)

A. _____

B. _____

3. We had warned Phil. (*whom*)
   Phil went ahead and tried the slope anyway. (*who*)

   A. _____

   B. _____

4. Father Egan is a charismatic priest. (*who*)
   The parishioners of St. James Church love Father Egan. (*whom*)

   A. _____

   B. _____

5. India owes much to Mohandas Gandhi. (*whom*)
   Gandhi dedicated his life to upholding human dignity. (*who*)

   A. _____

   B. _____

EXERCISE E

Combine each of the following sets of sentences using *who, which, that, whom,* or *whose.* In some cases, you may be asked to give two different versions of the sentence, each emphasizing a different idea. Remember to put commas around the interrupting word groups to focus attention on the base sentence.

EXAMPLE:

Henry James wrote about Americans in Europe.

Henry James lived most of his life in England.

A. (subordinate where he lived)

   Henry James, who lived most of his life in England, wrote about Americans in Europe.

B. (subordinate what he wrote about)

   Henry James, who wrote about Americans in Europe, lived most of his life in England.

1. Lydia was heavily tattooed.
   Lydia became the subject of a famous song.

   A. (Subordinate her being tatooed.)

   _____

   _____

B. (Subordinate her becoming the subject of a song.)

_____

_____

2. Harold's parents don't approve of gambling.
    Harold has taken a job in Atlantic City's biggest casino.

_____

_____

3. The Amazon starts high in the Andes.
    The Amazon is the world's second longest river.

    A. (Subordinate its origin)

_____

_____

    B. (Subordinate its length)

_____

_____

4. I met Herbie in a biology lab. (_whom_)
    Herbie is our star quarterback.

_____

_____

5. The Himalayas were pushed up when India collided with Asia.
    The Himalayas include some of the highest mountains on earth.

    A. (Subordinate how the Himalayas were formed.)

_____

_____

    B. (Subordinate what the Himalayas include.)

_____

_____

6. The Dog-Star rises with the sun in August.
    The ancients thought the Dog-Star was the cause of the scorching heat.

_____

_____

7. Old Fez has changed little since feudal times.
    Old Fez is in Northern Morocco.

    A. (Subordinate the location of Old Fez.)

_____

_____

B. (Subordinate the lack of change.)

_____

_____

8. The moon's surface is covered with craters.
   The moon is too small to have a protective atmosphere.

_____

_____

9. The tiny room was filled with people.
   The room's atmosphere was stifling.
   The people wanted to audition for the part.

_____

_____

10. St. John wrote the Apocalypse.
    Many scholars call St. John a mystic.
    The Apocalypse tells of a new creation at the end of time.

_____

_____

PUNCTUATING SUBORDINATE WORD GROUPS

As you saw in earlier exercises, you can use punctuation to keep the reader's attention focused on the base sentence. Thus, you put commas around any subordinate word group that interrupts the flow of the sentence. Some subordinate word groups, however, do not interrupt even though they come in the middle of the base sentence. They are, in fact, necessary parts of the base sentence. They narrow or make particular the meaning of some part of the base sentence they modify, as in this sentence:

> People who have violent tempers shouldn't marry.

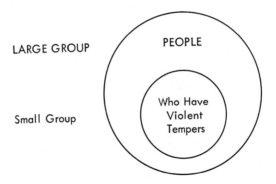

The subordinate word group *who have violent tempers* narrows down the meaning of *people* from a broad group to a smaller group. It is not an interruption, but an important, necessary part of the sentence. Without it, the sentence does not mean the same thing.

Subordinate word groups that narrow rather than interrupt *do not* get set off by commas.

Interrupting and *narrowing* word groups are not always easy to distinguish. You must look closely at the purpose of their use. Compare these two sentences:

Alcatraz, which is in San Francisco Bay, was a famous federal prison.
Any team that loses three games in a row needs more practice.

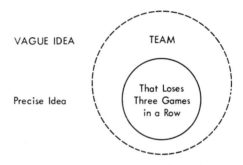

In the first, the word modified, *Alcatraz*, doesn't need narrowing down to be identified correctly: there is only one Alcatraz; no confusion is possible. The subordinate word group, therefore, is extra information *interrupting* the sentence. (Read it out loud; you will hear the interruption.)

In the second sentence, the word modified, *team*, is vague. You have to explain what kind of team you are talking about, so you *narrow* down to a particular kind of team: one that has lost three games in a row. This word group is not an interruption but a meaningful part of the flow of the sentence. (Read this one without the subordinate word group. Is the meaning the same as before?)

Look at another example.

Penguins that live in Antarctica are relatively large.
Penguins, which are flightless birds, have unusual nesting habits.

In the first sentence, you have taken the general group of penguins and narrowed it down to the smaller group of penguins that live in Antarctica (as opposed to Tierra del Fuego, New Zealand, or the Falklands—other penguin habitats). Only penguins in this group are large. Penguins living elsewhere may be small. In the second sentence, you are not narrowing down: *all* penguins, the whole group, are flightless birds. You are simply choosing to get in the information about flightlessness by interrupting the sentence.

As you may have noticed in the examples above, the signal *that* is usually used with narrowing subordinate word groups. The signal *which* is used with interrupting subordinate word groups.

When a narrowing subordinate word group has its object replaced by *whom* or *that*, the signal is often omitted from the sentence as the examples below illustrate.

The messenger never came.
You were expecting the m~~essen~~ger. *whom*

The messenger (whom) you were expecting never came.

The boots cost plenty.
She bought the b~~oot~~s yesterday. *that*

The boots (that) she bought yesterday cost plenty.

In sentences like these, where *whom* or *that* replaces the object in a narrowing word group, you can omit the signal word as long as no confusion results from the omission.

To summarize, when the subordinate word group is used to narrow a vague word or a general group down to a specific case, you are *not* interrupting the sentence and *no* commas should be used.

EXERCISE F

Identify the subordinate word groups in the following sentences and label each as *I* (Interrupting) or *N* (Narrowing) in the blank. Insert commas in the sentences that are interrupted.

_____ 1. Mary who can't stand the sight of blood fainted.

_____ 2. Paintings that are done on walls are called murals.

_____ 3. My cousin Arthur who lives in Dubuque flies jumbo jets.

_____ 4. Only shells that are unusual fetch high prices.

_____ 5. The news that Jane had left him broke his heart.

_____ 6. *The Wizard of Oz* which was made in 1939 is a classic musical.

_____ 7. Our team which has a winning record may go to a bowl game.

_____ 8. People who live in glass houses shouldn't throw stones.

_____ 9. Trees that lose their leaves in winter are deciduous.

_____ 10. Anyone who wants to run for political office should have her head examined.

EXERCISE G

In Exercise E, all the subordinate word groups were interrupting. In the following combining exercise, you are given both kinds of groups. You must decide what kind you are dealing with. Combine the following sentences and punctuate appropriately.

1. Claudia tried to stay calm.
    Claudia's face showed her surprise.

    _____

    _____

2. The party lasted three days.
    We had the party to celebrate our wedding.

    _____

    _____

3. The song drives me crazy.
    Burger King uses that song in its advertising.

    _____

    _____

4. Utah prairie dogs are an endangered species.
    Utah prairie dogs are small, burrow-building rodents.

    _____

    _____

5. Elmer Fudd always got the worst of the deal.
    Elmer Fudd tried endlessly to capture the "wabbit."

    _____

    _____

6. People love to visit the park.
    The people live in Baltimore.
    The park looks over the Inner Harbor.

    _____

    _____

7. Mozart was an infant prodigy.
    Mozart wrote operas.
    The operas make fun of human foibles.

    _____

    _____

8. The book is full of pictures.
    You gave me the book for Christmas.

The pictures remind me of my childhood dreams.

_____

_____

9. In the TV series, Carl Sagan projects the future.
Sagan made the series last year.
Humanity can look forward to the future in the twenty-first century.

_____

_____

10. Nineveh is now dust and ruins.
Nineveh was once the center of a great empire.
The empire ruled the Near East when Rome was a village.

_____

_____

USING VERBAL SUBORDINATION SIGNALS

Another way of subordinating an idea is to use one of the three verb forms that don't show time. These verb forms are called VERBALS.

Every verb has three verbal forms, that is, forms that don't indicate the time of an action:

_to_ + verb	To speak
verb + -ing	Speaking
past participle	~~Have~~ spoken

Any of these forms may be used to make a subordinate word group.

Look at these examples:

A. My friend Sara ran to catch the bus.
   She met Jeff.
   Running to catch the bus, my friend Sara met Jeff.
   My friend Sara, _running to catch the bus,_ met Jeff.

B. Pete Thorpe was gunned down in cold blood.
   He was buried at Boot Hill.
   Gunned down in cold blood, Pete Thorpe was buried at Boot Hill.
   Pete Thorpe, _gunned down in cold blood,_ was buried at Boot Hill.

C. Mark got downtown.
   He took a cab.
   To get downtown, Mark took a cab.

First, notice the forms of the verbals. In each sentence, the subject is eliminated and the verb is changed. In the first example, the verb changes from *ran*, which tells the time of the action (in the past), to *running*, which does not. The verb in the second example, *gunned*, takes the form used with the helping verb *have*, called the past participle. (For example, in the verbs *have shown* and *have gone*, *shown* and *gone* are past participles.) Used alone, the past participle does not show when the action happened. In the last example, the verb is put in the form used with *to* (*to get*), which does not indicate any time relationship.

Second, notice the relationships among ideas in these sentences. The sentence, "Gunned down in cold blood, Pete Thorpe was buried at Boot Hill," emphasizes where Thorpe was buried by putting that idea in the base sentence. The sentence, "Buried at Boot Hill, Pete Thorpe was gunned down in cold blood," emphasizes how Thorpe died by putting that idea in the base sentence. Like other forms of subordination, a verbal modifies some part of the base sentence as an adjective or adverb. Both *buried* and *gunned down* in these examples modify *Pete Thorpe*.

Finally, notice the punctuation. As with other patterns of subordination, verbals need commas when you use them to introduce or interrupt the base sentence.

EXERCISE H

Identify the verbal subordinate word groups in each of the following sentences. Be prepared to explain how each verbal group relates to the base sentence.

1. Ardith, finishing the crossword puzzle in an hour, was bored for the rest of the day.
2. To register for classes, go to Caldwell Hall.
3. Passed over for promotion, Lewis was furious.
4. The marines killed in action received a state funeral.
5. Booming over the loudspeaker, the music excited the crowd.
6. Esteban had to study for years to become a physician.
7. Gracie will spend the evening proctoring the exams.
8. Married fifty years ago, the O'Neills are celebrating their golden anniversary this month.
9. The mosquito, buzzing in my ear, kept me awake for hours.
10. The Amish seek the freedom to preserve their simple lifestyle.

EXERCISE I

Combine the following sentences by changing one sentence to a subordinate word group that uses a verbal. Be prepared to explain which idea gets the main emphasis in your new sentence.

EXAMPLES:

A. Marcia felt like death warmed over. (*-ing*)
    Marcia dragged herself to work.
    Feeling like death warmed over, Marcia dragged herself to work.

B. *The Odyssey* was composed when Greece was young. (*composed*)
    The Odyssey is still as fresh as dawn.
    The Odyssey, composed when Greece was young, is still as fresh as dawn.

C. Tom developed his physique. (*to —*)
    Tom took hormones.
    To develop his physique, Tom took hormones.

1. The town sweltered in the heat. (*-ing*)
    The town lay open to the sun.

    _____

    _____

2. Melvin had been lost since the Blizzard of '78. (*lost*)
    Melvin wandered home yesterday.

    _____

    _____

3. Jo marked her place. (*to —*)
    Jo stuck an envelope in the book.

    _____

    _____

4. The rock had been worn by the ocean for centuries. (*worn*)
    The rock was smooth and shaped to the hand.

    _____

    _____

5. Lester sang to himself. (*-ing*)
    Lester jogged through the autumn leaves.

    _____

    _____

6. You make great lasagne. (*to —*)
    Use fresh cheese.

    _____

    _____

7. The Fertile Crescent runs from Iraq to Egypt. (*-ing*)
    The Fertile Crescent nourished the first agricultural states.

    _____

    _____

8. The University of Virginia was designed by Thomas Jefferson. (*designed*)
   The University of Virginia is a model of classical architecture.

   _____

   _____

9. Bentley inherited Lady Emmilina's fortune. (*to —*)
   Bentley slipped cyanide in Lady Emmilina's tea.

   _____

   _____

10. Lucy was detained for questioning. (*detained*)
    Lucy spilled the beans.

    _____

    _____

11. Amos published his autobiography. (*-ing*)
    Amos started a few myths.

    _____

    _____

12. Tivoli was built as an adult amusement park. (*built*)
    Tivoli stands in the center of Copenhagen.

    _____

    _____

13. Monet captured the essence of light. (*to —*)
    Monet painted with contrasting, isolated spots of color.

    _____

    _____

14. Dempsey leaped for the ball. (*-ing*)
    Dempsey made a spectacular catch.

    _____

    _____

15. Radio telescopes sweep the skies in precise patterns. (*-ing*)
    Radio telescopes listen for messages from other civilizations.

    _____

    _____

ARRANGING WORD GROUPS
WITH VERBALS

Subordinate word groups with verbals define or describe parts of the base
sentence. Since these word groups have no subjects, you must be particularly
careful about arranging them. Place them as close as possible to the part of

the base sentence they describe. If you don't, your reader may have difficulty seeing precisely what these word groups are describing, as in the following sentences:

> Growing in the front yard, we saw a rose bush. (What was growing—we or the rose bush?)
> Running down the street, my English book fell in the gutter. (Who was running—the English book?)

In the first case, all that is needed is some rearranging. Put the subordinate word group next to rose bush, and the sentence becomes clear:

> We saw a rose bush growing in the front yard.

The second is harder. No part of the base sentence performed the action. You must change either the subordinate word group or the base sentence:

> As I was running down the street, my English book fell in the gutter.
> Running down the street, I dropped my English book in the gutter.

EXERCISE J

Expand each of the following word groups either by completing the idea with a base sentence or by making the idea more precise with an appropriate verbal subordinate word group. Be very careful that every verbal group can attach itself logically to some part of the base sentence. Place the verbal subordinate word group next to the part it modifies.

EXAMPLES:

A. Filling two notebooks . . .

Filling two notebooks, Dr. McFarland's journal explained his theory in detail.

B. *The animals died in a matter of moments.*

Exposed to the dangerous drug, the animals died in a matter of moments.

1. To explore space, _____.

2. Preparing for war, _____.

3. _____, they moved the furniture into the den.

4. Signed by the governor, _____.

5. _____, Meredith was named Most Valuable Player.

6. To save the city, _____.

7. Swinging on the gate, _____.

8. Created by George Lucas, _____.

9. _____, the knights prepared for the battle.

10. To double his investment, _____.

11. Loaded with 150 pounds of groceries, _____.

12. _____, he waited for silence in the room.

13. Loafing all afternoon, _____.

14. Founded in 1927, _____.

15. _____, her father shouted encouragement.

16. To raise his grade, _____.

17. Handing over the money, _____.

18. _____, several companies bid on the job.

19. Leaping over the net, _____.

20. _____, I had trouble seeing.

REVIEW OF METHODS OF SUBORDINATION

When you use the technique of subordination, you often have a choice of one or more of the methods discussed in this chapter. For example, suppose you wanted to write about these two ideas:

Walter intends to climb the face of El Capitan.
Walter practices every weekend.

You could combine these ideas with an adverb subordination signal:

Because Walter intends to climb the face of El Capitan,
he practices every weekend.

You could also combine these ideas with an adjective subordination signal:

Walter, who intends to climb the face of El Capitan,
practices every weekend.

Or you could combine these ideas with a verbal subordinate word group:

Intending to climb the face of El Capitan, Walter prac-
tices every weekend.

Each of these sentences is built on the same base—Walter practices every weekend—but the subordinate idea can be expressed in a number of ways.

WAYS TO SUBORDINATE IDEAS

1. **Attach an adverb subordination signal to the front of a sentence:**

   The defendant lost the case.

   ↓

   because the defendant lost the case

   ↓

   Because the defendant lost the case, he was ruined.

2. **Replace one word in the sentence with *who*, *whose*, *whom*, *which*, or *that*:**

   The defendant lost the case

   ↓

   who lost the case

   ↓

   The defendant, who lost the case, was ruined.

3. **Remove the subject and change the verb to a verbal:**

   The defendant lost the case

   ↓

   losing the case

   ↓

   Losing the case, the defendant was ruined.

EXERCISE K

Combine each of the following sets of sentences in two different ways. Each version of your sentence should use a different method of subordination. Be prepared to identify the base sentence in each version and to explain the relationship between the base sentence and the subordinate word group.

1. The summer session lasts six weeks.
   The summer session requires a lot of work.

A. _____

_____

B. _____

_____

2. Godzilla has grown to full size.
   Godzilla can devour whole skyscrapers.

   A. _____

   _____

   B. _____

   _____

3. Anne pushed the wrong button.
   She erased two months' work.

   A. _____

   _____

   B. _____

   _____

4. We want to boast about humanity to possible audiences in space.
   We could transmit the music of Bach.

   A. _____

   _____

   B. _____

   _____

5. *The New English Bible* is written in a clear, elegant style.
   The New English Bible is the work of scholars from around the world.

   A. _____

   _____

   B. _____

   _____

6. The pyramids are one of the Seven Wonders of the World.
   Generations of Egyptians worked on the pyramids.

   A. _____

   _____

   B. _____

   _____

7. Timbuktu became a great trading center.
   It lies on the caravan route to North Africa.

   A. _____

   _____

   B. _____

   _____

8. Television has great potential.
   Television has remained disappointing.

   A. _____

   _____

   B. _____

   _____

9. Juana left home at an early age.
   She wanted independence.

   A. _____

   _____

   B. _____

   _____

10. A hideous scream filled the air.
    It came from the dungeon.
    No one had opened the dungeon's door for twenty years.

    A. _____

    _____

    B. _____

    _____

11. Life is wrung from the sea with endless work.
    Life is hard for the villagers.
    The villagers live on this treeless island.

    A. _____

    _____

    B. _____

    _____

12. Claire worked day and night.
    Claire finished her report.
    The report points out several marketing opportunities.

    A. _____

_____

    B. _____

_____

13. Salmon swim upstream.
Salmon find their birthplace.
Salmon spawn and die.

    A. _____

_____

    B. _____

_____

14. Cuthbert's work was shoddy.
The boss couldn't fire him.
Cuthbert knew too much.

    A. _____

_____

    B. _____

_____

15. Alma loves mystery stories.
Alma is suspicious of everybody.
The mystery stories involve deep intrigue.

    A. _____

_____

    B. _____

_____

EXERCISE L

Combine the following sentences using any techniques of coordination or subordination you think are appropriate. Underline the base sentence or sentences in each finished version.

1. Sabrina lowered her paw.
She stared at the window.
She was rapt.

_____

_____

2. Lester and Laura Hicks settled in this valley.
    They came in 1848.
    They cleared the land for an orchard.
    They raised their children.

    _____

    _____

3. Joyce has trouble reading.
    She passed English.
    She is a hard worker.
    She showed the teacher she cared.

    _____

    _____

4. Moslem armies swept out of Arabia.
    They were motivated by faith.
    They reached southern France.
    They were beaten by Charles Martel.

    _____

    _____

5. Knife blades used to be made from carbon steel.
    Carbon steel holds a sharp edge.
    Carbon steel rusts.
    Carbon steel pits.
    Carbon steel stains.

    _____

    _____

6. Later knife blades were made from stainless steel.
    Stainless steel will remain shiny through years of use.
    Stainless steel cannot hold a sharp edge.

    _____

    _____

7. The best blades today are made from high-carbon stainless steel.
    It will hold an edge.
    It is easily resharpened.
    It will not rust.

    _____

    _____

8. Itzhak Perlman is a concert violinist.
    He wants to be photographed.

He enters the stage on crutches.
He wants to encourage other physically handicapped people.

_____

_____

9. Most contractors are honest.
    They are hardworking.
    They are highly skilled.
    A few are con artists.
    They prey on unsuspecting homeowners.

_____

_____

10. The Pioneer spacecraft sent back pictures.
    The pictures were marvelous.
    The pictures were of Jupiter.
    Jupiter hung like a huge ball.
    The ball was orange.
    The hanging was in the sky.
    The sky was black.

_____

_____

EXERCISE M

Expand the following sentences by adding a second sentence to each.
First coordinate the two ideas. Then subordinate the sentence you added.

EXAMPLE:

Toni was an ideal candidate.

Coordinate: *Toni was an ideal candidate, but Martin's views were too radical.*

Subordinate: *Although Martin's views were too radical, Toni was an ideal candidate.*

1. Robert Frost wrote about New England.

    CO _____

    _____

    SUB _____

    _____

2. I signed the petition.

   CO _____

   _____

   SUB _____

3. Sue wrote the report on the marina.

   CO _____

   _____

   SUB _____

4. The shoes were expensive.

   CO _____

   _____

   SUB _____

5. The pastor announced the next hymn.

   CO _____

   _____

   SUB _____

6. Hearst's blue eyes were cold.

   CO _____

   _____

   SUB _____

7. It took a month to unpack the books.

   CO _____

   _____

   SUB _____

8. The accident victim recovered.

   CO _____

   _____

SUB _____

_____

9. Last year, the parts division showed a 15 percent increase in profits.

CO _____

_____

SUB _____

_____

10. The Norwegian skiers placed third in the cross-country race.

CO _____

_____

SUB _____

_____

EDITING PRACTICE

Read the following paragraphs carefully, checking for any errors in using the writing techniques presented thus far. Make sure that each sentence is complete. Make sure that subjects and verbs agree. Make sure that coordinate and subordinate word groups are correctly punctuated.

Underline any errors you find and then recopy the paragraph, correcting those errors.

1.   Max who is trying to win the Mr. Teenage New Mexico title go to the gym every day. After changing into his workout clothes his routine for the day begins. Mondays Wednesdays and Fridays, he works his calves thighs back and arms, Tuesdays Thursdays and Saturdays he concentrates on his stomach. Which is his weakest feature and his chest. The exercises, that he does for his stomach definition, involves repeated twisting. With a bar across his shoulders. Either his arms or his chest take an award in every contest, he enters, if he can just improve his stomach he will have a good chance at the title, he covets.

2.   Almost no other city in the world to match the incredibly rich cultural life, of New York. Art abound here. The vast Metropolitan Museum of Art whose collection covers 5,000 years of culture demands several return visits in addition, the Museum of Modern Art the world's most outstanding modern art exhibits. New York's visual art treasures being truly dazzling however the performing arts sparkle too. From the Metropolitan Opera and the New York City Ballet to the Newport Jazz Festival and the Alvin Ailey Dance Company. Music and dance lovers will find something in New York to satisfy every taste. New York's theaters as everyone know, are also unrivaled.

Although the Broadway plays are the most famous the off-Broadway stages often present exciting and innovative drama. For people, who are interested in culture, a trip to New York is like a visit to paradise.

WRITING PRACTICE

1.   For its special Back-to-School issue, *Family Circle* magazine has asked a number of people, including you, to contribute a short piece about a first-day-of-school memory.

Before you write, close your eyes and think about your first day of kindergarten, elementary school, high school, or college. What scene comes to your mind? What do you see, hear, taste, touch, and smell in that scene? Make some notes about the details of that scene. What is the main impression you want your readers to have of the scene you are describing? Use those sensory details in your writing to make the scene vivid for the readers of *Family Circle.* Try to use the techniques of coordination and subordination to keep your readers' attention focused on one main impression of the experience.

When you have written a draft of your memory of a first day of school, go back and check your sentences to see that they are complete and correctly punctuated.

2.   In your psychology class, you have been discussing inheritance of personality traits. Your teacher has asked you to show how this applies in your family by comparing yourself to some other member of your family with whom you think you share personality traits. Or you may show a case where the theory doesn't apply by contrasting yourself with some member of your family.

Before writing, make a list of some of your main personality traits. Then try to match each quality with a similar or an opposite quality of another person in your family. Choose three or four of your best examples to develop your paragraph. Try to use the techniques of coordination and subordination to focus your reader's attention on the similarities or differences you are discussing.

When you have composed a draft of your paragraph, go back and check your sentences to see that they are complete and correctly punctuated.

5

Practice in Sentence Combining

In the preceding chapters, you have practiced various ways of constructing sentences to express thoughts more precisely and to make the relationships between ideas clearer to your reader. You have practiced modifying the different elements in a sentence (subject, verb, complement); you have coordinated sentences and parts of sentences; you have tried out different kinds of subordination.

This chapter contains more exercises in writing sentences. The first sections provide a review of the techniques you have studied. Since you are already familiar with these various kinds of combining, the models provided in these sections are *not* intended to show you all the techniques reviewed in the exercises, but rather to remind you of some of them.

If you run into a type of sentence combination not shown in the model and you are unsure of the options you have, turn back to the chapter where the related techniques were introduced and review the models and exercises to discover the choices you can make. Compare your choices with those of your classmates.

ADDING TO THE BASIC SENTENCE

EXERCISE A

MODELS:

A.   ADJECTIVES

John sent a message.

The sending was to his neighbor.

The message was threatening.

The neighbor lives next door.

John sent a threatening message to his next-door neighbor.

B. ADVERBS

Salome danced.

Her dancing was provocative.

Her dancing was before Herod.

Salome danced provocatively before Herod.

1. A *black hole* is an object.
   The object has density.
   The object is mysterious.
   Its density is almost unbelievable.
   The object is in space.

2. Neon gives streets a look.
   The streets are in the city.
   The look is flashy.
   The look is unreal.
   The giving is at night.

3. American cars grew.
   They grew faster.
   They grew longer.
   They grew gaudier.
   All this happened during the fifties.

4. The archeologist said he saw things.
   The things were wonderful.
   He saw them through a hole.
   The hole was in the door.

5. Autumn turns the woods to colors.
   The colors are bright.
   The colors are reds.
   The colors are golds.
   The colors are yellows.
   This happens in one week.
   The week is magic.

6. General Washington used ink.
   It was used during the Revolutionary War.
   The ink was invisible.
   He used it for messages.
   The messages were secret.

7. Greece gave ideas to civilization.
   Greece was ancient.
   The civilization was Western.
   The ideas were important.
   The ideas were many.

8. Spiders dissolve.
> Their prey is dissolved.
> The dissolving is done with juices.
> The juices are poisonous.
> The dissolving takes place before eating.

9. The empire had vanished.
> The empire was enormous.
> The empire belonged to Genghis Khan.
> The vanishing happened within a few generations.
> The generations were after Khan's death.
> Khan's death was in 1227.

10. The beach stretches.
> The beach is below Assateague.
> The stretching goes for miles and miles.
> The beach is white.
> The beach is clean.
> The stretching is under a sky.
> The sky is cloudless.

MORE PRACTICE IN COORDINATION

EXERCISE B

MODEL:

A. It was only January.
> Winter seemed eternal. (*and* – *but*)

It was only January, and winter seemed eternal.

It was only January, but winter seemed eternal.

Analysis: Both sentences are making a comparison between the *actual* time (only January) and the length of time that it *seems* (eternal). *But* emphasizes the contrast between real time and felt time.

B. Harold's aunt is very rich.
> Harold does what she says. (; – *so*)

Harold's aunt is very rich; Harold does what she says.

Harold's aunt is very rich, so Harold does what she says.

Analysis: Both sentences express a cause and effect. The semicolon only implies the relationship. The *so* makes it explicit.

1. Winter teaches us about hope.
> Spring gives us satisfaction. (; – *so*)

2. Money talks.
> Hunger is quiet. (*but* – *so*)

3. Kevin likes herbal shampoo.
   Denise buys only fruit-scented shampoos. (*and – however*)

4. My sister always said I should marry a Gemini.
   Geminis are so tolerant. (*; – for*)

5. Morning rush hour is awful.
   Evening rush hour is just as bad. (*; – but*)

6. The Declaration says, "All men are created equal."
   The Constitution originally allowed slavery.

7. Biology is the science of life.
   Physics is the science of matter.

8. Evolution is a long, painstaking process.
   Revolution is quicker and sharper.

9. Africa is old.
   It is divided.
   It is changing.

10. According to legend, Jesse James was an American Robin Hood.
    In reality, he was a thief and a callous killer.

MORE PRACTICE IN SUBORDINATION

EXERCISE C

MODELS:

A. George drove for 48 hours straight. (*after, while-ing*)
   George fell sound asleep.

After George drove for 48 hours straight, he fell sound asleep.

While driving for 48 hours straight, George fell sound asleep.

Analysis: Both sentences deal with cause and effect. In the first, George may have made it to the rest stop *before* dozing off. In the second, he is in serious trouble: he is sleeping *while* driving.

B. John likes Margo. (*because*)
   Margo likes John. (*because*)

Because John likes Margo, she likes him.

John likes Margo because she likes him.

Analysis: Both sentences deal with cause and effect. In the first, Margo is the one responding to John's affection; in the second, John is the one responding to affection.

1. My cat adores me. (*because*)
   I feed her specially prepared meals. (*because*)

2. He spent his lifetime working in a bank. (*since, although*)
   He never made much money.

3. Joe selects his ingredients carefully. (*who*)
   Joe knows his stew is worth the trouble. (*-ing*)
4. Envy reared its ugly head. (*-ing*)
   Envy ruined everything. (*-ing*)
5. Nellie liked nice things. (*even though, -ing*)
   Nellie married Stanley.
6. Ulysses wandered for ten years. (*-ing*)
   Ulysses searched for his home island of Ithaca. (*-ing*)
7. Winston has lived in Italy for thirty years.
   Winston loves spaghetti.
8. Middle Eastern cities controlled the caravan routes to Asia.
   Middle Eastern cities were ruined by the discovery of new sea routes.
9 Sharp cold freezes the sugar in the leaves.
   The leaves change from green to the colors of fall.
10. Lydia has always spoken her mind.
    Lydia is an assistant manager.
11. Galileo perfected the telescope.
    Galileo made many important discoveries about the planets.
12. Romantic heroines are always beautiful and helpless.
    Romantic heroines are popular with romantic heroes.
13. Mr. Harrison owns several apartments in the city.
    Mr. Harrison is fairly wealthy.
14. Thelma fell lifeless beside the corpse.
    Thelma saw the serpent.
    The serpent had bitten Brent.
15. Franklin boiled over.
    Franklin screamed at the kid.
    The kid's car had crushed Franklin's fender.

COORDINATION / SUBORDINATION

EXERCISE D

MODEL:
The Nile waters the Valley of Egypt.
> The Nile flows out of the heart of Africa. (*-ing*) (*;*)

The river's flooding deposits soil along the banks.
> The depositing makes agriculture possible. (*-ing*)

Flowing out of the heart of Africa, the Nile waters the Valley of Egypt; the river's flooding deposits soil along the banks, making agriculture possible.

Note: The signal for coordinating the sentences is given after the first set of sentences. Thus, in the model, the ; appears to the right of the sentence "The Nile flows out of the heart of Africa" and appears *after* the whole first sentence, joining it to the second.

1. Evelyn lives in a big house.
    The house is near the woods. (*so*)
Evelyn is able to keep a kennel.

2. The swordsmith strikes the steel.
    He keeps time with a gong. (*-ing*) (*;*)
A priest sounds the gong.
    He chants to set his rhythm. (*-ing*)

3. Some small, feathered dinosaurs survived.
    The big dinosaurs died. (*when*) (*;*)
Scientists think these creatures were the ancestors of birds.

4. Brandon left Marilyn.
    Brandon was aware of her cheating. (*because*) (*but*)
Brandon went to Barbara.
    Barbara was worse than Marilyn was. (*who*)

5. Linda wanted a clone.
    The clone resembles her completely. (*-ing*) (*however*)
Many thought one Linda was enough.

6.   Ms. Brown has watched Yvonne. (*after*)
    Yvonne has sashayed in late all semester. (*-ing*)
Ms. Brown won't get mad. (*;*)
Ms. Brown will get even.

7. The Sahara was once a great savanna.
    The savanna was filled with antelope and ostriches.
    The Sahara stretches from the Red Sea to the Atlantic. (*-ing*)
(*but*)
The Sahara dried out slowly.
    The drying out trapped many animals. (*-ing*)

8. Mr. Mikulski runs a bakery.
    The bakery is on Lombard Street.
Mr. Mikulski has served his neighborhood.
    He has done this for forty years.
    His neighborhood is Polish and Lithuanian.

9. Harper stared along the barrel of his gun.
    Harper sighted Dandridge.
    Dandridge tried to scramble up the hillside.
Harper fired.
    The shot hit home.
    The shot started a small avalanche.

10. The Snow Queen put a splinter of ice in Hans's eye.
    The Queen wanted to keep him.
    The splinter made Hans completely unemotional.
Hans left home.
    Hans forgot his family and friends.

11. Atlanta has become the finance capital of the South.
    Atlanta has grown rapidly since the Depression.
Atlanta's first big money came from Coca-Cola.
    Coca-Cola is the world's most popular drink.

12. Many colleges are pinched.
    The pinching is financial.
Evening courses generate income.
    Part-time instructors teach these courses.
    These instructors receive no fringe benefits.

13. *Hamlet* is one of the world's most popular plays.
    It is long.
    It is difficult to stage.
Certain theatergoers like Shakespeare's drama.
    These theatergoers enjoy a challenge.

14. The Appalachians are among the oldest mountains on Earth.
    They run from New England to Alabama.
They are low, rounded, and tree-covered.
    They have been eroded by wind and water.

15. The panda has an unusual thumb.
    The thumb has evolved from a bone in the wrist.
It is used to strip leaves from bamboo shoots.
    Bamboo shoots are the panda's main food.

FREE EXERCISES

EXERCISE E

Use these sets of sentences to practice different ways of showing relationships among ideas. Be prepared to explain why you made the choices you did.

1. The National Road runs from Maryland to Ohio.
   It helped open the Old Northwest to Americans.
   This happened after the Revolution.
   The Road goes through the Cumberland Gap.

2. Copernicus was a Polish scientist.
   He moved the Earth.
   It was moved out of the center of the universe.
   He replaced it with the sun.

3. The Red Shift is a natural phenomenon.
   It measures the speed of some stars.
   These stars are moving away from Earth.

4. Evelyn takes wonderful pictures.
   The pictures are of animals.
   The animals are in the wild.
   The animals are in captivity.

5. Francis Scott Key wrote the National Anthem.
   He was imprisoned in Fort McHenry.
   The King's troops were shelling the fort.
   They wanted to capture Baltimore.

6. Immigrants came to this country.
   They came from every part of the world.
   They came to escape famine and unemployment.
   American farmlands and industry offered them hope.

7. There was no spring for centuries.
   This happened in Europe and much of Asia.
   This happened during the Ice Ages.
   No buds opened.

8. Dante wrote the *Divine Comedy*.
   He was in exile in Ravenna.
   He describes a journey through Hell to Heaven.
   The *Comedy* is the greatest poem of the Middle Ages.

9. Tides are caused by the moon's gravity.
   The gravity tugs at the oceans.
   The gravity makes a huge bulge of water.

10. *The Twentieth Century* was a train.
    It ran from New York to Los Angeles.
    It brought stars to Hollywood.
    Many stars made their names on Broadway.
    This happened back in the thirties.

11. It is still possible to get lost in Toledo.
    Toledo is the ancient capital of Spain.
    It is one of the most romantic cities in the world.
    Its streets are narrow.
    Its streets are winding.

12. Vincent wants to be a carpenter.
    He loves working with his hands.
    His mother wants him to be an ophthalmologist.
    She dreams of calling him doctor.

13. An early civilization was built on the Indus River.
    We know little about it.
    It had an advanced plumbing system.
    It employed a network of dams and canals.

14. Many science fiction writers lack political imagination.
They fill the future with emperors and princesses.
They can't picture democracy among the galaxies.

15. The mustang ran swiftly.
He led the herd.
They galloped in terror.
The hunters pursued them.
Their hoofbeats echoed off the canyon walls.

16. The Museum is next to the Brandywine.
It is in an old mill.
It has paintings by the Wyeths.

17. Alice told Bill about Carol.
Carol had left George.
George was Bill's best friend.
Carol took all George's record albums.

18. Twenty inches of snow fell.
It fell in 8 hours.
It blocked the city streets.
It brought all traffic to a halt.

19. Somewhere a dog was barking.
A shadow crept along the wall.
A shot rang out.
A woman's voice screamed.

20. The evil sisters laughed at Cinderella.
She was dressed in rags.
She was miserable.
They were going to a ball.

21. Venice is sinking.
It is sliding into the lagoon.
The lagoon once protected it from enemies.
Venice is built on islands in a marsh.

22. The tumbleweed rolled.
It ran into the steps of the old church.
The church's windows had been shot out.

23. They were giant ants.
Nuclear radiation made them monsters.
They got into the drains under Los Angeles.

24. The woman played the guitar.
She sang.
Her mother beat on a bucket turned over her knee.
They won the talent show.

25. The rain splattered on the window.
The cat purred.
The fire glowed.

The writer ran a pencil down the paper.
A poem appeared.

26. The figure walked in the rain.
The car headlights lit the figure.
The figure turned.
The figure stuck out its thumb.

27. Michael plays the guitar.
Michael sings sad songs.
Michael paints vaguely obscene pictures.
Life has passed Michael by.

28. Taos is a small town.
It is in the New Mexico mountains.
It is north of Santa Fe.
It is an artists' colony.

29. Arctic foxes scavenge across hundreds of miles.
They look for food.
The miles are of frozen waste.
Scientists are not sure how they survive.

30. Paris stole Helen.
She was the wife of the king of Sparta.
The king followed them to Troy.
Troy was destroyed.

31. The pendulum swung closer.
It cut the air.
It whistled.
The victim listened.
The pendulum had a knife-edge.
The victim was terrified.

32. Reading makes an informed mind.
Conversation makes a quick mind.
Writing makes a precise mind.

33. Danny owns a diner.
He serves cheeseburgers.
He serves soda.
He can't boil water.

34. Cows are sacred in India.
Cows provide labor.
Cows provide milk.
Families sometimes eat cows.
This happens in famines.
Afterwards, these families are poorer.

35. The rain is falling.
The snow is melting.
Our basement is flooding.
Our washer just floated by.

36. Christopher was an orphan.
He was nasty.
A snake ate him.
Everybody was relieved.

37. Julie loves Dennis.
She cooks for him.
She keeps house.
She works full-time.
Dennis never considers Julie's feelings.
Julie is leaving Dennis.

38. China has a 4,000-year history.
Historians study China's history.
They find that every year a disaster occurred.
The disasters were famines.
The disasters were plagues.

39. The batter swung hard.
He twisted his body.
He let go of the bat.
The bat almost hit the umpire.
The umpire called, "Strike three!"

40. Crocuses bloom.
They thrust above the snow.
They are yellow and blue.
The snow is half-melted.
This all happens in the spring.

PATTERN IMITATION

EXERCISE F

In the following exercise, you will create your own sentences, on any subject of your choosing, imitating the sentences given.

EXAMPLE:
When winter comes, the bears hibernating in their warm caves sleep like contented children.

Imitation: When night comes, the taxis cruising the city streets scatter like frightened birds.

1. In the middle of this family party lay a cat with its paws tucked under its chest and its eyes closed in complete relaxation.

2. Spencer was a big spender, but when he died, the funeral was cheap.

3. During the night there fell a fine snow, which covered the clearings and stretched out on the branches of the pines.

4. We valued our days for their activity and our nights for their freedom.

5. From time to time, she closes herself in her room, types furiously, and creates a children's story.

6. Vic wanted to get away from home not because he disliked his family, but because he longed for experience.

7. Jazz is loose and it is unplanned, but it is not shapeless and it is not senseless.

8. Children aren't easily impressed; special effort is required to catch their imaginations.

9. I hum a bit and croon some, but when I go for a high note, my voice cracks.

10. The great wars and tyrants get all the press coverage, but it is the millions of quiet lives that shape history.

PROFESSIONALS' SENTENCES

EXERCISE G

The following sentences are taken from the writings of professionals. The originals have been broken down so you can try reassembling them. Compare your results with the professionals' solutions found at the end of the chapter. What are the differences? Can you account for the choices you made and those the professionals made? If your solutions differ from those of the professionals, yours are not necessarily *wrong*. The professionals are responding to particular situations, and their choices are offered as possibilities, not *answers*.

1. A man sat.
   His hands were clenched.
   His hands rested on his knees.
   His eyes were bent.
   The bending was on the ground.
   The sitting was amidst a scene.
   The scene was sordid.

2. Sage brush is a very fair fuel.
   Sage brush is a distinguished failure.
   Its failure is as a vegetable.

3. There stood a geranium.
   It stood on the window seat.
   It was diseased with yellow blotches.
   The blotches had overspread its leaves.

4. The songs told a tale.
    The tale was of woe.
    The tale was then altogether beyond comprehension.
    The comprehension was mine.
    The comprehension was feeble.
They were tones.
    The tones were loud.
    The tones were long.
    The tones were deep.
They breathed the prayer of souls.
They breathed the complaint of souls.
    The souls were boiling over with anguish.
    The anguish was the bitterest.

5. Significant events are measured in years or less.
    These events are in our personal lives.
Our lifetimes are measured in decades.
Our family genealogies are measured in centuries.
All of recorded history is measured in millenia.

6. They were careless people.
    The people were Tom and Daisy.
They smashed up things.
They smashed up creatures.
Then they retreated back into their money.
They retreated into their vast carelessness. (*or*)
They retreated into whatever it was.
    It kept them together.
They let other people clean up the mess.
    They had made the mess.

7. I went to Walden.
    My purpose was not to live cheaply there.
    My purpose was not to live dearly there.
    My purpose was to transact some business.
    The business was private.
    I wanted the fewest obstacles.

8. A city is stones.
A city is people.
It is not a heap of stones.
It is not just a jostle of people.

9. The mass will never have any zeal.
    The mass is of mankind.
    The zeal is ardent.
    The zeal is for seeing.
    The seeing is of things.
    The things are as they are.

Ideas will satisfy them.
> The ideas are very inadequate.
> This is always true.

10.   Elizabeth had no expectation of pleasure.
> Elizabeth had the strongest curiosity.

Elizabeth opened the letter.
> Her wonder was still increasing.

Elizabeth perceived an envelope.
> The envelope contained two sheets of letterpaper.
> The paper was written quite through.
> The paper was written in a very close hand.

PROFESSIONALS' CHOICES

1. Amidst this sordid scene sat a man with his clenched hands resting on his knees, and his eyes bent on the ground.

    —Charlotte Bronte, *Jane Eyre*

2. Sage brush is a very fair fuel, but as a vegetable it is a distinguished failure.

    —Mark Twain, *Roughing It*

3. On the window seat there stood a geranium diseased with yellow blotches, which had overspread its leaves.

    —Nathaniel Hawthorne, "The Birthmark"

4. The songs told a tale of woe which was then altogether beyond my feeble comprehension; they were tones loud, long, and deep; they breathed the prayer and complaint of souls boiling over with the bitterest anguish.

    —Frederick Douglass, *Narrative of the Life of Frederick Douglass, an American Slave, Written by Himself*

5. Significant events in our personal lives are measured in years or less; our lifetimes in decades; our family genealogies in centuries; and all of recorded history in millenia.

    —Carl Sagan, *The Dragons of Eden*
    Copyright © 1977 by Carl Sagan. Reprinted by permission of Random House, Inc.

6. They were careless people, Tom and Daisy—they smashed up things and creatures and then retreated back into their money or their vast carelessness, or whatever it was that kept them together, and let other people clean up the mess they had made.

    —F. Scott Fitzgerald, *The Great Gatsby*
    Charles Scribner's Sons, 1953.

7. My purpose in going to Walden Pond was not to live cheaply nor to live dearly there, but to transact some private business with the fewest obstacles.

—Henry David Thoreau, *Walden*

8. A city is stones and a city is people; but it is not a heap of stones, and it is not just a jostle of people.

—Jacob Bronowski, *The Ascent of Man*
Little, Brown and Company, 1973

9. The mass of mankind will never have any ardent zeal for seeing things as they are; very inadequate ideas will always satisfy them.

—Matthew Arnold, *The Function of Criticism*

10. With no expectation of pleasure, but with the strongest curiosity, Elizabeth opened the letter, and to her still increasing wonder, perceived an envelope containing two sheets of letterpaper, written quite through, in a very close hand.

—Jane Austen, *Pride and Prejudice*

6

Sentences in the Context of Paragraphs

So far, you have looked at various ways of putting ideas into a single sentence. However, most writing situations require more than one sentence. Therefore, you should be aware of some of the special problems of writing a series of sentences on the same subject.

PRONOUNS

As soon as you write more than one sentence on the same subject, you will probably use pronouns. Instead of *"Pete Ross* is the best coach the Thunderbolts have ever had. *Pete Ross* demands a lot of hard work from *Pete Ross's* players," you would probably write: *"Pete Ross* is the best coach the Thunderbolts have ever had. *He* demands a lot of hard work from *his* players."

The pronoun *he* can substitute for the noun *Pete Ross.* The possessive pronoun *his* can substitute for the possessive *Pete Ross's.* A pronoun, in other words, is a word that can substitute for a noun.

When you use pronouns, you have to be careful of three things:

1. A pronoun must use the form that fits its function in the sentence. (Pronoun Function)
2. A pronoun must have the same number and gender as the word it replaces. (Pronoun Agreement)
3. A pronoun must refer clearly and specifically to one word. (Pronoun Reference)

Although you don't always need to follow these rules in informal or conversational situations, most readers expect you to observe them when you write.

As you can see, then, pronouns can have many forms. Which form you use depends on what word the pronoun is replacing and how the pronoun functions in the sentence. The chart below shows the various forms that pronouns can take.

Number / Function	Singular	Plural
Subject/ Subject Complement	I, you, he, she, it	we, you, they
Object Complement/ Object of Preposition	me, you, him, her, it	us, you, them
Possessive Modifier	my, your, his, her, its	our, your, their
Possessive Subject or Complement	mine, yours, his, her, its	ours, yours, theirs

Pronoun Function

When you replace a subject or a subject complement, you must use a subject pronoun; when you replace an object complement or the object of a preposition, you must use the object form; when you replace a possessive complement, you must use the possessive complement form. For example:

$\overset{s}{Henry}$ gave the $\overset{oc}{best\ years\ of\ his\ life}$ to $\overset{op}{Sylvia}$.

$\overset{s}{He}$ gave $\overset{oc}{them}$ $\overset{op}{to\ her}$

The Danish *invaders* settled the *Danelaw* in the ninth century.
[s over invaders, oc over Danelaw]

They settled *it* in the ninth century.
[s over They, oc over it]

The *champion* was *Stella.*
[s over champion, sc over Stella, with connecting arc]

It was *she.*
[s over It, sc over she]

Those gloves are *Bruce's.*
[s over gloves, pc over Bruce's]

They are *his.*
[s over They, pc over his]

EXERCISE A

In each sentence below, replace the underlined words with an appropriate pronoun. Be prepared to explain what function the pronoun has in the sentence: subject, complement, or modifier.

EXAMPLE:

Fred picked up Lila's umbrella by mistake.
He picked up hers by mistake.

1. The pitcher twisted his knee running for the ball.
2. Students usually dislike pop quizzes.
3. My book was next to Sandy's book.
4. The winner was Alma.
5. Debbie found Debbie's sweater, but Bill couldn't find Bill's.
6. Albert and Angela lowered your and Winnie's boat carefully.
7. Don cooked a wonderful ragout for Joanne.
8. Great-aunt Constanza left the entire estate to Lucille.
9. The first reader was Mr. Teel.
10. Members must pay members' dues before members can use the club's facilities.
11. The next house is the Cohns'.
12. The monster's head was turned the other way.
13. Chin-Li and I supervised the camping trip.
14. So changed were Alice and Peter that John and I hardly recognized Alice and Peter.
15. The proposal of Becky and me would cost $10,000 less than the proposal of Elaine and you.

EXERCISE B

Rewrite each sentence below using the verb shown in parentheses. Be sure to choose an appropriate pronoun form for each new sentence.

EXAMPLE:

Joel and I have been selected by the coach to represent the team.

(has selected) *The coach has selected Joel and me to represent the team.*

1. She and Mary Lou will be escorted by Mike and him.

(will escort) _____

2. They and the Farrells were approached by the sales staff.

(approached) _____

3. We are asked by the church to give 10 percent of our income.

(asks) _____

4. The finalists will be chosen by you and me.

(will choose) _____

5. The police have rewarded Carla and him.

(have been rewarded) _____

6. She and I were trained by Morrocco the Magnificent.

(trained) _____

7. An agreement has been reached today by the Council and them.

(have reached) _____

8. The snow kept Janet and us home.

(were kept) _____

9. For the next shift, he and Steve are listed on the duty roster.

(lists) _____

10. She and Pat wrote the prize-winning articles.

(were written) _____

Pronoun Agreement

The second problem in using pronouns correctly involves matching the pronoun to the noun it refers to. For instance, a feminine noun like *the girl*, as a subject, would require the feminine pronoun *she*. A plural noun like *the cars* would require the plural pronoun *they*.

With some indefinite words, you may have trouble deciding if they are singular or plural. Words like *another, anybody, anyone, each, either, everybody, everyone, neither, nobody, no one, one, somebody,* and *someone* are considered singular. Except in some informal situations, you need to use a singular pronoun when you refer to one of these words. For example:

No one opened *his* package.

Words like *all, both, few, many, most, others,* and *several* are considered plural. You need to use a plural pronoun when you refer to one of these words. For example:

Few opened *their* packages.

When using these indefinite words or other nouns that do not have an obvious sex, like *student* or *driver* or *doctor,* writers have traditionally used the pronouns *he, him,* or *his.* Recently, however, some people have suggested that this practice gives writing a masculine bias. One solution is to use *his or her,* but this can become rather clumsy if it is overused. The National Council of Teachers of English recommends that when you are using singular nouns of indefinite sex, you alternate the pronoun sex to avoid the impression that every person is a *he.*

Here are some examples of sentences that have nouns of indefinite gender.

Each member of our club owes the balance of *his or her* dues by Monday.

When a criminal seeks rehabilitation, *she* should get it.

Every child must be allowed to grow into *his* own person.

Another way of handling the masculine/feminine pronoun problem is to make the noun plural and use a plural pronoun. For instance,

When criminals seek rehabilitation, *they* should get it.

EXERCISE C

Rewrite each sentence below using the new subject given. Be sure that the pronouns in the new sentence agree with the subject.

EXAMPLE:
Most of the pilots check *their* own planes before take-off.
Each of the pilots checks *his (her)* own plane before take-off.

1. Both schools lost their accreditation.

Another _____

2. Phyllis and I turned in our papers on time.

    I _____

3. The members voted for their favorite candidate.

    Each _____

4. Bach has earned his place in music history.

    He and Bach _____

5. Neither said she would go.

    Both _____

6. Only Carolyn took her family with her.

    A few _____

7. The children said they could do it by themselves.

    Nobody _____

8. I promised I would clean my room on Saturday.

    My brother and I _____

9. Apollo believes he is smarter than his father.

    Everyone _____

10. Nobody wanted to read his paper first.

    Several _____

EXERCISE D

Fill in each blank in the following sentences with an appropriate pronoun. Draw an arrow back to the word or words that each pronoun agrees with.

EXAMPLE:

James and Kim wrote the script. ___They___ worked every weekend to finish ___it.___

1. The museum curator spent over a million dollars for the painting.

    Ten years later, _____ learned _____

    was a forgery. The museum fired _____ for

    _____ mistake.

2. This recipe was handed down to Dottie by _____

    grandmother. _____ calls for sixteen eggs and takes

    all day to make. Therefore, _____ saves

_____ for special occasions.

3. The clerk was nearly bent double by the sack of mail.

   _____ must have weighed more than

   _____ did. Everyone in the office felt sorry for

   _____ .

4. Word games, with _____ challenging use of language,

   are a snap for Andy. _____ combines a photographic

   memory and a keen intellect to put together _____

   winning performance.

5. The rocker was delicately carved. _____ had roses

   across the back, and _____ arms were decorated with

   swans. The matching ottoman was equally elaborate. I held

   _____ breath when _____ came up for

   auction.

6. You and Marcie have tied for the championship.

   _____ will both be awarded medals for

   _____ efforts. The whole school is proud of

   _____ .

7. Rabbi Stanley is a great favorite with the children.

   _____ always has a funny story to tell

   _____ , and _____ pockets always

   seem to have an extra piece of candy in _____ .

8. Dr. Graham and _____ wife disagreed with the Com-

   mission's report. _____ said _____

   overlooked some obvious facts and _____ recommen-

   dations would not solve the double taxation problem. Several others

   also expressed _____ opinions.

9. Michelangelo was primarily interested in sculpture. All

   _____ work, even _____ painting,

   shows _____ influence. Many wealthy Italians com-

   missioned _____ to create statues for

   _____ .

10. When we had finished the practice, the coach told

_____ to get a good night's sleep.

_____ wanted _____ to be ready for

the big game. _____ obeyed _____ in-

structions.

Pronoun Reference

Look at these sentences:

> My father and my brother visited my grandpar-
> ents. *He* told *them* about *his* trip to Canada.

In the second sentence, it is not clear who *he* is or who *they* are. A pronoun doesn't convey any meaning unless your reader knows what the pronoun stands for. The second sentence above would have to be rewritten to make the pronouns clear:

> <u>Dad</u> told <u>them</u> about <u>his</u> trip to Canada.
>
> *or*
>
> <u>Jerry</u> told <u>them</u> about <u>his</u> trip to Canada.
>
> *or*
>
> <u>Grandpa</u> told <u>Dad and Jerry</u> about <u>his</u> trip to Canada.

Note the use of pronouns in these sentences:

> Sheila wants to be a doctor. She thinks *it* is a very
> lucrative profession.

The pronoun *it* has no noun that it can refer back to. To correct this fault, you have two options: put in a noun that *it* will stand for (Sheila wants to enter the medical profession. She thinks *it* is very lucrative.) or eliminate the pronoun (Sheila wants to be a doctor. She thinks medicine is a very lucrative profession.)

EXERCISE E

Rewrite the following pairs of sentences so that each pronoun refers clearly to one word.

1. Monica wrapped the gifts for her sister. She had an eye for artistic effects.

_____

_____

2. Ray enlisted in the Air Force last week. It surprised all his friends.

   _____

3. I have known Jessica much longer than I have known Mark. We met at a New Year's Eve party.

   _____

   _____

4. After the rain, the whole forest looked fresh. They spread their leaves to make a cool shade.

   _____

5. The nursing home looked bright. They had just painted the halls.

   _____

   _____

6. Frances drove with Mary to the airport. She was going to Duluth.

   _____

   _____

7. Miguel sings beautifully. They seem to be a way of expressing his own private emotions.

   _____

   _____

8. Fred told his dad that he had been cheated.

   _____

   _____

9. Walt, for instance, missed seventeen questions. It was just too hard for most of them.

   _____

   _____

10. When Doris congratulated Keren, she smiled.

    _____

    _____

EXERCISE F

After each of the following sentences, add two more sentences that use the pronouns you have been practicing. Be sure that the pronouns refer clearly to one noun and that they agree with the nouns they refer to. Circle the pronouns you use.

1. The *Enterprise* shot out into space with the incredible power of warp drive.

_____

_____

_____

2. Stan bought Ethel a new mink.

_____

_____

_____

3. The new Tigermobile is like no other car on the road.

_____

_____

_____

4. We left a message for our agent in Bonn.

_____

_____

_____

5. Sharon took only half an hour to hang the new light fixture.

_____

_____

_____

6. The baby cried when I couldn't find his yellow blanket.

_____

_____

_____

7. Running wildly away from the house, North suddenly tripped over a body sprawled across the driveway.

_____

_____

_____

8. Mr. Falston and I have been in charge of the paint department for twenty years.

_____

_____

_____

9. Your grocer is having a special this month on avocados.

_____

_____

_____

10. Louise and Tom had everyone laughing at the story of their trip to Alaska.

_____

_____

_____

CONSISTENCY

When you begin to write a series of sentences, you have to be careful to be consistent from one sentence to the next in verb tense and in point of view.

Consistency in Verb Tense

If you were telling a story about something that happened to you in the past, you would confuse your reader if you jumped around in time like this:

> I have never forgotten my first plane ride. I (was) four years old, and I (am) terrified of the noise of the engines. My mother (drags) me down the aisle and (strapped) me into my seat. Even the stewardess's offer of a piece of gum (does) not calm me down. I (was) convinced that the monster (will eat) me.

Written this way, the story moves from the past to the present to the future without any logical reason. All these actions happened in the same time period, but the verb tenses don't show that. It would be correct to tell this story in the past tense since it happened in the past, but you could also tell it in the present tense as if you were reliving the events as you were describing them. You have to be sure, though, that you tell the story consistently in the present or the past tense. Both of the versions shown below use verb tenses consistently.

A. PRESENT TENSE

> I (am) four years old, and I (am) terrified of the noise of the engines. My mother (drags) me down the aisle and (straps) me into my seat. Even the stewardess's offer of a piece of gum (does) not calm me down. I (am) convinced that the monster (is) going to eat me.

B. PAST TENSE

I (was) four years old, and I (was) terrified of the noise of the engines. My mother (dragged) me down the aisle and (strapped) me into my seat. Even the stewardess's offer of a piece of gum (did) not calm me down. I (was) convinced that the monster (was) going to eat me.

Generally, if you start a series of sentences using one verb tense, you should stay with that verb tense through the whole series. The only time it's all right to change tenses is when the time reference really changes. For instance:

New Year's Eve (is) traditionally a big party night. Tonight (will be) no exception. Nearly every club in the city (has planned) some special entertainment for New Year's revelers.

The first sentence uses the present tense to show that New Year's Eve is always "a big party night." The second sentence refers to time that has not yet arrived—tonight. The third sentence uses verb tense to show that the planning began in the past and continues into the present.

If the article above went on to list the plans of the various clubs, it would use the future tense since all the action would be happening at some later time. For example:

At the Cross Street Club, the music of the Freemen (will be featured.) The party here (will last) from 9 P.M. to 5 A.M. The Sandlot, on Western Avenue, (will provide) jazz by the Ravens. The $15 cover charge will entitle patrons to a cold buffet. All drinks (will be) $1.50 at the cash bar.

EXERCISE G

Identify the verbs in the following sets of sentences. What time frame does each verb indicate: past, present, or future? Rewrite the sentences as necessary to make the time frame consistent in each set of sentences.

1. In 1908, by the time Willa Cather becomes editor of McClure's Magazine in New York City, she had lived in Virginia, Nebraska, and Pennsylvania. She will be strongly influenced by her years in Pittsburgh. Later, Cather writes novels such as *O Pioneers!* and will win a Pulitzer Prize.

_____

_____

2. Many teachers say that there are four kinds of writing. One kind was narration; another will be description; a third type is exposition, and last there was argument. Other teachers will emphasize only the last two kinds.

3. At first, the princess refused to marry the handsome prince because he wears polka-dot ties. The princess hated polka dots. Later, however, she changes her mind. She will realize that his clothes didn't matter as long as he is a kind person.

4. For millions of years, the Grand Canyon is a huge sea. Several layers of the canyon showed fossils of marine plants and animals who will live there. Later, the region will be a desert. And still later, volcanoes erupted creating lava dams. Finally, about five million years ago, the Colorado River began to cut a channel through the rocks. The forces of erosion gradually widen the channel to today's spectacular canyon.

5. Television camera crews are probably the least well known part of news reporting. Although filming took great technical skill and artistic sense, many people will not realize how much of their news they owe to the camera team. Camera crews had to be fearless to finish their job. They risked anything from a torrential downpour to a burst of machine-gun fire to get the pictures that will appear on the nightly news. Despite the camera team's skill and courage, though, their names were rarely known by television viewers.

EXERCISE H

Show the time connections in the following sentences by a consistent use of verbs. If you use more than one tense, make sure there is a logical reason for doing so. You may use the verbs given in parentheses or use verbs of your own choice.

1. Holography, a form of photography, _____ photo-
   (to use)
   graphic film and laser light to create three-dimensional images. It

   _____ developed in the 1960s by two scientists from
   (to be)
   the University of Michigan.

2. Embassy guards _____ an elite branch of the Marine
   (to be)
   Corps. The guards _____ at a special school in Vir-
   (to train)
   ginia where they _____ everything from the social
   (to learn)
   graces to the latest alarm systems.

3. Racing across the Russian tundra, hunters _____
   (to look)
   for wolf tracks in the snow. When they _____their
   (to spot)
   prey, they _____ in for the kill. Sometimes they
   (to close)
   _____ helicopters, which _____ down
   (to use)   (to swoop)
   on the pack.

4. In her Nobel Prize acceptance speech, Mother Teresa

   _____ on poverty. The Western world, she
   (to speak)
   _____, _____for love far more than the
   (to say)   (to hunger)
   poor _____for rice.
        (to hunger)

5. Scripture scholars _____ that each Gospel writer
   (to say)
   _____ us a slightly different portrait of Christ. Each
   (to give)
   evangelist _____ a somewhat different purpose in
   (to have)
   writing.

6. Rodgers' and Hammerstein's *Oklahoma* _____the
   (to establish)
   American musical. The 1943 show _____ plot, music,
   (to combine)
   and dance to produce a hardy new breed, a musical with well-
   rounded characters and some tough social problems. *Oklahoma*

   _____ the beginning of the truly *American* musical
   (to mark)
   theater.

7. College athletic programs _____ very vulnerable to corruption. Coaches sometimes _____ high school transcripts to qualify promising athletes for college. Some players _____ credit for courses they _____. Other athletes _____ money or cars to stay at certain schools and play football or basketball.

8. They _____ black robes and lace scarves. They _____ $66,500 tax-free, every year. They _____ the ideal of peace through world law. They _____ the fifteen judges of the International Court of Justice.

9. Joel Poinsett, James Madison's confidential agent to Mexico, _____ poinsettias to America. When Poinsett _____ Mexican gardens filled with the wonderful plant, he _____ cuttings home for his garden in Charleston, South Carolina.

10. By the year 2080, if computer technology _____ at its present pace, a single computer _____ a memory equal to 16,000 human memories. In the next hundred years or so, computers _____ our children, _____ our transit systems, and _____ our health.

Consistency in Point of View

In writing a series of sentences, you have to be consistent about the point of view you use. There are three points of view—the first person, the second person, and the third person.

With the first-person point of view, you focus the reader's attention on yourself, the speaker, by using the first person pronouns: *I, me, mine, my, we, us, ours, our.* The paragraph below, for example, is written from a *first-person point of view.*

> *My* garden gives *me* many hours of enjoyment, even before *I* set foot in it. Early in the winter, *I* gather together *my* new seed catalogs and read about this year's developments in vegetables and flowers. Then *I* list the varieties *I* think *I'd* like to plant, usually two or three new ones each year plus a lot of *my* old favorites. *I* really enjoy planning *my* garden every winter.

With the second-person point of view, you focus attention on the audience, the person or persons being spoken to, by using the pronouns *you, your,* and *yours.* This paragraph, for example, is written from the *second-person point of view.*

You can begin to enjoy *your* garden even before *you* start to plant it. Gather up *your* seed catalogs early in the winter and read about the new vegetables and flowers developed this year. Then pick out a few that *you'd* like to try along with *your* old favorites. *You* can then begin to anticipate *your* delicious rewards while snow is still on the ground.

With the third-person point of view, you focus attention on the subject you are discussing by using nouns that refer to the subject, as well as the third-person pronouns: *he, she, it, him, her, his, hers, its, they, them, their, theirs.* Words like *anyone, someone, several,* and *each* are also third-person words. The paragraph below, for example, is written from a *third-person point of view.*

An enthusiastic *gardener* enjoys *his* garden even before the planting season begins. *He* or *she* gathers up seed catalogs early in the winter to read about the latest in vegetables and flowers. Experienced *gardeners* usually try one or two new varieties each year along with *their* old favorites. For many *gardeners,* planning is as much fun as planting.

Which point of view you choose depends largely on the kind of relationship you want to have with your audience. The important thing is that you have to stick with a point of view once you have chosen it. Otherwise, your audience will become uncomfortable with your shifting perspective.

EXERCISE I

Identify the point of view in each sentence below. Then rewrite the sentence from the point of view indicated. Reword each sentence as necessary to change the point of view.

EXAMPLE:

When you look at Rodin's sculptures, you can almost see them breathe. (second person)

(first person) *When I look at Rodin's sculptures, I can almost see them breathe.*

1. Moviegoers are usually sympathetic to Woody Allen's sweet, sentimental characters.

   (second person) _____

   _____

2. If you read *Gulliver's Travels* as a children's story, you are missing most of Swift's genius.

   (third person) _____

   _____

3. The Buckhorn Bar entices you with exotic dishes like rattlesnake stew and roast moose nose; of course, you have to pay handsomely for this gastronomic experience.

(first person) _____

_____

4. Students must have their instructor's approval before beginning their research projects.

(second person) _____

_____

5. I have such fond memories of my Saturday afternoons at the Pratt Library; I can't believe it is gone forever.

(third person) _____

_____

EXERCISE J

Rewrite the following paragraphs so that each one maintains a consistent point of view.

1. The technology exists right now to make driving safer. If we simply used our seat belts and buckled our children into safety seats, you could prevent thousands of injuries and deaths. The installation of airbags would give us even more protection in a crash. Safety engineers estimate that a higher brake light centered on the back of your car would cut your rear-end collisions by 40 percent. We have also developed a new plastic-backed windshield glass that can prevent many of your facial injuries. By using existing safety devices and asking for more safety options in your cars, drivers could have safer cars very soon.

2. By following a few simple suggestions, almost anyone can improve his or her photography. First of all, know what your camera is capable of. Shoot a few practice rolls before you try to capture a vacation or a sister's wedding on film. I would also recommend taking more close-up pictures. I always come as close as I can to my subject without eliminating any important part of the background. Finally, a good photographer tries to compose each picture so that there is a natural frame. He also tries for unposed shots of people doing things rather than stilted, formal poses. These ideas can make the difference between an "Oh!" and an "Uhh . . ." when you show off your pictures.

3. The alligator, Florida's leading reptilian citizen and the animal you are probably most interested in seeing, is not the same as the crocodile. You can find the alligator all along the Atlantic coastal plain, whereas the crocodile is found only in a limited section of southern Florida. Each species generally prefers a different territory: 'gators inland in fresh water and crocs along the

coast or just offshore. Even their physical characteristics mark the two animals as different. Alligators are blackish with broad, shovel-shaped snouts as opposed to the greenish crocodile with its narrow, tapering snout. Now, I don't think you should have any trouble telling the difference between an alligator and a crocodile.

SENTENCE VARIETY

In the earlier chapters of this section, you have seen that most sentences are built on a few patterns, all of which rely on the basic subject–verb unit:

s — v
Turner won.

s — v (passive)
The prize was awarded.

s — v —   oc
Turner accepted the prize.

s — LV — SC
Turner was excited.

When you begin to write a series of sentences, you need to think about varying the patterns occasionally. You can use variation to call attention to a particular point or just to make your writing more interesting to a reader. For instance, look at the following series of related sentences:

West Point owes its distinctive character to Sylvanus Thayer.
Thayer became its superintendent in 1817.
He transformed the school.
The new military academy started as a shaky enterprise.
Thayer made it supreme in science and engineering.
Thayer studied French military schools.
Thayer imbued West Point with the best of the military tradition.

Can you see how similar these sentences are? Every sentence is short; the longest is only eleven words. Every sentence begins with the subject, which is immediately followed by the verb. Although these sentences are perfectly correct and contain useful information, nothing in the series particularly stands out, and the sameness of the sentences could make the paragraph boring to read. What the paragraph could use is more variation in its sentence structure.

Methods of Variation

Varation I: The Question   A simple statement can be turned into a question in order to suggest uncertainty rather than certainty.

> The truck stopped.
> *Has the truck stopped?*
> The truck hit the wall.
> *Did the truck hit the wall?*
> The wall was hit.
> *Was the wall hit?*
> His truck was expensive.
> *Was his truck expensive?*

Notice that the question is formed by using a helping verb in front of the subject.

Variation II: Reversing Word Order   You can call special attention to some part of a sentence by putting it out of its normal position. For instance,

> The wind was wild.

could become

> *Wild was the wind.*

In this second version, the descriptive word, *wild*, gets extra emphasis because it isn't where the reader would expect to find it.

Another example,

> An ugly beast was watching from the window.

could become

> *Watching from the window was an ugly beast.*

In this variation, the subject, *beast*, gets special emphasis. Again, the additional impact comes from the word's being out of its normal position.

Variation III: Introducing or Interrupting the Base Sentence   You can call special attention to an adjective, adverb or a subordinate word group by using it to introduce or interrupt the base sentence.

For instance,

> The lawyer presented her case skillfully.

can become

Skillfully, the lawyer presented her case.

The second version calls more attention to *how* the lawyer presented her case, *skillfully,* by opening the sentence with the adverb.

The untrained tenor sang badly.

can become

The tenor, untrained, sang badly.

In the second version, the reader is forced to pause over the adjective *untrained,* and so it gets more emphasis.

Notice that any construction that introduces or interrupts the base sentence is set off with commas.

Here is one way these techniques could be applied to the paragraph above so that the sentence patterns are more interesting.

> S   V   OC
> West Point owes its distinctive character to Sylvanus Thayer. *After studying*
> INTRODUCTION   S   V   OC   S
> *French military schools,* Thayer transformed the academy. Thayer, *who became*
> INTERRUPTION   V   OC
> *superintendent in 1817,* made the shaky new military enterprise supreme in the
> INTRODUCTION   S   V   OC
> fields of science and engineering. Overall, Thayer imbued West Point with the
> best of the military tradition.

Here the sentence patterns are varied by introductory and interrupting word groups. Because some sentences have been combined, there is also a greater variety in the lengths of the sentences.

Besides making your writing generally more interesting, variation can also be used to call attention to one point. When there are several sentences in a row that use the same pattern, one different sentence will stand out to the reader. For example, a short sentence following several long sentences will get more emphasis in a reader's mind.

Look at the way this paragraph uses sentence patterns:

> The average cadet has scored better on the S.A.T. than the average American college freshman. (15) More significantly, most cadets have been "A" students in high school, with one out of ten having been class valedictorian or salutatorian. (22) In one recent year, over 200 of the plebes had been Eagle Scouts. (13) Cadets are, in short, overachievers. (5)

The last sentence in this paragraph should get the reader's full attention because its pattern is significantly different from the sentences that came before it.

Repetition

It is also possible to use pattern repetition to emphasize a point, if the point is that two ideas are quite similar or quite different. For instance, look at the way repetition is used here:

> My two uncles are completely different in temperament. *While Bob is* thoughtful and slow to show emotion, *Randy tends* to speak his feelings before he has thought about them. *While Bob is* home-loving and has never been farther than 50 miles from home, *Randy* is a wanderer who has visited forty states and six foreign countries. Most telling of all, *while Bob has* few friends and keeps mainly to himself, *Randy is* always accompanied by half a dozen of the friends he has acquired in his travels. How can twin brothers be so different?

(Notice how variation is used in the last sentence. A question stands out from all the direct statements.)

The important thing to remember in using any variation of the basic sentence pattern is:

NEVER WRITE A SENTENCE THAT WILL CONFUSE YOUR READER.

EXERCISE K

Write one variation for each basic sentence below. Try to use all the patterns of variation in this exercise.

EXAMPLE:
Oil company profits have risen by 200 percent.
Have oil company profits risen by 200 percent?

1. Gutenberg's printing press was invented in the fifteenth century.

    _____

2. That morning was beautiful.

    _____

3. His delicate photography captured the peace of the scene.

    _____

4. Arnold's Bakery is famous for its pastry.

    _____

5. Thirty thousand acres of wilderness have been preserved by the efforts of the Sierra Club.

    _____

6. A fast strawberry picker can earn $30 in one day.

    _____

7. Some very ancient myths form the basis of many modern television shows.

_____

8. Comunity college students want career education by and large.

_____

9. Good laws make good government.

_____

10. The fire raced through the house hungrily.

_____

EXERCISE L

Rewrite the following paragraphs so the sentences show more variety in length and structure.

1. The pony limped. Her head hung down. Her mane was wet. She had run. She had come down from the high mountains. It was raining. The pony was tired. Her sides heaved. Her breath smoked in the cold night air.

2. To the south, the Plank Road ran eastward to the capital of the Confederacy. To the north, the Union Army spread its camp. To the west, the Blue Ridge rose in the haze. To the east, the sun rose over the fields. In an hour, the Battle of the Wilderness would begin.

REVIEW

Basic Sentence Patterns

S-V	Evalina frowned.
S-V-OC	The manager was observing her.
S-V (passive)	She was observed by the manager.
S-LV-SC	Evalina's anger was deep.

Variations

Question	Was Evalina's anger deep?
Reversal	Observing her was the manager.
Introduction/	Deeply angry, Evalina frowned.
Interruption	Evalina, deeply angry, frowned.

EXERCISE M

Combine each of the following sets of sentences to produce an effective paragraph. You may use any form of modification, coordination, or subordination in putting together your paragraphs. You may follow the suggested groupings of ideas, or you may set up groups of your own. Either way, be sure that your finished paragraph uses verb tenses and pronouns consistently. Also try to use appropriate repetition and variation of sentence patterns.

THE CYCLONE STATE

1. Kansas has long been known as the "Cyclone State."
2. This distinction is sometimes credited to the Irving tornado.
    I believe this.
    This tornado was exceptionally violent.
    This tornado occurs nearly a century ago.
3. Others will credit the distinction to authorities on tornadoes.
    These authorities were your early ones.
    These authorities live in Kansas.
    These authorities work in Kansas.
4. Or this name is given because of Dorothy.
    Dorothy's flight to Oz begins in Kansas.
    You remember Dorothy, of course.
5. Or this name was given because twisters are photogenic.
    I have found the photogenic quality was exceptional.
    The twisters will be in Kansas.
    Kansas had an open sweep of prairie.
6. We don't know exactly how Kansas got this name.
    The "Cyclone State" certainly fits Kansas.

CLEAN-UP

1. Our troop had a service project.
    Eighteen scouts took part.
    The project is the first one of the year.
    The project will be a clean-up.
    The clean-up was at Emerson Park.
2. We arrive at 9 A.M. on Saturday.
    The scouts brought rakes, shovels, and wheelbarrows.
3. We will pick up trash.
    There are forty-seven bags of trash.
4. The scouts raked the grass.
    The scouts weeded the flower beds.

We swept the paths.
We painted the benches.

5. You will really get tired after a few hours of cleaning.
    We relax with a cookout.
    The cookout comes after your morning's work.

6. Our troop receives an award.
    The award will be from your mayor.
    The award was for this clean-up project.

MARJORAM

1. Marjoram came from Western Asia.
    Marjoram comes from the Mediterranean.
    The scent of marjoram has always been highly prized.

2. In some countries, marjoram is the symbol of honor.
    In some countries, marjoram is the symbol of happiness.
    I have discovered this.

3. The Greeks will use marjoram.
    The Romans will use marjoram.
    Marjoram was used to create crowns.
    The crowns are worn by couples.
    The couples were young.
    The couples were happy.

4. You planted marjoram on graves.
    The planting was to delight the souls.
    The souls belong to your loved ones.

5. In England, marjoram is a charm.
    In Germany, marjoram is a charm.
    We used the charm against witchcraft.
    People believed.
    Our belief was that witches will not endure the fragrance.
    The fragrance belongs to the happy herb.

6. Marjoram is my favorite herb.

HONEYMOONING

1. The industry begins in 1945.
    The industry is for honeymoons.
    The industry is mighty.
    The industry is in the Poconos.

2. Rudolf van Hoevenberg will open a resort.
    The resort was specifically for honeymooners.
    The hideaway was called The Farm on the Hill.

3. You want to go to The Farm.
You had to submit a statement.
The statement was informal.
The statement was about yourself.
The statement included a description.
The description was of the future plans.
The plans were of the couple.

4. The couple will be evaluated.

5. You were found easy to get along with.
The couple will get a small cottage.

6. Each couple was surrounded.
The surrounding was by other couples.
The other couples shared your anxiety.
The anxiety was about being newly married.

7. The resort will reduce the possibility for surprise.
The resort will reduce the possibility for error.
The possibilities were on the wedding trip.

8. We crave this security.
A new industry was born.

EDITING PRACTICE

Review the following paragraphs for any errors in using the sentence patterns you have learned. Be sure that all sentences are complete and correctly punctuated. Make sure there are no inconsistencies in point of view or verb tense that might distract a reader. See that pronouns are used correctly. Rewrite each paragraph to correct any sentence problems you find.

1. The New York Giants battling the Cleveland Indians for the 1954 World Series title. The score is tied, 2–2, in the eighth inning of the first game, and Cleveland had two men on base. Vic Wertz who already have three hits in the game steps up to the plate swings, and connects. You knew that ball was heading out of the park. As the ball left the bat the Giants' center fielder is racing toward the bleachers he reaches up over his head at the last minute and catching the ball. Even more amazing he throw the ball to the infield so fast that the runner on second doesn't make it to home plate. Every Giants' fan leaped to their feet cheering. Willie Mays who was in his first full season in the major leagues. Breaks the back of the Indians. After Mays's spectacular catch, they go on to win the championship in four games.

2. The ancient Greeks believe, that Prometheus who was the cleverest of all the Titans, make all living creatures. Wandering around the newly made earth, little bits of clay were shaped into worms snakes crocodiles and all kinds of fantastic reptiles. Prometheus as he will become more skillful made

birds and animals. Last of all Prometheus inventing human beings he will mix into this final creature pieces of all the other animals. Perhaps this story explained sometimes why human beings will behave so strangely.

WRITING PRACTICE

1.   You are about to leave Earth for a newly established moon colony. Because of limited space, you are allowed to take only one personal item with you to your new home. Write a statement of 200 words or less for the NASA archives explaining what item you have decided to take and why you have chosen it. Before composing the statement, you may want to explore your choices in a private journal entry. After you have composed a draft of your statement, check your writing (or have a classmate check it) to see that your sentences are sufficiently varied and that they are complete, consistent, and correctly punctuated.

2.   It is now thirty years after you joined the moon colony. The colony has prospered and so has your family. You now have several lovely grandchildren who, unfortunately, know very little about your home planet, Earth, and its customs. Because you don't want knowledge of the old traditions to die out completely, you have decided to write a book for your grandchildren and great-grandchildren about your memories of Earth. Prepare a short article for your book about some traditional celebration that you were familiar with on Earth, for instance, Thanksgiving or the Fourth of July.

Before writing, try to recreate the celebration in your mind. Make notes about the sights, sounds, smells, and tastes associated with this celebration. See if you can focus your article to create one dominant impression of the scene.

After you have composed a draft of your article, check your writing (or have a classmate check it) to see if your sentences are sufficiently varied and if they are complete, consistent, and correctly punctuated.

Part Two

Basic Paragraph Patterns

A sentence, clear and well-constructed, can be a very useful tool for communicating ideas. Through the use of modification (adjectives and adverbs), coordination, and subordination, all of which are presented in the first part of this book, you can express some fairly complicated ideas and also show a precise relationship between one idea and another within the same sentence.

However, sentences do have limits. If you try to push too much information into one sentence, you can easily confuse or distract your readers. If you try to relate too many ideas in one sentence, your readers may not be able to figure out which idea you really want them to pay the most attention to. So the paragraph, a series of sentences carefully developing one idea, can be even more useful than a single sentence for sharing your idea with someone else.

This section of the book will present a basic model for paragraphing and then show you some strategies for arranging the ideas that go into paragraphs. You will also be able to practice shaping paragraphs from series of sentences.

7

Basic Paragraph Structure

In some ways, paragraph structure is an extension of sentence structure. In a sentence, one subject–verb unit serves as the focus, and all the other ideas are arranged around it. In a paragraph, one sentence gives the focus, and all the other sentences are arranged to explain, expand, and generally clarify that idea.

Although there are many possible forms for a paragraph, in this book you will concentrate on one basic pattern for paragraph construction: a *topic sentence*, which focuses the main idea; *support*, an arrangement of subordinate ideas; and a *conclusion*, which coordinates with the topic sentence by restating the focus.

Here is a typical paragraph that uses the pattern of a topic sentence, followed by supporting detail, followed by a concluding sentence.

(main idea)
>According to our study, then, the change from 24-hour to 8-hour shifts for firefighters would not benefit the city.

(subordinate details)
>At the least, three shifts each day instead of one are more difficult to schedule for overtime salaries. In addition, to keep all stations fully staffed under the new system, the city would have to hire and train an additional 200 men and women, at a cost that would be prohibitive. Equally undesirable alternatives for implementing the change would be the closing of some stations, staffing stations below minimum standards, or floating crews from station to station, any of which would make the city's fire protection service less efficient.

(restatement of main idea)
>In the light of these drawbacks, therefore, the Commission on Fire Protection recommends that the city retain the present system of 24-hour shifts for fire-fighters.

147

In this paragraph, which is being used to summarize a longer report, the focus idea is stated in the topic sentence. Then three reasons, which are subordinate to the topic sentence, are given to show why the focus idea is valid. Finally, the conclusion, coordinating with the topic sentence, restates the main point in slightly different words.

LEVELS OF GENERALITY

To construct this kind of paragraph, you need to understand how ideas relate to one another on a scale of generality.

To borrow some mathematical terms, you can think of "books" as a set that includes many members. However, "books" itself is but one member of a larger set of "reading materials," which includes even more members than the set "books." "Reading materials," therefore, is more general than "books" because it includes more members. Likewise, "novels" is one member of the set "books." Although you may have a set called "novels," that set will not have as many members as the set called "books." "Novels," therefore, is more specific than "books" because it has fewer members in its set. The chart below illustrates one example of such a scale of generality.

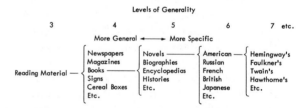

In writing a paragraph, you are moving back and forth on a scale of generality. Your topic sentence makes a relatively general statement. Your support moves across the scale one or two levels. And then your conclusion moves back to the level of your topic sentence. You might visualize your paragraph something like this:

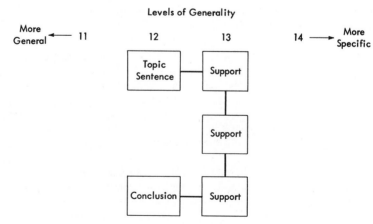

When you have mastered this form of paragraphing, you may wish to develop other paragraph structures, as many professional writers do. In the meantime, however, this basic three-part paragraph can be used for many different kinds of writing, from letters to term papers to professional reports.

EXERCISE A

Supply an appropriate term for each blank in the following scales of generality.

1. Living things → _____ → dogs → Great Danes → my dog Metro → _____ → Metro's cute pointy ears

2. _____ → grains → wheat → _____ → a slice of Wonderbread

3. Means of transportation → _____ → Fords → _____ → the mechanical systems of my car → _____

4. Government → _____ → legislative branch → senate → Senator Goodtime → _____ → _____

5. _____ → Christian → _____ → Presbyterian → _____ → Rev. Brimstone → Rev. Brimstone's knowledge

EXERCISE B

Identify the topic sentence, support sentences, and conclusion in each of the following paragraphs. Be prepared to explain how these parts relate to each other on a scale of generality.

1. Although eyeglasses were invented in the thirteenth century, the problem of how to keep them on comfortably wasn't solved until nearly 350 years later. The first spectacles, two lenses in metal or leather frames riveted in an inverted V-shape, balanced precariously on the bridge of the nose. These rivet spectacles pinched the nose, and wearers had to hold their heads at an odd angle to keep the contraption from falling off. By the fifteenth century, the Italians had rigged a wire hat with the glasses dangling down over the forehead. The Spanish later experimented with silk ribbons that tied behind

the wearer's ears. The Chinese attached small weights to strings that ran behind the ears. Around 1730, a London optician named Edward Scarlett perfected the use of rigid sidepieces. Finally, eyeglass wearers could enhance
their vision in relative comfort.

2.   My first day of college left me thoroughly confused. I drove around the
campus for what seemed like hours before locating a parking space. Then I
had to dig out my campus map to figure out where I was and where I had to
go for my first class. Heading in what looked like the right direction, I soon
reached the main highway without catching a glimpse of anything that
looked like the Rankin Building. When I asked a group of students for directions, I got three conflicting sets of instructions on how to find the place. I
finally stumbled into the right building through sheer luck, only to find a sign
on the classroom door announcing that the class had been moved to some
building that wasn't even shown on my campus map. Thoroughly bewil-
dered, I decided to return to the parking lot and start over. I haven't felt so
confused since I was lost in a shopping mall at the age of five.

TOPIC SENTENCE

The topic sentence in a paragraph has two main purposes: to identify the
subject of the paragraph and to show the focus you are going to use in discussing that subject. Look at the topic sentence in the sample paragraph at
the beginning of this chapter. What is the subject of the paragraph, according
to the topic sentence? *The change from 24-hour to 8-hour shifts for firefighters.* That
subject could be written about from a number of different angles: costs, advantages, comparison to other cities. But, in a paragraph, you really can't do
justice to more than one of these. You have to choose one aspect to focus on.
What focus does this sentence give for the subject? *Would not benefit the city.* In
other words, the topic sentence tells the reader right away what to expect
from this paragraph. It will present the ways in which a particular change
would not be beneficial.

SUBJECT + FOCUS = TOPIC SENTENCE

EXERCISE C

Circle the subject and underline the focus of each of the following topic

1. Compared to nuclear energy research, solor energy research is underfunded.
2. Sacajawea, the guide for Lewis and Clark's expedition, led a dramatic life.
3. The full consequences of the Civil War were not understood until the twentieth century.
4. Bridge is one of the most difficult card games to master.
5. Living on a farm can be just as stressful as living in a large city.
6. Prof. Kinsey's image of San Francisco was more sedate than mine.
7. Laslow's proposals mean several major changes in corporate policy.
8. Fictional detectives frequently appear smarter than ordinary human beings.
9. The use of coupons can save shoppers 40 percent of their weekly food bills.
10. If it is done on a regular schedule, home maintenance is simple.

As you were doing the exercise above, you may have observed some characteristics of topic sentences. The box below shows some important qualities of a useful topic sentence.

TOPIC SENTENCES

a. **A topic sentence must be a complete sentence, not a fragment.**

b. **A topic sentence is usually a direct statement, not a question.**

c. **The subject of the topic sentence is usually the subject idea of the paragraph.**

d. **The verb and complement of the topic sentence usually show the focus of the paragraph.**

e. **The focus part of the topic sentence usually presents a judgment or attitude about the subject.**

f. **A subordinate word group is sometimes used in the topic sentence to define the focus still further.**

EXERCISE D

Keeping in mind the characteristics shown above, combine each of the following sets of sentences into one effective topic sentence. Identify the subject and focus of each topic sentence. (Refer to Chapters 3 and 4 if you need to review sentence combining strategies.)

Compare your topic sentences with those of your classmates and discuss any differences in wording or arrangement. Does one version of the sentence seem better to you than another? Can you explain why?

EXAMPLE:

Americans have attitudes.

Their attitudes are toward John F. Kennedy.

These attitudes have changed.

The change has occurred since JFK's death.

Americans' attitudes toward JFK have changed since his death.

Since JFK's death, Americans have changed their attitude toward him.

1. Teaching is a job.
    The teaching is in kindergarten.
    The job demands great patience.

    _____

2. A bride should begin.
    Planning should be begun.
    The bride wants a perfect wedding.
    The planning should be in advance.
    The advance should be at least six months.

    _____

3. Arson is a crime.
    It is detected.
    The detection is difficult.
    The difficulty occurs often.

    _____

4. I stood before the platoon.
    The platoon was of 'droids.
    The 'droids were in the service of the Empire.
    I felt a sense.
    The sense was of despair.

    _____

5. People have endangered.
    Their health has been endangered.

The people want to seem fashionable.
The endangering was to achieve the "right" look.
This has happened for thousands of years.

_____

_____

6. Quality is determined.
   The quality is of chocolate candy.
   The variety of the cocoa beans determines quality.
   The degree of kneading determines quality.
   The amount of cocoa butter determines quality.
   A chocolate connoisseur can make this determination.

_____

_____

7. A college wants support.
   The support is continuing.
   A college must maintain relations.
   The relations are with its alumni.
   The relations are good.

_____

_____

8. I am looking for three things in a car.
   The car is new.
   The car should be easy to maintain.
   The car should be safe.
   The car should be comfortable.

_____

_____

9. Dentists go into debt.
   The dentists are opening new practices.
   The going into debt almost always happens.

_____

_____

10. The character has been preserved.
    The character is special.
    The character is of the French Quarter.
    The French Quarter is in New Orleans.
    Laws havé preserved the character.
    The laws are strict.

_____

_____

Limiting the Subject and Focus

Each of the topic sentences below contains some sort of a subject and a focus, but one of each pair presents these two basic parts more clearly than the other. Which one in each pair gives the reader a clearer idea of what to expect in the paragraph that will follow?

1. A. I like music.
   B. A folk song called "Simple Things" saved my job for me one summer when I was sixteen.
2. A. My hometown is nice.
   B. Frenchman's Point is the ideal place for a young family.
3. A. My hometown was nice.
   B. Twenty years ago, Frenchman's Point was an inexpensive place to live.
4. A. That book is interesting.
   B. Richard Lattimore's translation of the Gospels is easier to read than the Knox version.
5. A. Democrats are better than Republicans.
   B. The Democrats on the County Council this year have shown more interest in the elderly than the Republicans on the Council.

In each case, you should have noticed that the second topic sentence gives the reader a more precise statement of the subject and the focus than the first topic sentence. Words like *nice, interesting,* and *better* don't work very well to focus an idea because they suggest so many different meanings that a reader isn't really sure what to focus on. Similarly, a broad subject like *music* or *Democrats* doesn't help your reader understand which particular aspect of that topic you want to tell about.

The terms of a topic sentence have to be placed very carefully on the scale of generality. Your subject and focus have to be general enough that they can include details from a more specific level, but not so general that they can't be dealt with adequately in a paragraph. A single paragraph usually starts near the more specific end of the scale rather than near the more general end.

EXERCISE E

Rewrite the word groups below so that each one is a topic sentence with a clearly limited subject and a well-defined focus.

1. Changing a tire.

_____

_____

2. He is a nice man.

   _____

   _____

3. Cats are better than dogs.

   _____

   _____

4. A time when I was embarrassed.

   _____

   _____

5. The room is beautiful.

   _____

   _____

6. Why should you vote for Jackson Browne?

   _____

   _____

7. Baseball is great.

   _____

   _____

8. Science is very interesting.

   _____

   _____

9. College is different from high school.

   _____

   _____

10. She looks good.

    _____

    _____

11. I don't like sports.

    _____

    _____

12. The show was pretty good.

    _____

    _____

13.   That restaurant was terrible.

_____

_____

14.   The best way to meet people.

_____

_____

15.   Do you have a future with the Army?

_____

_____

SUPPORT

The second important part of a paragraph is the support. You write a paragraph so that someone else can understand and perhaps accept your idea. Therefore, you have to do more than just present a general statement of your idea. You have to move to a more specific level of reasons, explanations, or examples that will clarify the idea for your reader.

For example, the paragraph on firefighting shown earlier in the chapter doesn't just keep making coordinate statements:

> This change would not benefit the city.
> This change would not be good for the city.
> This change has many disadvantages.

Instead, it moves from a general statement that a change in shifts would not be beneficial to specific, subordinate details of scheduling, costs, and efficiency.

Just as subordinate parts of a sentence help to clarify and define the base sentence, so does the support part of a paragraph help to clarify and explain the topic.

Look at the paragraphs below. Which one more effectively supports the topic sentence?

> Roberto Montoya deserves to receive this year's Citizen of the Year Award.

A.   For one thing, Bob is an all-around nice guy. There is really no better choice for this award. Bob is always willing to help. He is a special person. Besides his good personal qualities, Bob has worked hard for our community too. He has served

B.   Since being elected to the City Council three years ago, Bob has worked tirelessly for our community's interests. He has established a tax credit system for the elderly and has made sure we got an appropriate share of the library and recreation

the town well through his many public activities. Bob has worked for the community's interests at the state level too. The town of Bradley can be proud of an outstanding man like Roberto Montoya.

funds. Bob has been the leader in our fight to have the Interstate rerouted around our community. Besides his public work, Bob has also served us in a private capacity. He devotes many hours to coaching soccer and teaching camping skills to the scout troops.

Because of his many years of public and private service to our community, Roberto Montoya should be named Citizen of the Year.

What differences do you see in the kind of support provided in the two paragraphs above?

Paragraph A provides almost no specific detail to back up the nomination of Montoya. Most of the sentences stay on the same level. Paragraph B, on the other hand, moves to a more specific level to mention five of Montoya's particular contributions to the community, such as his legislation and his coaching activities.

Paragraph B, then, shows two important qualities of support: there should be enough support, without padding, to make your point convincingly (the more difficult the point, the more support is needed), and it should be as specific and as factual as possible. A few vague generalizations will not make your ideas clear to an audience.

Topic sentences, as you have seen, tend to present attitudes or opinions about which people may disagree. Support, on the other hand, tends to be more factual. The facts used for support may be details observable by your senses, such as what a person looks like or sounds like. Or you may use the events of your own life and those of your family and friends as facts to support some idea. Or you may use the written experiences of others as facts for support. (Historical fact and the attitudes of experts in various fields, for instance, are frequently presented in books and magazines, which are good sources of factual support.)

EXERCISE F

Decide which sentences in the following list would be appropriate statements of factual support and which are statements of opinion. Where would you place these statements on a scale of generality? Be prepared to explain your choices.

1. The Nile begins at Lake Victoria in central Africa.
2. Great enterprises often have obscure beginnings.
3. Linda has paid more than $2,500 in medical expenses this year.

4. Medical care has become too expensive for the average person.

5. More than one million people lined the streets of Paris for Victor Hugo's funeral.

6. Joe made only 74 on the grammar test.

7. The stove was over 20 feet from the sink.

8. The kitchen was poorly designed.

9. Fresh-water fishing is a relaxing recreation for many people.

10. Last summer in Quebec, I caught a rainbow trout 13 inches long.

11. This pair of designer jeans cost Wade $60.

12. The Baltimore–Washington area is the fourth-largest marketing region in the United States.

13. Every day, I seem to make a serious mistake about money.

14. The record holder stayed ten days in a cage with twenty-seven poisonous snakes.

15. Michelangelo's dome on St. Peter's is 132 meters high.

EXERCISE G

For each topic sentence shown below, select the three best supporting details from the list under it. Be prepared to explain your choices.

1. Over the centuries, human beings have devised many different ways of telling time.

_____ Time is an elusive and tricky concept.

_____ Sundials rely on shadows cast by the sun to tell time.

_____ There are dozens of different kinds of clocks.

_____ Mechanical clocks used a coiled spring to mark the passage of time.

_____ Today's quartz crystals have helped produce small but accurate wrist watches inexpensive enough for almost everyone to own.

2. My paycheck never seems to cover all my expenses.

_____ I have to pay rent of $400 a month on my apartment.

_____ Money just doesn't seem to go as far as it used to.

_____ I need $150 a month for groceries.

_____ Utilities payments take close to $100 a month.

_____ I'm trying to learn to manage my money better.

3. Because his plays were acted without scenery, Shakespeare could move his characters easily from one geographical location to another.

_____ The action of *Anthony and Cleopatra* shuttles back and forth between Egypt and Rome.

_____ *Othello* moves effortlessly from Venice to Cyprus.

_____ Shakespeare did not have to worry about the geographical confines of the action.

_____ *Pericles* travels easily around the coastal lands of the Aegean.

_____ Shakespeare's plays often move from one side of the world to the other in the space of one scene.

4. Apple has developed several new strategies to take over a larger share of the microcomputer market.

_____ Apple has built a highly automated computer-assembly plant to reduce its labor costs.

_____ Apple's new marketing techniques should give it some advantages over its competitors.

_____ Apple has lined up contracts with dozens of major universities to purchase its equipment for their students.

_____ Apple is really challenging other computer manufacturers with its new procedures.

_____ Apple has courted over a hundred software manufacturers to induce them to produce more programs for its new machines.

5. Prof. Riley is a more demanding teacher than Prof. Swanson.

_____ Prof. Riley asks more from her students than Prof. Swanson.

_____ While Prof. Swanson's students write only one paper, Prof. Riley's students write four.

_____ Although Prof. Swanson rarely calls on students for discussion, Prof. Riley frequently asks students to explain material from the text.

_____ Prof. Swanson almost never gives homework; Prof. Riley, however, assigns additional work after every class.

_____ Prof. Riley is considered a tougher teacher than Prof. Swanson.

EXERCISE H

Each topic sentence below makes a general statement about a subject. Supply three more specific details that could support each topic sentence.

EXAMPLE:

Many classic children's books involve fantasy.

A.   *Alice's Adventure's in Wonderland*
B.   *The Wind in the Willows*
C.   *Winnie the Pooh*

1.   Our state capital has many historic buildings.

A. _____

B. _____

C. _____

2.   Organized sports are (not) good for children.

A. _____

B. _____

C. _____

3.   Today's television shows are presenting a more positive (negative) image of the family than those of a few years ago.

A. _____

B. _____

C. _____

4.   Three distinct types of students attend our college.

A. _____

B. _____

C. _____

5.   My father is (not) a very organized person.

A. _____

B. _____

C. _____

6.   The success of the American Revolution depended on the work of several key people.

A. _____

    B. _____

    C. _____

7. My room reflects my personality.

    A. _____

    B. _____

    C. _____

8. To be effective with children, parents need three basic qualities.

    A. _____

    B. _____

    C. _____

9. Owning a car is expensive.

    A. _____

    B. _____

    C. _____

10. A successful party is easy if you plan ahead.

    A. _____

    B. _____

    C. _____

CONCLUSION

The final part of paragraph structure is the concluding sentence. This sentence should bring the discussion of the main idea to a close by returning to the general level of the subject and the focus of the paragraph. For example, in the paragraph on firefighters presented earlier, the topic sentence states: "... the change from 24-hour to 8-hour shifts for firefighters would not benefit the city." The conclusion coordinates by restating that idea in slightly different langauge: "... the Commission on Fire Protection recommends that the city retain the present system of 24-hour shifts for firefighters."

The conclusion also brings the discussion to a close by means of the phrase "in the light of these drawbacks," which asks the reader to recall the arguments that have been made.

Notice the relationship between the topic sentence and the conclusion of the Montoya paragraph earlier in this chapter:

Topic Sentence: Roberto Montoya deserves to receive this year's Citizen of the Year Award.

Conclusion: Because of his many years of public and private service to our community, Roberto Montoyo should be named Citizen of the Year.

The conclusion repeats the key words of the topic sentence and uses the phrase, "because of his many years of public and private service to our community," to sum up the points made in the paragraph. The conclusion moves back to the same level of generality as the topic sentence.

EXERCISE I

From the list below, select a concluding sentence that would fit with each topic sentence given. Write your choice for a conclusion underneath each topic sentence. Be prepared to explain the relationship between each topic sentence and conclusion.

CONCLUDING SENTENCES

I regret, then, that I cannot recommend Gail for this assignment because her administrative abilities are too limited.

By the forties, movies had again begun to approve of being rich.

Greek plays often showed the gods' actions in human lives.

The filmmakers of the thirties tried to emphasize ordinary human values more than wealth as a source of happiness.

When there are a hundred neuro-physiologists to every one general practitioner, the health profession is in trouble.

So speakers not only have to be careful of their words, they have to be careful of their body language too.

Intense competition in the medical field accounts for much of this specialization.

For the Greeks, drama was an especially powerful way of honoring the gods.

Finally, Gail was totally disorganized in her handling of the office move last year.

When a speaker communicates with an audience, a lifted eyebrow can contradict a thousand words.

1.   Movies of the Depression era suggested that being rich was not that much fun.

Conclusion _____

_____

2. Many hospital professionals make the mistake of overspecializing.

   Conclusion _____

   _____

3. Although Gail is a hard worker, I don't think she has the administrative abilities for this job.

   Conclusion _____

   _____

4. Body movements and facial expressions often convey a speaker's attitude better than words.

   Conclusion _____

   _____

5. In ancient Greece, the theater was closely tied to religion.

   Conclusion _____

   _____

EXERCISE J

Study the following paragraphs, particularly the topic sentences, and then try to write for each one a concluding sentence that coordinates with the topic sentence.

1. Even if you are a nonmechanic you can do some things to keep your car running efficiently. For one thing, you can check the oil level. First, pull the dipstick out of the engine and wipe it off with a rag. Then put it back in the engine again. This time, when it is pulled out, see where the oil level is on the stick. If it is low, add however many quarts of oil it will take to make it full. Another thing you can check is the water level in the radiator. First, make sure the radiator is not hot when you take the cap off. As long as the water level is within 1 inch of the top of the radiator, it is fine. Finally, you can make sure the tires are properly inflated. Most gas stations have an air pump. Set the air pump for the number of pounds of pressure shown on your tires. When the bell on the pump stops ringing, your tires are fully inflated.

    _____

    _____

2. Our inspection team found incredibly unsanitary conditions at Fred's Restaurant. The counters and floors were littered with scraps of meat and vegetables, some of which were starting to rot. The garbage cans were uncovered and overflowing. Insects and rodent droppings were discovered in sev-

eral boxes of flour and crackers. Milk and butter were left standing at room temperature because the refrigeration system was broken. The kitchen staff did not observe the hand-washing rule.

_____

_____

3.   As I looked out over the huge audience, I was overwhelmed with nervousness. First, my throat became clogged, and no amount of coughing could clear it. Then my hands began to shake. When I tried to steady myself against the podium, I just succeeded in scattering the pages of my speech across the stage. I thought my legs would collapse as I tried to collect them. Once I finally began to speak, my voice was so soft it could hardly be heard over the loud BA-BOOMP of my heart.

_____

_____

4.   Ocean Beach in October can still be a great vacation spot. You don't have to worry about not finding a room. All the major hotels stay open until December. And most of them offer big discounts for late fall visitors, sometimes as much as 50 percent. You can also find good prices on resort clothes in the fall. Your savings on next summer's wardrobe could finance another vacation next fall. During the fall, too, the cool weather is perfect for exhilarating walks along the ocean. And, perhaps best of all, you won't have to share all these benefits with a crowd of other vacationers.

_____

_____

5.   If your child doesn't seem to respond to your questions, perhaps you need to raise the level of the conversation. First level conversations begin with a question that asks for a factual reply: "Do you have any homework, dear?" There's no real opportunity for give-and-take here. The second level of conversation asks for opinions: "Did you like that movie?" This kind of question can lead to a more interesting discussion since more thought is required to reply. However, the third level, abstraction, can lead to the most rewarding conversations because it requires the use of imagination. "What do you think it would be like to be a pilot?" Here is a chance for stimulating discussion both for your child and for you.

_____

_____

EXERCISE K

Combine each set of sentences below to produce a paragraph with a well-defined topic sentence, specific support, and a conclusion that echoes the topic sentence. In each paragraph you will be asked to supply one part.

SWIM MEET

Topic Sentence: You supply this.
>
> We always arrived early.
> We were early by at least an hour.
> We arrived for a warm-up.
> The warm-up was before our swim meet.
>
> We changed into our suits.
> We got out our goggles.
> Some of us headed for the lanes.
> We swam 400 to 600 yards.
> We limbered up.
> Others headed for the sprint lanes.
> They worked on starts.
> They worked on turns.
> They got the feel of the water.
> The whistle blew.
> We retired to our bench.
> We waited for our events.

Conclusion:
>
> We had a good warm-up.
> We felt less nervous.
> We felt more ready.
> The readiness was for competition.

TIFFANY'S ART

Topic Sentence:
>
> Louis Comfort Tiffany lived from 1848 to 1933.
> He brought the art to heights.
> The art was of stained glass.
> No one else has reached these heights.
>
> Tiffany did not paint on the glass.
> Colors were not painted.
> He made his own glass instead.
> The glass was in colors.
> The colors were the ones he wanted.

He used a special kind of glass.
The glass was mottled.
He portrayed leaves and flowers.
He invented "drapery glass."
"Drapery glass" is folded.
It gives an appearance.
The appearance is fabric-like.
He also developed a new technique.
The technique was for putting glass together.
The technique allowed him to create detail.
Details were created with small pieces.
The pieces were of glass.
Tiffany also achieved.
Effects were achieved.
The effects were unique.
He layered one piece of glass over another.

Conclusion: You supply this.

COLLEGE INDEPENDENCE

Topic Sentence:

College demands.
Independence is demanded.
This independence is great.
The greatness is in comparison to high school's demands.

Support: You supply three examples to support the topic sentence.

Conclusion:

A student wants to succeed in college.
A student must learn.
Independence must be learned.

EXERCISE L

Combine the group of sentences below to produce a paragraph that follows the topic sentence–support–conclusion format. When you have finished, you will have the first of a pair of paragraphs. Using this one as a guide, write the second paragraph on your own.

The shadow glided along the wall.
It was silent.

The wall belonged to the old castle.

The shadow continued until it reached a window.

A hand opened the sash.

The hand was gloved.

The opening was carefully done.

A figure slipped into the room.

The room was where Sabrina usually slept.

The shadowy figure moved toward the bed.

There was no sound.

The hand reached for the bed-curtain.

A voice said, "Don't move."

The voice added, "I have a pistol."

The voice was soft.

The voice was cool.

FROM PARAGRAPH TO ESSAY

Longer pieces of writing are built on the same basic principles as single paragraphs. In many ways, an essay is just a larger version of a paragraph. Just as you related individual sentences in a paragraph, moving from general to specific to general, so you relate paragraphs to one another in an essay.

In an essay, you still need to provide your reader with a general statement of your subject and the focus you are taking on this subject (a *thesis*). You also need to move to a more specific level and provide examples, reasons, and details to explain your point about this subject. At the end of an essay, you need to restate the general point you made in your writing.

Here is an essay of several paragraphs that follows the pattern of introducing the subject with a thesis, supporting it, and then summarizing the main idea.

thesis (fo-cuses main idea)

Being divorced has caused me financial, emotional, and parenting problems that I did not face when I was married.

support (pre-sents subor-dinate details)

Since the divorce, my financial situation has certainly changed. Before, I could depend on my husband's salary to pay the rent, buy groceries, and clothe the three of us. The extra money that I made as a part-time bookkeeper could be used for extras like a vacation or new dining room chairs. However, since Ben and I separated, my full-time salary is barely enough to rent a small apartment, buy groceries and gasoline, and pay for babysitting for my son, Mark.

The financial strain has not made my emotional adjustment to divorce any easier, either. The divorce raised all kinds of frightening questions for me about my value as a person. Instead of Ben telling me that I'm lovable, I have to convince myself that I am. The loneliness is hard, too. There's no one but my four-year-old to confide my problems in. I often feel depressed because I don't think I can handle all the responsibilities I have now.

Of course, my chief responsibility is raising Mark, and the divorce has made parenting more difficult. Ben was able to be firm with Mark, while I find discipline very hard to maintain. Since I'm working all day, I find I have less energy at night to play with Mark. In fact, sometimes I'm just plain irritable with him. I never realized before how much easier it is to be able to share the responsibility for child raising. A single parent doesn't get much time off from parenting.

conclusion
(coordinates
with thesis)

All in all, the first few months after my divorce have caused great changes in my financial situation, in my emotional situation, and in my relationship to my son. But, as each day passes, I'm more and more sure that I'll make a good life for Mark and me.

Notice how the thesis of this essay tells the reader that it will deal with three main problems: financial problems, emotional problems, and parenting problems. The essay then devotes one paragraph to each kind of problem.

Each individual paragraph within the essay has its own topic sentence, which focuses on one aspect of the larger subject raised in the introduction. These individual paragraphs supply specific details about a financial, emotional, or parenting problem the writer faced. However, each paragraph does not have its own conclusion. Instead, the writer uses some linking phrases to move a reader from one paragraph to another and uses one paragraph at the end of the essay to sum up the points she has made.

The outline below shows one way of visualizing the structure of this essay.

PROBLEMS OF DIVORCE

Thesis: General Statement about kinds of problems faced.
  I.   First kind of problem (more specific than thesis)
       A.   Supporting detail about problem I (more specific than topic sentence I)
       B.   Supporting detail about problem I (about as specific as detail A)
  II. Second kind of problem (about as specific as problem I)
       A.   Supporting detail about problem II (more specific than topic sentence II)
       B.   Supporting detail about problem II (about as specific as detail A)
  III. Third kind of problem (about as specific as problem I)
       A.   Supporting detail about problem III (more specific than topic sentence III)
       B.   Supporting detail about problem III (about as specific as detail A)
Conclusion: General statement about problems of divorce (about as general as thesis)

The diagram below is another way you can visualize the relationship between the parts of an essay.

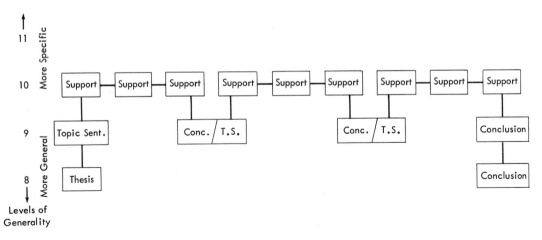

In general, any comment made in this book about paragraphing can be applied equally to longer pieces of writing.

EXERCISE M

Study the multiparagraph essay shown below and find its major parts. Be prepared to explain how the parts of this essay fit together using the general pattern described above.

TEA TRANSFORMS ENGLAND

Although tea has a reputation as a mild-mannered beverage, its remarkable effects on the economy, sociology, and politics of eighteenth-century England show it to be a rather potent brew.

For one thing, tea led to the rapid development of the British pottery and porcelain industry. In the 1700s, with tea the principal beverage in England, there was an enormous demand for teapots and tea cups. At first the delicate teaware was imported from China, but gradually British manufacturers such as Wedgwood took over the market.

Tea is also credited with lowering the death rate in eighteenth-century England. At the beginning of the century, cheap gin was London's most popular beverage. At the height of the gin era, when anyone could get dead drunk for two pennies, burials outnumbered baptisms in London by two to one. As tea shops replaced the gin shops, the death rate came down dramatically.

However, probably the most significant effect of Britain's passion for tea was the loss of its American Empire. The transplanted Englishmen in the Colonies made America a most profitable tea market. In 1765, the British Parliament began its unfortunate effort to tax the Americans for their tea. With "Tea Parties" in Boston, Annapolis, and other ports, the Americans signaled their unwillingness to pay the tax. The British tried to press the point, and everyone knows where that led—straight to the American Revolution.

So the English have a great deal to contemplate as they sip their tea and ponder the great changes these innocent-looking leaves have brought to their country.

EXERCISE N

Each set of topic sentences shown below represents the paragraphs of an essay. Compose a thesis that might introduce each essay and a conclusion that might close each essay.

EXAMPLE:

T.S. A On the one hand, King David was a fearless warrior.

T.S. B But David was also a gifted poet and musician.

Possible Thesis: King David had an unusual combination of military genius and artistic gifts.

Possible Conclusion: Through his genius for military strategy and his artistic talent, David became one of the greatest kings of Israel.

1. *Thesis:* _____

_____

T.S. A In the first stage of remodeling, we will make major structural changes in the building.

T.S. B During the next three weeks, we will take care of the utility services necessary to support the new structure.

T.S. C Finally, we will make the cosmetic changes to the interior of the building.

Conclusion: _____

_____

2. *Thesis:* _____

_____

T.S. A Reducing the speed limit would be one way to make Rt. 3 safer.

T.S. B We should also consider adding several traffic signals.

T.S. C As a last alternative, we could ban trucks from the road altogether.

Conclusion: _____

_____

3. *Thesis:* _____

_____

T.S.   A   Many homebuyers choose Hillendale because of its great location.

T.S.   B   Others are interested in the excellent design and construction of the homes.

T.S.   C   Still others move here because the houses are so affordable.

Conclusion: _____

_____

EXERCISE O

For each thesis–conclusion pair shown below, write appropriate topic sentences as indicated for the supporting paragraphs of the essay.

1. *Thesis:* In just two months, Barbara's new diet changed her from a sullen, withdrawn child to a cheerful, outgoing one.

    T.S.   A _____

    _____

    T.S.   B _____

    Conclusion: The elimination of certain foods from Barbara's diet worked an almost miraculous change in her personality.

2. *Thesis:* Because of Ms. O'Casey's outstanding performance in the classroom, in her department, and in the college as a whole, I would enthusiastically recommend her promotion to Associate Professor.

    T.S.   A _____

    T.S.   B _____

    T.S.   C _____

    Conclusion: State College is fortunate to have such an effective teacher who works well with her colleagues in the Mathematics Department and serves the whole college with such generosity.

3. *Thesis:* What kind of computer you should buy depends on what you want to do with it, how much technical knowledge you have, and how much money you want to spend.

    T.S.   A _____

T.S.   B _____

_____

T.S.   C _____

_____

Conclusion: If you shop for a computer with your needs, your level of expertise, and your budget clearly in mind, you should find your way more easily through the confusing computer market.

WRITING PRACTICE

1.   You have a work-study job at the Public Relations Office of your college. The college is hosting a group of Chinese high school students for a week, and your boss has asked you for some recommendations about what activities should be planned for the visitors. Write a memo to your boss laying out your top choice of an activity for the visitors. Explain why you think this activity should have a high priority in the visitors' schedule.

Before you draft your memo, list about ten possible activities you think the students might enjoy. Then choose your top priority from the list.

After you have drafted the memo, look over your paragraphing or trade papers with another student in the class and comment on each other's work. Is the main point clearly stated and adequately supported? Did you close with a strong restatement of your recommendation? Check your sentences to make sure they are complete and correctly punctuated. When you have made any necessary revisions or editing changes in your memo, complete a final draft.

2.   Because of your excellent suggestion for the visiting students, the head of the Public Relations Office has asked you to plan a 2-or-3-hour tour of your area (may include campus and/or surrounding city or region) for the husbands and wives of some deans who will be attending a conference at the college. Write a one-page description of the tour you have planned. This flyer will be mailed to all conference participants. For your work in setting up the tour, you will receive a commission for each person who signs up, so make your tour sound as interesting as possible.

While you are planning your tour, you might want to confer with relatives or friends familiar with your area to get suggestions about sights to visit. You might also consult the college library or the public library or call your local Chamber of Commerce or Tourist Bureau for suggestions.

In planning your tour, it might be helpful to have a theme—for instance, famous historical events, unusual natural features of the region, ethnic cultures in your area.

When you have composed a draft of your flyer, review your paragraphing or trade papers with another student and review each other's work. Have you stated the main idea clearly? Have you given enough supporting details to make the nature of the tour clear? Also check your sentences to see that they are complete and correctly punctuated. When you have made any necessary revisions or editing corrections, make a final copy of your tour description.

8

Basic Paragraph Strategies

Chapter 7 showed you a general structure for paragraphs (and, by extension, for longer pieces of writing): a topic sentence, followed by supporting detail, followed by a conclusion. Within that general format, however, you can arrange information in dozens of different ways. In this chapter, you will see five of the most common strategies for arranging information within the basic topic sentence–support–conclusion framework. The discussion of each strategy shows you some guidelines for using that strategy effectively. (These general guidelines are covered in greater detail in separate chapters elsewhere in this book.)

BASIC PARAGRAPH STRATEGIES

telling a story
describing physical characteristics
listing examples, reasons, or steps
breaking down into parts or categories
showing similarities or differences

EXERCISE A

The paragraphs below illustrate the use of these five strategies. The new management of Starr's Department Stores has hired five people to shop in the various branches of the store and report on the conditions, service, and merchandise they find. These paragraphs are taken from the shoppers' reports. Can you identify the strategy each writer has used? Be prepared to show the parts of each paragraph's structure.

1.   from Carl's report:

The Men's Department at the Westside Mall Starr's projects an image of quiet elegance. Soft, diffused lighting gives the whole area an atmosphere of understated luxury. The rich, dark burgundy of the upholstery and carpeting and the gleaming mahogany of the furniture also reinforce the air of polished sophistication. Accent pieces such as an antique globe and medieval brass rubbings further suggest the good taste and refinement customers should associate with Starr's. In sum, the decorating scheme of the Men's Department seems to complement perfectly the high quality of the mechandise sold there.

Carl's strategy: _____

2.   from Pat's report:

When compared to Brannigan's, Starr's at Harbour View offers less satisfactory customer services. In the first place, while the customer service area at Brannigan's is conveniently located on the first floor and marked with prominent signs, Starr's has hidden its customer service center in a corner of the basement with very few signs to guide shoppers in finding it. And even if customers do locate the service area, they won't find as many services offered at Starr's as at Brannigan's. Brannigan's, for example, provides clothing alterations and jewelry repair, neither of which is available at Starr's. Although Starr's provides boxes for customer purchases, it does not have a gift-wrap counter as Brannigan's does. In the Harbour View shopping area, customers looking for convenient service would do better at Brannigan's than at Starr's.

Pat's strategy: _____

3.   from Rita's report:

Trying to buy a popcorn machine at the Starr's downtown was an exercise in frustration from start to finish. When I arrived in the Housewares Department at about 6 P.M. on Friday, the 10th, there seemed to be no salespeople on the floor. I wandered through the rows of merchandise for about 20 minutes before I found the popcorn machines that had been advertised in that week's sale booklet. It then took me 10 more minutes to spot an open cash register on the other side of the floor in the Furniture Department. When it was finally my turn, the clerk rang up my purchase at the regular price instead of the sale price. I politely pointed out his mistake, but he insisted quite rudely that this was not the machine that was on sale. Finally, I pulled out my copy of the advertisement, and he grudgingly redid the sale. Meanwhile, I had discovered that the butter melter was missing from my popcorn machine. When I asked if I could exchange that popper for another one, the clerk insisted that I had to go down to the customer service area to get an exchange ticket. If Starr's wants to prevent the kind of frustration I experienced, it needs to take a close look at its staffing patterns and staff training procedures.

Rita's strategy: _____

4.   from Hannah's report:

The salespeople I observed at Starr's Memorial Plaza store ranged from aggressive to indifferent in their attitudes. The aggressive clerks began to bear down on me if I so much as looked in the direction of their sales area. One woman in Electronics even took me by the arm and almost pulled me over to her televison sets. These pushy salespeople made me so uneasy I wanted nothing except to escape from their clutches. Fortunately, a very large percentage of the sales staff was genuinely helpful and friendly. They allowed me to look around at my own pace, but immediately offered assistance when I asked for it. I also came across a few clerks who seemed to be afraid of me. These timid souls would scurry out of sight if I looked as if I might ask a question. The last, and, I am happy to report, the smallest group of sales clerks was the indifferent ones. They would keep me waiting while they finished up conversations with their buddies in the next department or be too busy fixing their make-up to find the merchandise I needed. I have attached a list of the salespeople I observed at the store, putting each into one of the categories described above. I think Starr's would do well to find more of the friendly types and dismiss or retrain the aggressive, the timid, and the indifferent clerks.

Hannah's strategy: _____

5.   from Wilma's report:

All things considered, then, I found shopping at the Starr's in Cedar Grove a pleasant experience. The selling areas seemed logically arranged, and the general look of the store was fresh and appealing, conducive to relaxed shopping. In the majority of departments, there was an adequate selection of merchandise in several price ranges. In addition, the salespeople, on the whole, seemed competent and polite in dealing with me, as did the managers and office personnel. With the few exceptions I have noted in my report, the Starr's in Cedar Grove seems like an excellent place to shop.

Wilma's strategy: _____

STRATEGY: TELLING A STORY

Guidelines

Focus

Focus on a limited series of events. Don't try to tell about your whole vacation, for instance, in one paragraph.

Topic Sentence

Be sure that your topic sentence explains the significance of the story.

> EXAMPLES:
> Last summer's weekend trip on the Bay turned into a *nightmare for our family.*
> Jerry's behavior at the party just shows *what a gentle person he is.*
> *I've never been so embarrassed* as I was the day I took my driver's test.

Organization

Arrange events in a logical time order, making sure that no important part of the story is left out.

Coherence

Use joining work like *after, next, while, then,* and *before* to emphasize time relationships between events.

Word Choice

Use sentences with strong verbs to emphasize action in telling a story.

> EXAMPLES:
> *Weak verbs*
> There *was* a certain tension in the air before the race.
> Millie *put* the package on the table.
> *Strong verbs*
> Tension *crackled* in the air before the race.
> Millie *slammed* the package down on the table.

Sentence Structure

Try to put an action in each base sentence.

> EXAMPLES:
> *Action not emphasized*
> *It was late summer* in 1963 when we set out for a sail in our new boat.
> *The sun shone cruelly overhead* as the drivers clocked mile after mile.
> *Action emphasized*
> In late summer 1963 *we set out in our new sailboat.*
> *The drivers clocked mile after mile* as the sun shone cruelly overhead.

Conclusion

Use a concluding sentence to reemphasize the significance of the story.

> EXAMPLES:
> At last, *the nightmare* was over.
> *Jerry's compassion* that night touched everyone in the class.
> With my family, I've never quite been able to live down *my "run in" with the Department of Motor Vehicles.*

EXERCISE B

Using the guidelines suggested above, evaluate each of the following paragraphs. Which one uses the story-telling strategy more effectively? Where could each paragraph be improved?

1.   Porter checked the paper to see if the item he'd seen yesterday was still there. It was. He called the number and made an appointment with the lady who answered. About two o'clock, he drove to the address she'd given him. She led him to the box in the corner of the kitchen. He looked in, and his heart beat hard. Oh yes, that was just what he needed. The tiny pup looked up at him with round, black eyes, and he knew he was lost— she would own him; his house would revolve around her; her every need would be met.

2.   Ruth climbed the dark staircase. She had come over on the ferry in the morning. It was raining. She stood for a time, watching the gulls. Later, back in London, she remembered the moment. The stairway was growing cold. Earlier, the weather had been warmer. The ferry had been comfortable. Her apartment in London seemed like paradise.

EXERCISE C

Keeping in mind the guidelines suggested above, combine the following groups of sentences to produce a paragraph that makes its point by telling a story.

1. I take Danny out to dinner.
   I take Bob out to dinner.
   Danny and Bob are my sons.
   We go to a nice restaurant.
   This is not my idea of an evening.
   The evening is one of enjoyment.

2. We have to struggle.
   The struggling is over baths.
   We have to tear the house apart.
   The searching is for two clean shirts.
   The seaching is for two clean pairs of trousers.
   The searching is for socks.
   The socks should match.
   All this happens before we can even leave the house.

3. Danny has to go to the bathroom.
   We arrive at the restaurant.
   We are seated at our table.

4. I am with Danny.
   Bob takes bites.
   The bites are out of all the rolls.
   The rolls are in the basket.
   He opens the sugar packages.

5. We order our dinner.
   Of course, the boys hate everything on the menu.
   They tell the waiter this.
   They speak in loud voices.

6. Finally, their hamburgers arrive.
   Danny insists that Bob's is bigger.
   Danny refuses to eat the "small" hamburger.

7. The clean shirts are covered.
   Chocolate sauce and mustard cover them.
   The clean faces are covered too.
   By this time, dinner is over.

8. My coffee is cold.
   My shrimp is untouched.
   My stomach is upset.
   I wonder.
   Does the zoo take reservations for dinner?

STRATEGY: DESCRIBING

Guidelines

Focus

Focus on the physical characteristics of one person, place, or thing.

Topic Sentence

Be sure that your topic sentence presents one central impression you want to give your reader.

> EXAMPLES:
> My brother's room is always *a mess.*
> Shirley looked *exhausted* after her first day at work.
> The kitchen is the *most cheerful* room in our house.

Support

Reinforce that central impression by using details that will appeal to the senses. Show your reader what the subject looks like, sounds like, smells like, tastes like, and/or feels like.

Organization

Arrange the descriptive details in a logical order, such as top to bottom, left to right, or far away to close up.

Coherence

Use transitions like *beside, under, against, where,* and *on* to emphasize the spatial relationships between details.

Word Choice

Use vivid adjectives to get your reader really involved in your description. Show your reader the exact color, size, shape, position, etc., of each detail.

Sentence Structure

Put these descriptive details into your base sentences.

> EXAMPLES:
> *Description not emphasized*
> Her desk, *which is covered with books, papers, and half-eaten food,* stands near
>   the door.

You walk in *as the tantalizing smell of pizza overwhelms you.*

Description emphasized

Open books, scattered papers, and half-eaten food littered her desk, which stood near the door.

The tantalizing smell of pizza overwhelms you as you walk in.

Conclusion

Restate the central impression in the conclusion.

> EXAMPLES:
>
> Fred's room is a *man-made disaster area.*
>
> Altogether, Shirley's fatigue *completely obscured her natural good looks.*
>
> With its bright colors and open layout, *the kitchen lifts everyone's spirits.*

EXERCISE D

Using the guidelines suggested above, evaluate each of the following paragraphs. Which one uses the description strategy more effectively? Where could each paragraph be improved?

1. The movie star was very pretty. Her acting was not bad, but it was her appearance that held my interest. She looked so young with her large, blue eyes. And her figure was delicate. Her blonde hair also made her look young. The costumes emphasized the star's girlish appearance and also suggested an appealing personality.

2. Davis's appearance conveyed lost youth. The over-bleached blonde hair tied up with a limp powder-blue bow looked out of place with her tired, wrinkled face. Her faded eyes gave only the faintest suggestion of a girlish sparkle that might once have lighted them. A frilly lace collar could not hide her drooping chins and baggy neck. The yellowed satin dress might have made its first appearance at a turn-of-the-century debutante ball. Everything about her suggested decayed beauty grasping vainly for its former glory.

EXERCISE E

Keeping in mind the suggestions above, combine the following groups of sentences to produce a paragraph that describes:

1. The face reveals suffering.
   The face belongs to Jim Wood.
   The suffering has marked his whole life.

2. His hair sticks straight up.
    His hair is short.
    His hair is graying.
    He looks like he is terrified.
    The terror is unending.

3. Eyes look out of his face.
    The eyes are pain-filled.
    The eyes are brown.
    The face is lined.
    The face is leathery.

4. A scar runs down.
    The scar is crooked.
    It is on his left cheek.
    His nose is bent.
    The bending is at an angle.
    The angle is queer.
    The nose has been broken.
    This has happened several times.

5. His mouth is half-open.
    His mouth displays rows.
    The rows are of teeth.
    The teeth are yellowed.
    There are many gaps in the rows.
    Teeth have rotted out.
    Teeth have been knocked out in fights.

6. A beard meanders.
    The beard is pathetic.
    The beard is scraggly.
    The meandering is over his chin.

7. Jim Wood's face tells the story.
    The story is of his life.
    The life is luckless.

STRATEGY: LISTING EXAMPLES, REASONS, OR STEPS

Guidelines

Focus

Focus on a process or event that you are familiar with so that you will know the examples, causes, or steps involved.

Topic Sentence

State the subject as clearly as possible in the topic sentence and try to indicate the examples, causes, or steps you will be discussing.

EXAMPLES:

The Drama Club's production of *As You Like It* failed *because of poor casting and poor directing.*

You can make a wreath for your front door *in five simple steps.*

Throughout American history, *women have had to struggle for educational opportunities* that men took for granted.

Support

Be sure that all necessary steps or significant causes have been mentioned. If you are giving examples, use enough to show your reader that there is a pattern present rather than just one isolated incident. Generally, three to five examples should be enough for one paragraph.

Organization

Arrange the examples, reasons, or steps in a logical order; either a time order or an order of importance works well with this kind of paragraph. If reasons or steps have been laid out in the topic sentence, they should be developed in the paragraph in the same order that they appear in the topic sentence. In the first topic sentence above, for instance, the two reasons for the play's failure are listed in chronological order. (Casting takes place before directing.) Therefore, in the paragraph, casting should be discussed before directing.

Coherence

Use transitions like *next, then, even more important, another example, a hundred years later,* and *most significant of all* to show the logical connections between your examples, causes, or steps.

Word Choice

Use specific, concrete statements rather than general or abstract ones.

EXAMPLES:

General

Cars today are more efficient.

Tighten the bolts.

The *Ohio* is a big submarine.

Specific

A 1985 Citation averages 35 miles per gallon.

Use an 8-centimeter torque wrench with a rubber handle to tighten the bolts.

The nuclear submarine *Ohio* is 560 feet long and has an 18,700-ton displacement.

Sentence Structure

Put important examples, causes, or steps into your base sentence.

EXAMPLES:

Unimportant idea emphasized

The first computers, which had vacuum-tube memories and occupied an entire room, *were developed in the 1940s.*

Next, a *medicated pad,* which should be wiped over the entire face, *can be very effective.*

Important idea emphasized

The first computers, developed in the 1940s, *had vacuum-tube memories and occupied an entire room.*

Next, *a medicated pad,* which can be very effective, *should be wiped over the entire face.*

Conclusion

Make the conclusion a restatement or summary of your main point.

EXAMPLES:

Although the sets were elegant, *poor casting and poor direction ruined this play.*

With little more than an hour's work, *you can hang this decoration on your door.*

So, little known women like these have *forced open the doors of American educational institutions.*

EXERCISE F

Using the guidelines suggested above, evaluate each of the following paragraphs. Which one uses the listing strategy more effectively? Where could each paragraph be improved?

1. There are three reasons we should change our work schedule rules to flex time. We could allow people to arrive at any hour they chose as long as they worked 8 hours, and we would get three benefits. People could run errands in the morning and still get in a day's work. The parking lot wouldn't undergo such terrible traffic jams. The elevators would work better, too. We would gain a lot.

2. Winter has several good points. For starters, there's skiing, sledding, and ice skating. Cold weather makes these sports possible, and they make the cold bearable. Then there's the beauty of the snow, the stripped, black trees, and the glory of the winter sky, clear of mist and full of blazing constellations. And finally, winter cleanses our senses, as chilled wine sharpens our taste, and prepares us to enjoy the richness of spring and summer. Without winter, after all, there'd be no spring.

EXERCISE G

Keeping in mind the techniques discussed above, combine the following sentences to produce a paragraph that lists reasons and examples.

1. I am qualified.
    The qualification is full.
    It is for the computer programming job.
    You advertised this job.
    The advertisement was in *The Times* yesterday.
2. Here is the first reason.
    I have the background.
    The background is in education.
    You require the background.
3. I graduated from Bayside College.
    I received my A.A.
    The degree was in computer programming.
    I mastered COBOL.
    I mastered Basic.
    I mastered FORTRAN.
4. I also have experience.
    My experience is extensive.
    My experience was gained on the job.
5. I worked for CompuData, Inc.
    I worked as a programmer.
    We handled the accounts of several large businesses.
    I worked there for two years.

6. I am working for the Social Security Administration.
    I have worked there for a year and a half.
    I work in Claims Verification.
    I am working there now.

7. My education gives me qualities.
    My experience gives me qualities.
    You need these qualities.

STRATEGY: BREAKING DOWN INTO CATEGORIES

Guidelines

Focus

Focus on a group of people or objects that you are very familiar with so that you will know the various types within the group. Find some principle that you can use to classify the members of the group you are writing about. Teachers, for example, might be classified according to how strictly they grade. Restaurants might be classified according to price or according to kind of food served. Be sure this classification principle reveals some *significant* similarities or differences among members of the group. (Most people would not be interested in a division of teachers according to height, for instance.)

Topic Sentence

If possible, name the major categories (usually three to five) in your topic sentence.

EXAMPLES:

Three kinds of students roam the halls of Southern High School: *the scholar,* *the jock,* and *the loner.*

Nervousness, calm, and *enjoyment* are the three stages in learning to dance.

Children's games require *varying degrees of athletic skill.*

Support

Explain each category and/or give examples of items that would fit in each.

Organization

Present the categories in a logical order: from smallest group to largest, from most expensive to least expensive, from first stage to last stage.

Coherence

Use transitions like *slightly more expensive, the highest degree of skill, most boring of all,* and *last* to emphasize your principle of classification.

Conclusion

Use a conclusion that will sum up the whole classification system, not just the last point.

> EXAMPLES:
>
> Though the actual students change from year to year, *the same types seem to appear again and again.*
>
> It is a rare dancer who does not pass through *each of these stages* in the course of his or her development.
>
> Children have devised games that *suit every level of athletic skill* from none at all to super jock.

EXERCISE H

Using the guidelines suggested above, evaluate each of the following paragraphs. Which one uses the categorizing strategy more effectively? Where could each paragraph be improved?

1.   In working on this collection of photographs, I have discovered various types of beaches, all beautiful in their own way. Tropical beaches create perfect crescents of white sand fringed with coconut palms and abutting an intensely blue sea. On the middle latitude coasts, the beaches tend to be dune-covered, tufted with coarse sea grass, and often shrouded in fog. Even more isolated are the craggy northern beaches with their coarse sand and towering cliffs. Although beaches may vary considerably depending on their location, each one provides unique photographic opportunities.

2.   There are three kinds of figure skaters. Elegant skaters stress line, stretch, and fluid motion. The finest examples of this group are the pairs team, the Protopapovs. The athletic skaters excel at triple jumps and bouncy rhythms. The East Germans produce a number of these. And then there are the great women skaters like Peggy Fleming and Dorothy Hamill. All these kinds of skaters contribute to the stature of their sports.

EXERCISE I

Using the suggestions above, combine the following groups of sentences to produce a paragraph that could introduce a study of architectural styles.

1. There have been four traditions.
   The traditions are in architecture.
   The architecture is of the West.
   The traditions are major.
   These traditions have influenced architecture.
   The traditions are from Egypt.
   The traditions are classical Greek and Roman.
   The traditions are Medieval.
   The traditions are of the Renaissance.

2. Architects learned about ornamentation.
   The ornamentation was decorative.
   The learning was from palaces, temples, and tombs.
   These structures were in ancient Egypt.
   Architects learned about the value of scale.
   This learning was also from palaces, temples, and tombs.

3. The effect can be felt.
   The effect is of classical Greece.
   The effect is of classical Rome.
   The feeling is in the practicality.
   The practicality is elegant.
   The practicality is of columns.
   The feeling is in walls.
   The walls are punctuated.
   The punctuation is with arches.

4. Architecture was enriched.
   The enrichment was by towers.
   The enrichment was by spires.
   The enrichment was by sculpture.
   The sculpture was used for decoration.
   These elements were developed mainly in cathedrals.
   The cathedrals were in Europe.
   They were great.
   This took place during the Middle Ages.

5. Architecture grew in richness.
   Architects developed skill.
   The skill was technical.
   The skill grew greater and greater.
   The Renaissance developed an architecture.
   The architecture was of expression.
   The expression was of individual architects.

6. Every aspect developed.
   The aspects are of architecture.
   The architecture is modern.
   The development has been out of these traditions.
   Or the development has been in response to these traditions.

STRATEGY: COMPARING
OR CONTRASTING

Guidelines

Focus

Focus on two subjects between which you see some clear differences or similarities that will interest your readers.

Topic Sentence

Name both subjects in the topic sentence and define the similarity or difference as clearly as you can.

> EXAMPLES:
>
> The *computer* **differs** from the *human brain* in its **speed of operation, number of components,** and **degree of free will.**
>
> *College* is **more academically demanding** than *high school.*
>
> *My mother* and *my father* share the **same easygoing temperament.**

Support

List several examples of the similarity or difference you are emphasizing. Make sure that your two subjects are developed in equal ways with just about the same space given and the same ideas developed for each subject. You can't, for example, compare two stories by writing two sentences about the plot of one story and ten sentences about the characters in the other.

Organization

Arrange the points of comparison or contrast in the block pattern or the alternating pattern.

EXAMPLE:

Block pattern

   I. High School
      A. Classwork
      B. Homework   block of information
      C. Long-term projects   on
                                  high school
  II. College
      A. Classwork
      B. Homework   block of information
      C. Long-term projects   on
                                  college

Alternating pattern
I. Classwork
   A. High school
   B. College
II. Homework
   A. High school
   B. College
III. Long-term projects
   A. High school
   B. College

Also consider the order in which you present the major points. High school, for instance, would logically be discussed before college; classwork might (since it is less demanding) logically come before long-term projects.

Coherence

Use transitions like *similarly, likewise,* and *compared to* to suggest similarity between ideas. Use transitions like *on the other hand* and *however* to suggest contrast between ideas.

Word Choice

Use concrete, specific language rather than vague or abstract words to point out similarities or differences.

EXAMPLE:

Vague language

Carol is nice like her mother.

Summer is pleasanter than winter.

Specific language

Like her mother, Carol always has a smile and a kind word for everyone who comes to her door, even salespeople.

With its drowsy, mint-julep evenings, summer in Atlanta is far more attractive to me than the cold, harried evenings up North when school is in session.

Sentence Structure

Put the similarities or differences you are trying to emphasize into the base sentence.

EXAMPLE:

Similarity emphasized

Although I like to think of myself as more liberated than my grandmother, *our ideas about marriage are remarkably alike.* While we disagree about the methods to use, we *both think that communication between spouses is crucial to a good marriage.*

Difference emphasized

Although our ideas about marriage are remarkably alike, *I consider my-self more liberated than my grandmother.* While we both agree that communication between spouses is crucial to a good marriage, *we disagree on the methods of communication.*

Conclusion

Restate the two subjects and the main points of similarity or difference in the conclusion.

EXAMPLES:

In **speed, complexity,** and **autonomy,** the *computer* is still not the equal of the *human brain.*

Anyone who says that *college* is just another four years of *high school* hasn't looked carefully at the **academic demands** of college.

Two more **evenly matched, unflappable** personalities than *Mom* and *Dad,* I could never hope to find.

EXERCISE J

Using the guidelines suggested above, evaluate each of the following paragraphs. Which one uses the compare/contrast strategy more effectively? Where could each paragraph be improved?

1. Sheila likes sapphires. She tells me they're prettier than rubies. Sheila doesn't look good in red. She likes them better than emeralds or amethysts. Sapphires, she felt, looked better against her tan. She even likes the blue gems better than diamonds. I like rubies myself.

2. Management Information Systems (MIS) address themselves to very different audiences than Decision Management Systems (DMS). MIS are designed to help shop managers control their planning by giving them accurate production statistics. Most of these statistics go into much more detail than the business managers need. DMS, on the other hand, help managers to see totals and trends. For example, DMS might display the total sales for each of the last three months in a bar graph so the difference between the forecast and the actual volumes can be seen at a glance. Although they provide different kinds of information, both systems are essential for a well-run business.

EXERCISE K

Keeping in mind the guidelines suggested above, combine the following groups of sentences to produce a paragraph that contrasts Baltimore and Washington, D.C.

1. Baltimore and Washington are only 45 miles apart.
   They share the Mid-Atlantic Piedmont.
   They are different.

2. Baltimore grew around a port.
   Its port is the second largest on the East Coast.
   It is the foundation of the city's economy.

3. Washington has no "natural" function.
   It was created to be a government center.
   It was deliberately put where no town had taken root.

4. Baltimore is mainly a blue-collar city.
   It works at heavy industry.
   One industry is steel.
   Another industry is automaking.
   Another industry is railroading.

5. Washington is primarily a white-collar city.
   It is dominated by huge office buildings.
   These buildings house the federal bureaucracies.

6. Baltimore is a city of ethnic neighborhoods.
   There is a large Polish population.
   There is a large Jewish population.
   There is a sizable Ukranian population.
   There is an established German community.

7. These groups live in areas.
   The areas are identifiable.
   Families have stayed there for generations.

8. The Washington area is peopled by professionals.
   They come from all over the country.
   They come to represent their hometowns and states.
   They come to work at the center of the government.

9. Baltimore belongs to its region.
   Washington belongs to the nation.

EXERCISE L

Combine each of the following groups of sentences to produce a complete paragraph. In some cases, you may have to add a topic sentence, a conclusion, or transition words. In other paragraphs, you may have to rearrange the sentences to get the most effective order. In writing these paragraphs, use whatever techniques are appropriate to the strategy being used.

EMERGENCY ROOM REPORT

1. The patient was admitted.
   The admitting was at 7:10 A.M.
   It was in the emergency room.
   The patient was complaining of severe pain in his ankle.

2. The region was swollen.
   The region was below the left distal fibula.
   The region was discolored.
   The discoloration covered an area.
   The area had a diameter of 7 centimeters.
   The area was circular.

3. The right side showed swelling.
   There was no discoloration.

4. The patient made a statement.
   He had pain when he moved the foot.
   The movement was from side to side.
   The pain was sharp.

5. The swollen area was tender.
   The tenderness was to the touch.
   The patient complained about it.

6. No signs appeared.
   The signs were of injury.
   The appearance was on the leg above the ankle.
   The appearance was on the foot.

7. X-rays were needed.
   The need was to determine the extent.
   The extent was of the injury.
   Bones might be broken.

BONING A TROUT

1. There is a way to bone a trout.
   The way is neat.
   The way is efficient.
   It can be learned in a few minutes.

2. Lift the fish by its tail.
   Make a cut on the underside.
   The cut should be small.
   It should be near the tail.
   This should be done first.

3. Hold the tail.
   Insert the tines of a fork into the cut.
   Separate the meat from the bones.
   The separating should be gentle.

4. You reach the gills.
   The filet will drop onto the plate.
   The filet will be unbroken.

5. Turn the fish over.
   Repeat the process.
   This may be done next.

6. You will have two filets.
   They will be perfect.
   You will have the backbone.
   The tail will be attached to the backbone.
   The head will be attached to the backbone.
   Head, tail, and backbone will be ready to throw away.
   You are done.

VISITING THE SIERRAS

1. We always drove.
   The drive was up the Owens Valley.
   Mt. Wilson was on the left.
   It was bare.
   It was stark.
   Death Valley was on the right.

2. We left early.
   We saw the dawn.
   The dawn moved down the slope.
   The slope belonged to Mt. Wilson.

3. We passed through Lone Pine.
   We passed through Independence.
   We passed through Bishop.

4. There was a chain of lakes.
   It was high in the mountains.
   The lakes were perfect for fishing.
   They teemed with trout.

5. The lakes mirrored crags.
   The crags were covered with snow.
   The lakes were rimmed with pine.

6. We would rent a boat.
   I would row.
   My grandfather would flyfish.

7. I can see him.
   He would stand in the back of the boat.
   He wore a flannel shirt.

8. He would catch the trout.
   My grandmother would cook them.
   The cooking was quick.
   They would be brown.
   They would be crisp.
   They would be delicious.

9. I will never forget those visits.
   The visits were to the Sierras.
   I went with my grandparents.

REGIONAL FOOD

1. American cooking is coming back.
   The cooking is regional.
   The coming back is into popularity.
   The popularity is with restaurant owners.

2. Nobody would have believed.
   The belief was that Tex-Mex chili could command a price.
   The price was nice.
   The commanding was in Manhattan.
   This belief was years ago.

3. Now restaurants compete.
   The competition is fierce.
   It is to prepare buffalo meat.
   The preparing is in a way.
   The way is new.
   The way is exciting.
   The restaurants are in Chicago.

4. Inns concoct recipes.
   The inns are in Vermont.
   The recipes use maple syrup.
   The recipes use fiddlehead ferns.

5. Long Island serves crabs.
   The crabs are Maryland style.
   Long Beach offers lobster.
   The lobster is from New England.

6. The restaurants serve food.
   The restaurants are in San Francisco.
   The restaurants are the newest.
   The restaurants are the chicest.
   The food is Creole.
   The food is from the Cajun country.
   The country is in Louisiana.

7. You see Americans.
   The Americans explore style.
   The style is their own.
   The style is American.
   The style is of cooking.
   This happens wherever you look.

EXERCISE M

In each of the following exercises, you are given a group of sentences to combine into an effective paragraph. When you have finished combining, you will have the first of a pair of paragraphs. Using it as a guide, write the second paragraph.

A.   There are reasons for exercising.
The reasons are two.
One reason is appearance.
The other reason is health.
Most people look better when fit.
Exercise keeps weight down.
Exercise burns up calories.
The calories are excess.
Exercise increases circulation.
Increased circulation improves complexion.
Exercise develops coordination.
Coordination gives precision and grace to movement.
Exercise tones muscles.
The tone improves posture.
Exercise has other effects.
These effects go beyond cosmetics.
Exercise also affects health.

B.   Movies tell their stories with moving, talking pictures.
TV dramas tell their stories with moving, talking pictures.
Movies and TV dramas are very different.
You have to go out to the movies.
Going out costs money.
Movies have to give something you can't get at home.
Movies don't have to worry about sponsors.
Movies don't have to worry about children watching.
Movies can be controversial.
Movies can deal with adult material.
People are willing to pay for these qualities.
Movies cannot serialize a story effectively.
Only TV can create long serials.

WRITING PRACTICE

1.   Your high school class is now preparing for its fiftieth reunion. As part of the celebration, the reunion committee is publishing a booklet with updated biographies of class members. Each biography can be no more than 250 words long.

Before composing your contribution to the booklet, take some time to imagine what you would like to have happen in the fifty years after your high school graduation. Make some notes of the major events or reflections that you think your classmates would be interested in. Try to focus your biography on some central theme of your life. In composing your biography, use whatever paragraph strategy seems appropriate to you.

When you have finished a draft of your biography, go back and review the sentence and paragraph structure, or have someone else review it for you. After making revisions and corrections, prepare the final copy of your biography.

2.   In applying for a part-time job as the entertainment editor of your community newspaper, you must submit a 250-word review of a recent movie, book, play, or recording.

Before you compose your review, you might want to look at similar reviews in local or college newspapers or magazines to get some ideas about the kinds of information reviewers need to give their readers. Then, as you watch the movie, read the book, or listen to the recording, take some notes on the kinds of details you observed in other reviews.

You may use whatever paragraph strategy seems appropriate for your review.

When you have a draft of the review ready, look it over, or have someone else look it over, to check the paragraph and sentence structure. After making whatever revisions or corrections you find necessary, prepare a final copy of your review.

Part Three

The Writing Process

In Parts 1 and 2 of this book, you looked at the relationships between ideas in sentences and between the parts of paragraphs and longer pieces of writing and started to get a feel for what a finished paragraph or essay looks like. It is important for you as a writer to have an idea of the overall structure you're aiming for in a piece of writing. But this kind of knowledge, all by itself, isn't necessarily enough to help you compose a well-written paragraph.

An architect, for instance, needs to have a basic knowledge of the structure of a building, needs to know the essential parts, needs to understand how these parts relate to one another. When she begins to design an actual building, however, the architect goes through a long process of considering all the factors in the design situation—what will the building be used for? where will the building be located? how much does the client want to spend on this building? and so forth. In other words, the architect adapts her basic knowledge to a particular situation.

Once she has gotten a feel for the situation, the architect begins trying out building designs, sketching a general shape, noting some particular features that might work well in this building, maybe reviewing other buildings that have been designed for a similar purpose or built in a similar location, consulting with the client about various options. In the course of her work, she may go through a dozen different versions of the building, adding or sub-tracting details as she gets a clearer sense of what will suit this situation. Only after a long process of exploring, drafting, and redrafting, does she come up with a design that satisfies her.

As a writer, you need to go through a similar process. Although you know the general shapes of sentences and paragraphs, you have to adapt them to a particular situation if you want to write well. A paragraph that has a topic sentence, support, and a conclusion is not necessarily a good paragraph any more than a building with a roof, walls, and a floor is necessarily a good building.

Writers usually go through several different kinds of activities in the process of composing. At various points in the process, writers explore, focus, organize, draft, revise, and edit, but not always in that order. A writer may move back and forth among these activities, skipping some, repeating others. In fact, the writing process tends to be somewhat messier than it looks when it is neatly laid out in a textbook. Shown below is one somewhat neatened-up way of visualizing the writing process:

The Writing Process

As you read the text's discussion of these various stages, you need to keep in mind that, although a book can deal with only one activity at a time, these activities may, in fact, overlap when you are actually writing.

9

Exploring

In the exploring part of the writing process, you are trying to see just what you have to work with in a particular writing situation. You want to consider as many options as you can for dealing with this situation, so when you are exploring, you want to stimulate the creative side of your brain and generate as many ideas as you can without being too concerned about how good each idea is. As that brilliant thinker Linus Pauling once noted, "the best way to have a good idea is to have a lot of ideas."

To explore a writing situation, you need to focus on the general areas of subject, audience, purpose, and writer's voice, as the box below shows. You don't have to explore them in any particular order; in fact, it's quite likely that thinking about any one of these factors will generate ideas about all of them. So don't worry if your exploration seems to jump around almost at random.

EXPLORING THE WRITING SITUATION

1. What is significant about the subject?
2. Who am I writing for?
3. What is my purpose in writing?
4. What image of myself do I want to project to my audience?

Although you may do some exploration of subject, audience, purpose, and voice early in your composing, you will be refining your ideas about them throughout the writing process. So stay alert for those sparks of inspiration that may flash as your ideas begin to rub against each other.

EXPLORING THE SUBJECT

All writing is *about* something. Sometimes you may have a completely free choice of your subject; more often, the subject is determined to a greater or lesser degree by someone else. Although you might want to write about your pet beagle, what your boss has asked for is an analysis of the county's proposed changes in utility rates. Although you may be dying to explain the intricacies of post-impressionistic art, what the community association needs is a good fundraising proposal.

Whatever the subject you are dealing with, you have three basic sources of information about it: your own memory, your immediate observations of the world around you, and the memories and observations of other people that you may discover through personal interviews, books, films, or tapes.

Many writers combine several of these sources by keeping a notebook where they record their own memories, observations, and responses, and also those of others that they have come across in their reading or conversations. Such a journal may suggest a subject that you would like to write about or may provide details about a subject that someone else has asked you to write about.

Since a writer's notebook is basically for your own use, you don't need to be particularly concerned about recording only completely formulated ideas or about such mechanical considerations as spelling and punctuation. One of the nice things about a journal is that it gives you a place to try out ideas on yourself before you try them out on someone else. If you do decide to keep a writer's notebook, that may be a good place to use some of the other exploration techniques suggested later in this chapter.

In using these techniques, remember that their main purpose is to prime the pumps of your thinking apparatus, to get your brain working on a subject. If one method doesn't help you come up with ideas, try another one. And be sure to allow yourself enough time to explore your subject. Ideas may seem to come very slowly at first. But gradually, as you activate your creative processes, ideas come faster.

Brainstorming

One way to begin exploring a subject is to brainstorm it with a friend or a group of people working on the same project. In a brainstorming session, the group pools its collection of memories, observations, and research on a certain subject. Everyone contributes ideas about the subject, and the whole group keeps working to expand the pool of ideas. Many times, one person's idea, even if it sounds strange at first, can jar another person's mind to come up with a new approach to the subject. So, in brainstorming, don't stop the flow of ideas to criticize; keep the flow moving. Each participant can then take whatever ideas seem useful and develop them.

Freewriting

Freewriting is a kind of private brainstorming. You just take a sheet of paper and write whatever comes into your head on the subject. You don't have to worry about organizing your thoughts or putting them into correct language. You just write until you've filled up a whole sheet of paper or until 10 minutes have passed. Don't stop to analyze your thoughts; just keep your pen moving on the paper. Later you can select, refine, and organize your thoughts. For now, generate as many ideas as possible. When you have filled a page, you might stimulate your thinking by rereading what you have written and putting a circle around what you think is your best idea.

Page 204 shows an example of some freewriting. This student has been asked to evaluate the education she received at her high school.

Webbing

Another technique that many writers find useful is webbing. Webbing is related to brainstorming and freewriting, but it is a little more visual. To use this technique, write your subject in the middle of a sheet of paper. Then draw a line leading out from your subject and write down the first thing you associate with your subject. Draw a line leading away from that idea and write down whatever you associate with that idea. Keep going with that line until you run out of associations. Then go back to your subject in the center of the page and start a new set of associations. Page 205 shows a web done by the student who was exploring the subject of her high school.

Self-Interviewing

Some writers prefer to explore their subjects in a little more structured way. For example, you can explore a subject by interviewing yourself. Make up ten questions about your subject and then write out your answers to your questions. Page 206 shows some self-interview questions for the student evaluating her high school.

Alphabet Cueing

You can also use a system of cues to force yourself to think about a subject from several different angles. You can even use the alphabet as a cue. You just write down one idea about your subject for each letter of the alphabet. Page 206 shows a sample of this technique.

Freewriting

<u>Mercy Villa High School</u>

small classes, everybody knew everybody else in
school — teachers all knew you too
same teachers every year — continuity —
strict discipline — Sister Gregory — very strict
order — you always had some place to be
every minute of the day and night — heavy
emphasis on academics — lots of homework —
rows of heads bent over desks in study hall
at night — I felt very close to these people
living with them for four years. sometimes we
had student teachers — also old retired nuns —
Sister Alberta must have been 80 and had
been teaching Latin at least 60 years — tiny little
person, we all towered over her. learned
responsibility — we all had cooking and cleaning
chores around the school and in the dorms.
Sunday afternoon walks — 150 of us trailing
off down the Blvd. looked like that kid's
book — Madelaine? or whatever. Overall, I
liked the school. I learned a lot, not all
in the classroom. Would I have liked a big
school? piano lessons with Sister Cecilia, I
hated it when it was my turn to play the chapel
music. all those little blue beanies on
everybody's heads. And the black row of
nuns in the back.

Webbing

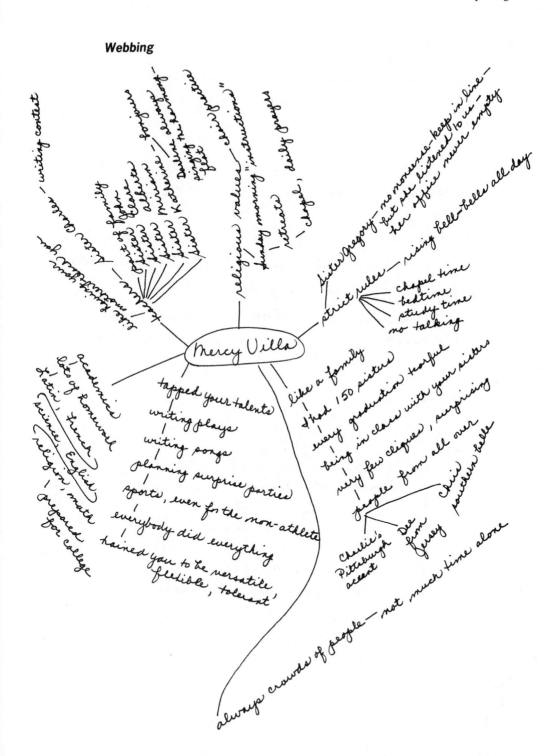

Self-Interviewing

1. What did I enjoy most about Mercy Villa?
2. What did I like least about Mercy Villa?
3. What picture comes to mind when I think of Mercy Villa?
4. What event do I remember best at Mercy Villa?
5. What is the most important thing I learned at Mercy Villa?
6. What person at Mercy Villa influenced me most?
7. How am I different because I attended Mercy Villa?
8. Why did I attend Mercy Villa?
9. Would I want my daughter to attend Mercy Villa?
10. What would I like to change about Mercy Villa?

Alphabet Cueing

Mercy Villa

a - academic program
b - basketball games / bus trips
c - community spirit
d - discipline / Darlene
e - everybody took same classes
f - friday night movies
g - going home for vacations
i - "instructions" on Sundays
j - "junior" teachers
etc.

Five W's Cueing

You can also cue yourself with the five W's as many journalists and other professional writers do. Using a cue world like *who*, you begin to write down all the *who's* you associate with your subject or any questions related to your subject that begin with *who*. When you run out of *who* associations or questions, move on to the next cue. Of course, you can always fill in more ideas if they occur to you while you're working on another cue.

Mercy Villa

who
- Sister Gregory, the principal
- 150 girls
- ten teachers: Sister Clare, Sister Katherine, Sister Peter, Sister John, Sister Miriam, ?

- sister classes
- who founded the school?
- who went there? who was a typical student?
    - not wealthy, mostly scholarships
    - East Coast area
    - smart girls

what
- private school, Catholic
- strict discipline
- emphasis on academics, Latin, French, 4 years
- also fun: parties, celebrations, songwriting, skits
- chapel, prayers, retreats
- what other subjects did we take?

where
- suburban Washington
- the Old Villa, the New Villa
- pretty campus, I liked to walk outside
- somewhat isolated

Five Senses Cueing

You may also find the five senses useful as cues for exploring. To use them, try to recreate in your mind some scene that you associate with your subject. Then review each sense in turn, making notes about what you see, hear, etc., in that scene.

<u>when</u>
- 1975/1979
- founded 1925
- I <u>always</u> knew I wanted to go there

<u>why</u>
- to give girls a good education
- created closeness
- emphasizes religious values
- traditional

Classroom at Mercy Villa

<u>See</u>
- rows of desks
- 30 girls in my class
- uniforms: blue jumpers, white blouses, saddle shoes
    shiny by the end of the year
- nun in black and white
- chart: the table of elements
- plain colors on floor, walls, ceiling — white, beige
- out the window: back driveway, kitchen area, trees
- stand up to recite
- old desks, shelf under seat;
  seniors got newer desks
- familiar faces

Hear
- creaking desks
- soft voices
- stomachs growling before lunch
- laughter; we laughed a lot
- thump, thud, splat as Janice's books fell out
  the side of the desk.
- rustle of papers
- singing in language classes
  or singing Sr. Clare's science jingles
- clicking of Sister's rosary beads
- texture of voices: Dee's tough New Jersey
                    Chris - smooth southern
                    Pat - "ott" west in Pittsburgh

Taste
- pencil between my teeth
- toothpaste, minty

Touch
- always a little drafty
- hard wooden seats
- scratchy wool knee-his
- sometimes too much starch in the blouses
  (or the underwear if a joker had laundry duty)

Smell
- soup for lunch, smell comes down the
  corridor
- chalk dust
- Sister Miriam's cologne
- Sister Clare's mouth wash

Observing and Researching

Any of these methods of exploring a subject can help you find out what is in your memory about that subject. Just as important, these techniques can help you discover what kinds of additional information you may need to find by observation or research.

For example, the student who has been exploring the subject of her high school might need to check the school yearbooks to find the name of a particular teacher, or call the principal's office to get an exact list of the courses she was required to take for graduation, or talk to some of her old classmates or teachers to get their thoughts on the school.

She might also decide to spend some time at the school observing what is happening now to see how it compares with what she remembers. The exploring techniques of the five senses or the five W's could help her organize her observations.

After she has done some reading and observing, she can try some further explorations to see what new ideas may have been stimulated by her new information.

EXERCISE A

Keep a writer's notebook for at least four weeks. You should make at least two entries per week, one based on something you have observed, the other based on something you have read. You may use the exploring techniques described in this chapter or any other format you choose for your notebook entries. The notebook entries should be about subjects that you might choose to develop into finished pieces of writing.

EXERCISE B

Using one or more of the methods described in this chapter, explore each of the following subjects. Use whatever combination of memory, observation, and research seems appropriate to you.

1.   My Family

Situation: The Kiwanis Scholarship will be awarded to the writer of the best essay on the subject of "What Does Family Mean to Me?"

Sources Used: *Techniques Used:*

_____ memory   _____ brainstorming

_____ observation   _____ freewriting

_____ research   _____ webbing

                                                      _____ interview

                                                      _____ five W's

                                                      _____ alphabet

                                                      _____ five senses

2. Television

Situation: *TV Guide* would like a student's perspective on current television programming.

Sources Used:	*Techniques Used:*
_____ memory	_____ brainstorming
_____ observation	_____ freewriting
_____ research	_____ webbing
	_____ interview
	_____ five W's
	_____ alphabet
	_____ five senses

3. Sports

Situation: You want a local company to sponsor a community athletic program.

Sources Used:	*Techniques Used:*
_____ memory	_____ brainstorming
_____ observation	_____ freewriting
_____ research	_____ webbing
	_____ interview
	_____ five W's
	_____ alphabet
	_____ five senses

4. Politics

Situation: Your political science teacher's first assignment asks you to define the term *politics*.

Sources Used:	*Techniques Used:*
_____ memory	_____ brainstorming
_____ observation	_____ freewriting
_____ research	_____ webbing

_____ interview

_____ five W's

_____ alphabet

_____ five senses

5.   Students at My School

Situation: You are working on an entertaining article for the student newspaper.

Sources Used:	*Techniques Used:*
_____ memory	_____ brainstorming
_____ observation	_____ freewriting
_____ research	_____ webbing
	_____ interview
	_____ five W's
	_____ alphabet
	_____ five senses

EXPLORING THE AUDIENCE

After doing some exploration of your subject, you will probably find yourself with lots of ideas, maybe even more ideas than you can use in one writing project. To help you select from among these ideas, you need to explore your audience. What you write has to be shaped to some degree by who will be reading it. Sometimes, you have no choice about your audience. You may know from the beginning, for instance, that the report you are preparing will be read by your supervisor. Other times, you are free to choose the most suitable audience for what you want to say. Would your ideas on solar power have more impact on your representative in the legislature or on a group of local business people?

In any case, to write well, you must consider who will be reading what you write. Is it a person you know well, like your brother? Or is it a group of people you don't know personally—the members of the City Council, for example? Is your audience already interested in the subject you are writing about—a group of fellow skindivers, perhaps? Or do you have to convince your audience of the importance of your idea—for instance, potential contributors to your club's fundraising project?

For each kind of audience—personal or public, knowledgeable or uninformed—you have to write in a somewhat different way. You would choose different arguments, use different words, take a different attitude, depending on your audience.

For example, if you were writing something about inflation for the local food co-op newsletter, you would want to choose examples that your audience could immediately recognize, like food prices. If you were writing about inflation for your economics class, though, you would have to choose other kinds of examples since members of this audience might not do the family grocery shopping.

Also, your language would be different for each group. For the food co-op members, you would try to use fairly nontechnical terms so that you could be easily understood by everyone. Your economics class, on the other hand, should be more familiar with the professional language of economists, and so you could use words like *commodities market*, *the Fed*, and *prime rate* and expect to be understood.

You can explore your audience using the techniques described earlier. The audience simply becomes another subject you want to explore. For instance, this writer is working on a letter to City Council members about the need for public day care facilities. Here is his private brainstorming on the audience.

Who are Council members?
- Clarke - chair
- Nolan - my district
- Barrett -
- Freeson (?)
- Ventre - woman
- one other?

how many have children?

Clarke said in newspaper he would introduce day care bill

don't know how others feel

all council members democrats

public hearing scheduled two weeks

all members know about proposal

professional backgrounds
- Barrett - tax lawyer
- Clarke - in insurance
- others - don't know

met Nolan once at high school graduation

he gave talk on necessity for future education
- relate this to need for day care?

only existing city center is in Clarke's district

This exploration has revealed several things that the writer needs to consider. First, there are some significant gaps in his knowledge of his audience. He is not sure of all the names. He doesn't know how many council members have children. He doesn't know the professional backgrounds of the council members. But he needs this information to compose an effective letter. Therefore, he is probably going to have to go down to the Public Library or call City Hall to get some more information about his audience.

Exploring has also shown that it may not be possible to write just one letter that will appeal to the interests of all six council members. So he may decide to write just one letter, addressed to the chairman and appealing to him, and to send copies to the other members. More time-consuming, but more effective, would be six different letters, each using what the writer knows about that recipient to gain his or her support.

For instance, since Nolan is from the writer's own district and he has heard him speak, he might make his appeal to him a little more personal than one to those members whom he does not know at all. Since Clarke is the sponsor of the bill, the writer knows he is already very interested in the subject. His letter to Clarke could be a simple statement of support and encouragement, or it might include suggestions for improving the bill. Barrett, a tax lawyer, might be appealed to on the basis of economic benefits to the city. If Ms. Ventre is a mother, the writer might appeal to a sense of fellowship with the plight of working women with children. And so on for each council member.

Knowledge of the audience can affect the content of writing.

You can vary the brainstorming technique by giving yourself a set number of things (say ten) that you will list about your audience. The Mercy Villa alumna might say, for example, that these were the ten most important characteristics of her audience, the Board of Trustees.

1. all Catholics
2. business-oriented people mostly
3. worried about finances of Villa Mercy
4. interested enough to call for student input
5. all older than I am
6. six men, four women, one is alumna ('63)
7. they think religious education is important
8. they are busy people with lots of other responsibilities
9. most have been involved with MV more than 5 years
10. some are parents of MV students (how many?)

Once you have made a list like this, you need to review each item to see how it will affect what you write. For instance, because the members of the Board all share the same religion, the writer can address religious values freely in her evaluation of the school. Because they are primarily business people and are concerned about the financial condition of the school, she may also choose to emphasize the practical benefits of the education given at Mercy Villa. And so on down the list.

An even more structured way to explore an audience is to use a set of questions like the one shown below.

QUESTIONS FOR EXPLORING AUDIENCE

1. What is the personal background of this audience? (age, sex, social status, education, religious and political affiliation, professional or work experience, etc.)

2. How much does this audience already know about the subject of my writing?

3. What else does this audience particularly need to know about this subject?

4. How favorably or unfavorably does the audience feel about this subject? Or is the audience neutral on this subject?

5. What is the audience's relationship to me, the writer? Am I writing to my peers or to those superior or inferior to me in some way? (older/younger, more/less educated, more/less experienced) Does the audience know me personally?

6. In general, what response do I want from this audience?

Again, your answers to these questions can help you determine, throughout the writing process, which ideas you will emphasize or de-emphasize in your writing, what kind of language you will chose, and how you will organize the material.

EXERCISE C

Assume that you are writing about your initial reactions to college. Using any of the techniques suggested above, explore each of the following potential audiences. After your exploration, list the three factors you consider most significant about this audience. Be prepared to explain how these factors might affect your writing in this situation.

1. The president of the college
    Most significant factors:

    A. _____

    B. _____

    C. _____

2. Your parents
    Most significant factors

    A. _____

    B. _____

    C. _____

3. Your best friend
    Most significant factors

    A. _____

    B. _____

    C. _____

4. The president of the Student Government Association
    Most significant factors

    A. _____

    B. _____

    C. _____

5. Your favorite high school teacher
    Most significant factors

    A. _____

    B. _____

    C. _____

EXPLORING PURPOSE

Closely related to your consideration of the audience for your writing is an analysis of the effect you wish to achieve with a particular piece of writing. As with audience, your purpose in writing may be given to you as part of the writing situation, or you may have some choice in what purpose you want to achieve.

Do you want members of the food co-op to understand what the term *inflation* means? Do you want to show them some ways they can get the most for their money? Do you want to convince them that inflation is not really a serious problem? Do you want them to support some piece of legislation designed to curb inflation? Each of these possible purposes for an article on inflation would demand a different selection and arrangement of material on the subject.

Most writing is aimed at achieving one of the four purposes shown in the box below.

GENERAL PURPOSES FOR WRITING:

To entertain: to make the subject enjoyable for the audience.

To inform: to fill in gaps in your audience's knowledge of the subject.

To interpret: to explain the meaning or significance of certain facts for your audience.

To persuade: to convince your audience to follow a certain course of action.

Many poems and stories and other types of imaginative writing have entertainment as their primary purpose. Academic writing, such as term papers, and business writing, such as annual reports, often aim primarily at providing information. Movie or restaurant reviews are examples of writing that tries to interpret information. Newspaper editorials and letters to government officials frequently try to persuade their readers to perform a certain action.

Whatever your purpose is, you should understand it clearly before you begin to write. If you understand why you are writing, you can better control what you say so that the paragraph does exactly and only what you intend. Of course, it frequently happens that you have more than one purpose in writing. You may want to entertain as well as inform or inform as well as persuade. In cases like these, you should decide which purpose is most important so that you will be able to emphasize it in your writing.

When you are exploring your own purpose in writing, you should consider each of the four general purposes and decide whether it is appropriate for what you want to do.

Suppose, for instance, that you are a member of the local Board of Education. One of your tasks this year has been to study the reading program in elementary schools. Now you want to write a report for your fellow board members, none of whom is too familiar with the reading program.

Your exploration of purpose might look like this:

entertain

limited entertainment possibilities here
maybe a story about kids learning to read?
use a story from one of the readers

inform

tell them what our reading program is like
describe typical reading class
use research about reading methods
compare one method of instruction to another

interpret

explain why our program is not effective
how did we get here – history of program
disadvantages of sight reading

persuade

get new texts

From a list like this, you would have to choose what you thought was your most important purpose, or which purpose you should deal with first. Should you just explain the instructional method being used? Or should you attack the present method? Or should you try to get the Board to act right away to solve the problems you discovered?

In a longer piece of writing, different sections of the paper may have different purposes, but your reader should be able to see how each individual paragraph contributes to the purpose of its section of the whole.

EXERCISE D

Here are several paragraphs that might be part of the report described above. Decide what purpose each of these paragraphs seems to aim at. Be prepared to explain your choice.

1.   The phonics method of instruction seems clearly superior to the sight-reading method. First of all, students learn more vocabulary and learn it more quickly with phonics instruction. While a year of sight-reading training develops an average vocabulary of 350 words, a year of phonics gives students a reading vocabulary of over 5,000 words. Even more important, though, phonics instruction gives students the ability to learn new words independently. Once students have mastered the basic sounds of the language, they can figure out unfamiliar words on their own. Sight-reading students, on the other hand, remain dependent on the teacher to identify new words for them, and they may be completely baffled by a letter combination they have not seen before. Because phonics produces better results both quantitatively and qualitatively, the Board should implement phonics instruction in all elementary schools.

Purpose: _____

2.   In implementing this change, the Board needs to provide for an orderly transition from one method of instruction to another. First, the Superintendent of Schools should inform all principals of the Board's decision. Then, a committee of reading teachers should prepare a plan for phonics instruction. Money should be set aside in next year's budget for the purchase of new textbooks. Finally, the Board should hold a series of informational meetings for parents and taxpayers to explain the reasons for the change in emphasis. With careful planning, the new instructional program can be introduced with minimal difficulty.

Purpose: _____

3.   Most children are taught to read by one of two basic methods: sight-reading or phonics. With sight-reading, children learn to read by reading. They are given short stories containing the most common English words. Gradually, through repetition, the students begin to recognize certain words. A sight-reading text might contain a sequence like this: "Here is Bob. Here is Rosa. Bob runs. Rosa runs. Run, Bob, run! Run, Rosa, run!" At the end of a year of sight-reading instruction, children should have a reading vocabulary of about 350 words. With the phonics system, on the other hand, children begin with letters rather than words. Children learn the twenty-six letters of the alphabet and the forty-four sounds those letters stand for. The letters and sounds are taught in a planned order, and students see only those words whose sounds they have already mastered. A beginning phonics reader who knew some basic consonant sounds plus the short *a* sound might be given a sentence like: "Dan can fan the man." At the end of a year of phonics instruction, children should have a reading vocabulary of about 5,000 words. Sight-reading and phonics are the basic choices the Board of Education has when it establishes a reading program.

Purpose: _____

EXERCISE E

Explore possible purposes for each of the following writing situations. List all the possible purposes you might want to achieve. What information would you need to achieve each purpose?

1. Your brother's Cub Scout troop has asked you to write something about your hobby for the next newsletter, which is going to be about various kinds of leisure activities.

2. Your English teacher has given you the topic, "How I Spent My Summer," for your first writing assignment. He encourages you to be creative in approaching this subject.

EXPLORING VOICE

In every writing situation, as in every speaking situation, you use a certain voice to communicate with your audience. You try to sound a certain way to achieve a certain effect. If this quality of voice is based on your analysis of the audience, purpose, and subject of your writing, you are more likely to achieve the effect you intend.

For example, suppose that an automobile accident has occurred. One car is badly damaged. The other has only a small dent. No one has been injured. If you were a police officer writing a report on this accident, you would choose a voice that was impersonal, unemotional, and serious. You would know that your purpose was to record the factual details of the accident as clearly as possible and that your audience (for instance, your superior officer, the participants, insurance claim adjustors, the courts) would not be interested in your personal feelings about the accident. In fact, allowing emotion to show in your report might obscure the facts or lessen the degree of confidence the audience could place in your observations. So your report might sound like this:

At approximately 9:10 P.M. on Sunday, January 29, the first car, a tan 1979 Aspen station wagon, approached the traffic signal at Howard and Monroe Streets at a speed of approximately 50 mph. . . .

However, if you were the driver of the damaged car and you had to write your brother, who is the car's owner, explaining the accident, you would probably want a different voice to suit your purpose and audience. In this situation, a more personal and emotional voice might be more appropriate. Here, it is your interpretation of events and your relationship with your brother that will determine the effectiveness of the writing. So your letter might sound like this:

> Dave, I'm sorry, but I have some bad news. Your Mustang has been damaged in an accident. Last Sunday, as I was going home after I had visited Dad in the hospital, some crazy driver ran the red light at the corner of Howard and Monroe. . . .

In the actual writing process, voice is created by such things as sentence structure (see Chapters 2–6) and word choice (see Chapter 13). But consciously thinking about voice *before* you write can help you choose the most effective voice possible.

QUESTIONS FOR CHOOSING VOICE

Do you want a personal voice (I, you, we, us) or an impersonal voice (he, she, it, they)?
An emotional voice or an unemotional voice? Which emotion—anger, sadness, joy, excitement?
A serious voice or a light voice?
A formal voice or an informal voice?
A knowledgeable voice or a questioning voice?

EXERCISE F

For each of the following writing situations, you are given two possible opening sentences. Decide which voice is better suited to the audience, purpose, and subject in each case, and be prepared to explain your choice.

1. The editor of the Hometown Senior Citizens Newsletter has asked the president of the Hometown Historic Preservation Society to write her a short piece explaining some of the problems of preservation. Which of these openings seems more promising?
   A. Ten dollars is a small price to pay for the many benefits of membership in the Hometown Preservation Society.

B. The current attempt to save the Sullivan Building on Crane Boulevard illustrates many of the difficulties, legal and financial, that historic preservationists have to deal with.

C. I am very concerned about historic preservation.

2. You want a position as assistant manager of the local department store. Which of these openings is more likely to get you an interview?

A. Hi! I'm Bobbi and I'd like to be an assistant manager.

B. I have all the qualifications you are looking for in an assistant manager. I am hungry and topnotch at everything I put my mind to.

C. My 15 years of experience in retail management and my familiarity with this community make me well-suited for the opening you advertised in the *Gazette*.

3. Your daughter's third-grade teacher has asked each parent to write a paragraph or so about his or her work for the student's unit on careers. You are a veterinarian. Which opening would be more suitable for your daughter's class?

A. If you like helping animals and don't mind working at some unusual hours of the night, you could be a good veterinarian.

B. Veterinary medicine is a good career for people who have a strong sense of other-directedness and the intellectual ability to master advanced principles of anatomy and physiology.

C. Dogs can have some unusual health problems.

4. Your credit-card company has just billed you for the fourth time for a round-trip ticket to Nairobi. You feel there has been a mistake and you want it straightened out. Which of these openings would be more effective?

A. I know your efficient computers hardly ever make mistakes, but I should respectfully like to suggest that there is (maybe) a possible error in the bill you recently sent me, although I must admit you have given me fine service for the last three years and I am reluctant to believe that you are mistaken, but I'm pretty sure I never spent that money.

B. On June 17, 1984, you billed my account #A-300-166 for $748.18 for a round-trip ticket to Nairobi, Kenya; however, I believe this billing is in error.

C. You guys had better do something about this foul-up with my credit card account #A-300-166.

5. Your final exam in American History asks you to discuss the major causes of the Civil War. Which of these openings will be more impressive to your history professor?

A. The Civil War has always fascinated me.

B. Although it is difficult to pin down exact events that caused a major historical phenomenon like the Civil War, we can see general causes of the war in the economic conditions of the North and the South and in the relative political power of the two areas.

C. Basically the Civil War was fought by infantry and cavalry troops who each performed a distinct military function.

EXERCISE G

Evaluate each of the following openings for its effectiveness in the situation presented for it. Which openings seem suited to the audience, subject, and purpose?

1. Since you teach guitar, *Folk Music* magazine has asked you to write a brief article on how to buy a guitar. Would this be a good opening?

   In buying a guitar, you should consider these five factors: resonance, type of wood, type of strings, string action, and tone.

2. A good friend who is visiting your city for the first time has asked you which of two restaurants she should take her client to for dinner. Is this an appropriate opening for your response?

   When evaluating a restaurant, you should consider the location, the type and quality of food, the price range, and the atmosphere.

3. You are spending your winter break backpacking through Europe. The college newspaper has asked you to write about your experiences in the various countries you visit. How would this be as an opening for one of your reports?

   The mean temperature in Belgium during January is a chilly −17° centigrade, and the precipitation is expected to total 20 inches for the month.

4. The adult education group at your church has asked each member to write a definition of *church* for the next meeting. Would this be a good opening?

   To me, the church is not a building of brick or wood, but rather the people caring for each other in God's love.

5. As part of your management-training program you have spent six weeks in the Customer Service department of an electronics firm. You are asked at the end of the period to discuss what you've observed. Would this be an appropriate opening?

   Customer Service requires constant managerial attention to maintain an efficient courtesy.

WRITING PRACTICE

1.   The president of your college has encouraged students to communicate with him about the things they like or don't like at the college. Write a 250-word letter to the president about what you consider to be your college's greatest strength or its greatest weakness. Before you write the letter, use the strategies discussed in this chapter to generate some ideas and explore the other aspects of this writing situation: audience, purpose, and voice.

2.   When you mention to your friend, the editor of the school paper, what you have written to the president, she is very impressed with your idea. She asks you to write it up as an opinion column or editorial for the paper. She has room for about 300 words. Before you prepare the article, use the techniques presented in this chapter to explore this writing situation.

10

Focusing, Organizing, and Drafting

When you have spent some time exploring each of the factors in a writing situation—subject, audience, purpose, voice—your mind really starts to become engaged with this problem. You have churned up lots of ideas, and now you can begin to sort through them and select the ones you want to use.

An incubation period can be very useful now. If you have enough time (and this is one reason for allowing plenty of time for a writing project), you should let your ideas simmer for a day or two and see which ones seem to float to the top. Your subconscious mind can do a lot of work for you if you give it the time and the material to work with.

Although this chapter is going to give you some suggestions for shaping this welter of ideas into a semicoherent whole, keep in mind that the writing process doesn't always happen in a nice, orderly progression. You may not do things in the same order in which they are presented in the text. You may find several of these operations happening at once. You may find yourself ready to go right into a draft of your paper without performing all these preliminary steps. So stay flexible.

NARROW THE FIELD

If you are lucky, your mind will have already begun the process of narrowing the field by the time you start reviewing your exploration sheets. One or two ideas will "grab" you as promising material. If you aren't already conscious of an emerging focus for your ideas, look at your exploration sheets to see what material is repeated. Are there any ideas that seemed to crop up in several different ways? Quite often, those are the ideas that you think are important. If none of the ideas particularly inspires you, go back anyway and circle two or three that you think you might be able to work with. (Face it, not every piece of writing will be inspired!)

EXERCISE A

In Chapter 9, you explored each of the subjects below. Review those explorations now in light of the writing situations shown, and narrow the field to two or three aspects of the subject that seem most promising.

EXAMPLE:

My High School

Situation: The Board of Trustees has asked recent graduates to evaluate the quality of education provided at the school.

Writing Possibilities: (based on explorations shown in Chapter 9)

1. the importance of discipline and order at Mercy Villa

2. the influence of a few of my teachers

3. how I used what I learned at Mercy Villa

1. My Family
   Situation: The Kiwanis Scholarship will be awarded to the writer of the best essay on the subject "What Does Family Mean to Me."
   Writing Possibilities:

   1. _____
   2. _____
   3. _____

2. Television
   Situation: TV Guide wants a student's perspective on current television programming.
   Writing Possibilities:

   1. _____
   2. _____
   3. _____

3. Sports
   Situation: You want a local company to sponsor a community athletic program.
   Writing Possibilities:

   1. _____
   2. _____
   3. _____

4. Politics

Situation: Your political science teacher's first assignment asks you to define the term *politics.*

Writing Possibilities:

1. _____

2. _____

3. _____

5. Students at My School

Situation: You are working on an entertaining article for the student newspaper.

Writing Possibilities:

1. _____

2. _____

3. _____

RELATE IDEAS AND FILL IN GAPS

When you have narrowed your field to a few possible topics, go back over your exploration sheets and look for connections among ideas. Which details or ideas seem to relate to each possible approach? Within the ideas for each narrowed topic, can you see any natural groups? What ideas seem to belong together?

This student, for example, was working on a report for a biology class. One topic in his narrowed field was muscles. In reviewing his initial exploration sheets, he found these details related to that topic. The lines show some of the initial connections he made.

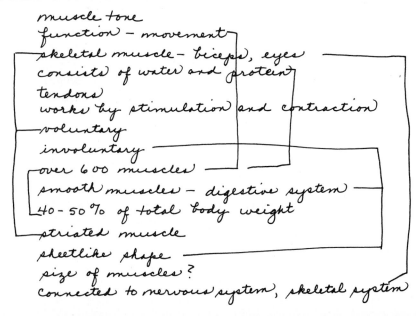

muscle tone
function – movement
skeletal muscle – biceps, eyes
consists of water and protein
tendons
works by stimulation and contraction
voluntary
involuntary
over 600 muscles
smooth muscles – digestive system
40 – 50 % of total body weight
striated muscle
sheetlike shape
size of muscles?
connected to nervous system, skeletal system

As he looked at these connections, he saw a pattern. He had details relating to two of the three different kinds of muscles: striated and smooth. He added the third kind, cardiac, to his list, and filled in some other ideas. Eventually, he came up with a rough grouping that looked like this:

STRIATED	SMOOTH	CARDIAC
skeletal muscle	digestive system	heart
voluntary	involuntary	involuntary
shape—cylindrical	shape—sheetlike	shape—hollow
size—(look this up)	size—?	size—?

ALL MUSCLES

function—movement

consist of protein and water

operate by stimulation and contraction

40–50% of total body weight

over 600 muscles

connected to other systems—skeletal, nervous

As this writer's experience shows, in grouping ideas, you will probably leave out some things from your exploration sheets and add other ideas to fill in gaps. You may also uncover places where you need to go out and find additional information.

REVIEW STRATEGIES

As you begin to establish connections between your ideas, you may see a clear pattern developing, as the writer of the muscle report did. At other times, you may need to consciously review various strategies (such as the five shown in Chapter 8: telling a story, describing, listing examples, breaking into categories, and comparing or contrasting) to decide on an appropriate way to develop your narrowed topic so that it suits your audience and purpose.

For example, the student evaluating her high school listed the influence of her teachers as one possibility for approaching her writing project. In order to discuss her teachers, she might tell the story of one particular incident that sums up her feeling about the teachers. Or she might list several examples of ways the teachers influenced her. Or she could categorize the kinds of teachers she had at the school.

In trying to move your writing to completion, look for a strategy that seems to suit your material. Again, if you are lucky, one strategy may stand out to you as absolutely right for this situation. If none seems particularly better than another, choose any one that you think you can work with. You can always revise if inspiration strikes later in the process.

EXERCISE B

Study each of the following lists of details. What connections can you see among the ideas on each list? For each list, suggest a possible set of groupings. Label each group of ideas. Feel free to add more ideas to any group.

When you have established a set of groups, consider possible strategies for developing this topic and choose the one that seems most appropriate for this subject, audience, and purpose. Be prepared to explain your choices.

EXAMPLE:

Writing Situation: The City Tourist Bureau wants to persuade people living in nearby counties to visit the city more often.

    Topic: Things to Do in the City

zoo	little restaurants	neighborhood bars
museums	symphony	specialty stores
parks	major-league sports	theaters
ethnic food	historical sites	historic district

    Groups:

I. *Stretch the Mind*
   * museums
   * symphony
   * theaters
   * art galleries (added)

II. *Relax Outdoors*
   * zoos
    parks
   * major-league sports
   * tour historic sites

III. *Eat*
   little restaurants
   neighborhood bars
   *ethnic food
   *elegant restaurants
   (added)
   gourmet food (added)

    * indicates unique city attractions

    Strategy: Compare city attractions to suburb attractions

  1. *Situation:* A feature article to entertain readers of *Silver Screen Magazine.*

      Topic: Famous Movie Monsters

Dracula	Godzilla	The Alien	Mr. Hyde
The Thing	Wolfman	The Mummy	King Kong
Frankenstein's Monster		The Creature from the Black Lagoon	

Group I:

Group II:

Group III:

Strategy:

2. *Situation:* As a PE instructor, you are making a presentation to a junior high school PTA explaining the physical education program at the school.

Topic: Kinds of Activities

basketball	gymnastics	field hockey
football	swimming	soccer
tennis	baseball	weight training
jogging	aerobic dance	archery
wrestling	first aid	track and field

Group I:

Group II:

Group III:

Strategy:

3. *Situation:* As a high school guidance counselor, you are preparing a letter for the seniors encouraging them to consider going to college.

   Topic: Reasons for Going to College

make more money   meet new people   better jobs
personal development   more social life   good sports
explore different fields   sense of independence
career promotion   satisfaction of greater achievement
participate in clubs   increase knowledge

   Group I:

   Group II:

   Group III:

   Strategy:

ARRANGE GROUPS LOGICALLY

When you have a sense of strategy for your writing and you have set up some groups within your list of ideas, you need to consider the arrangement of those groups. Which details should come first in your paper? Which should come later? Which should you end with?

The report on muscles, for instance, used the strategy of showing different categories of muscles, and the writer had broken his material into four general groups.

One logical way to arrange the four points would be to use the information about muscles in general as an introduction and then present the three kinds of muscles in an orderly pattern.

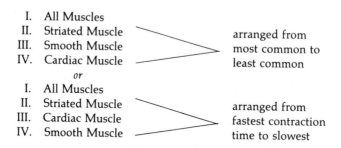

I.   All Muscles
II. Striated Muscle
III. Smooth Muscle   arranged from
IV. Cardiac Muscle   most common to
                            least common
or
I.   All Muscles
II. Striated Muscle
III. Cardiac Muscle   arranged from
IV. Smooth Muscle   fastest contraction
                            time to slowest

Logical patterns of arrangement can be based on time (earliest event to latest event), space (farthest away to closest, top to bottom), or size (smallest to largest). If no other pattern of arrangement seems obvious to you, you can arrange points in order of importance, always beginning with the least important and ending with the most important.

Of course, the order in which you present your ideas depends, to some extent, on your audience and purpose. For instance, in the example shown above on muscles, an arrangement from most common type to least common would be suitable for an audience whose knowledge of muscles was not very specialized. The arrangement from fastest contraction time to slowest would be suitable if your audience had more detailed knowledge or if your purpose were to explain some research related to the contraction time of muscles.

Knowledge of audience is particularly critical when you arrange items in an order of importance. The most important point to one audience may not be the most important point to another. Suppose, for instance, that your employee group has three complaints about the job: low pay, poor working environment, and the difficulty of the work. If you were writing to the plant manager about these complaints, you might choose to end with (that is, emphasize) poor working environment because that is the area that the plant manager can do the most about. A letter to fellow workers, on the other hand, might make low pay the item of greatest importance.

Whatever pattern of arrangement you choose, be sure that it is as clear to your reader as it is to you. This may require some use of signals in your writing to tell your reader what the organizational structure is. In the example above about muscles, you could say, "Striated muscle, which is the most common type, . . ." and "a smaller group is smooth muscle." Phrases like these would indicate to your reader the direction in which you were moving. (Chapter 12 on Coherence presents a full discussion of connectives between major ideas.)

EXERCISE C

Arrange each of the following lists of major supporting points in a logical order and explain briefly what principle you have used to organize them. For what audience and purpose would your arrangement be best suited?

1. Description of Jane's face

nose   I.

chin   II.

hair   III.

eyes   IV.

lips   V.

cheeks   VI.

Explanation _____

_____

2. Superiority of a cat

is independent   I.

uses litter box   II.

catches pests   III.

cleans self   IV.

purrs   V.

Explanation _____

_____

3. Major American fiction writers

Nathaniel Hawthorne   I.
  (1804–1864)

Edgar Allan Poe   II.
  (1809–1849)

William Faulkner   III.
  (1897–1962)

F. Scott Fitzgerald   IV.
  (1896–1940)

Herman Melville   V.

  (1819–1891)

Ernest Hemingway   VI.

  (1898–1961)

Explanation _____

_____

4. Tour schedule

New York   I.

Los Angeles   II.

Denver   III.

Chicago   IV.

Boston   V.

Dallas   VI.

Explanation _____

_____

5. Restaurant review

	Rating	
food	★★★★	I.
atmosphere/decor	★	II.
price	★★★★	III.
service	★★	IV.

Explanation _____

_____

When the major groups have been arranged satisfactorily, you can arrange any supporting detail within each category. For instance, look at the details you saw listed earlier under muscles:

STRIATED	SMOOTH	CARDIAC
skeletal muscle	digestive system	heart
voluntary	involuntary	involuntary
shape—cylindrical	shape—sheetlike	shape—hollow
size	size	size

The supporting points under *Striated* could be related into two groups, like this:

APPEARANCE	FUNCTION
shape	skeletal
size	voluntary

The supporting points in the other two categories could be arranged similarly. This organization of supporting details ensures that you will cover the same points for each kind of muscle.

STATE THE FOCUS

At some point in this organizing process, you should be ready to state the focus of your paper. You may do this after you have chosen a strategy and begun to arrange supporting details or even after you have worked out a draft of the paper. Or you may choose to do this early in the process.

The focus statement, whenever you compose it, helps to clarify in your mind the main point you want to make in this piece of writing. It serves as the basis for a topic sentence and/or a thesis statement in your finished paper.

For instance, suppose that you work for an office furnishings company and want to interest potential clients in your new product line. You have decided that your strategy will be to describe an office filled with your products. You have this list of details related to the description:

open rooms
few walls : free-standing partitions / file cabinets
upholstered desk chairs
chrome
sculpture
carpeting
no regular rows of desks
work modules
clean-looking desks
lighting
earthy colors : orange, yellow, brown

Now, looking at this list, you can try to decide on one word that most clearly defines the central impression you want your clients to have about the office you are describing. Brainstorming can be useful in this process. Just list the words you think might fit:

> flexibility
> economy
> ✓ openness
> spacious
> freedom

Then consider your audience. Which word will your clients respond to most favorably? Try creating a focus statement that will emphasize whatever word you have chosen. Try using the key idea in several different positions in the sentence:

Subject	— *Openness* is the key in an office designed by Modern Furnishings, Inc.
Verb	— Modern Furnishings, Inc., *can open up* your office to the look of the eighties.
Complement	— An office designed by Modern Furnishings, Inc., will have *a feeling of openness.*

EXERCISE D

Choose one topic from each subject you developed in Exercise A. After doing whatever grouping of details you can, select an appropriate strategy for your topic and compose a focus statement that will show the main point you would try to get across in this paper.

> EXAMPLE:
>
> *Subject:* My High School
>
> *Topic:* The Influence of My Teachers
>
> *Strategy:* Tell a story about one influential event
>
> *Focus Statement:* More than anything else, Sister Charles's patient work with me on my entry for the Atlantic Writing Competition taught me to think of myself as a creative person.

1. My Family

   Topic: _____

   Strategy: _____

Focus Statement: _____

_____

2.   Television

    Topic: _____

    Strategy: _____

    Focus Statement: _____

    _____

3.   Sports

    Topic: _____

    Strategy: _____

    Focus Statement: _____

    _____

4.   Politics

    Topic: _____

    Strategy: _____

    Focus Statement: _____

    _____

5.   Students at My School

    Topic: _____

    Strategy: _____

    Focus Statement: _____

    _____

OUTLINING

A formal way of presenting the organization of a piece of writing is an outline. In the drafting stage of a piece of writing, you can use it to clarify the planning you have done, clearly showing the coordinate and subordinate relationships among your ideas. Later, it can also be useful to your readers, especially for a long piece of writing like a term paper, by showing them what to expect from your essay.

An outline uses Roman numerals (I, II, III) to show major points. Capital letters (A, B, C) show supporting details for each major point. Arabic numerals (1, 2, 3) show any further examples under an A, B, or C.

Here is an outline of the report on muscles:

Topic Sentence: Although all muscles have certain properties in common, muscles can be divided into three distinct types: striated, smooth, and cardiac.

   I. All Muscles
      A. Function—movement
      B. Operation—contraction and relaxation
      C. Composition—protein and water
  II. Striated
      A. Appearance
         1. Size
         2. Shape
      B. Function
         1. Skeletal
         2. Voluntary
 III. Smooth
      A. Appearance
         1. Size
         2. Shape
      B. Function
         1. Digestive System
         2. Involuntary
 IV. Cardiac
      A. Appearance
         1. Size
         2. Shape
      B. Function
         1. Heart
         2. Involuntary

Conclusion: Each of the three types of muscles is ideally suited to its own particular movement function in the body.

Notice that an outline moves from the most general idea, expressed in the topic sentence, to the most specific idea, here expressed as Arabic numerals 1 and 2. In an outline that goes only as far as Arabic numerals, you usually will not have a I without a II or an A without a B. Sometimes, if you are using only one example, there may be a 1 without a 2, but this is not the norm.

Be careful that your outline accurately reflects the weight to be given to each point. All Roman numeral items should coordinate. Similarly, all capital letter items should be of equivalent weight, but subordinate to the Roman numeral points. (For coordination, see Chapter 3. For subordination, see Chapter 4.)

What is wrong with this outline?

Topic Sentence: Good fishing can be found in both fresh and salt water.

   I. Salt Water
      A. Barracuda

II. Water that is Fresh
   A. Trout
   B. Carp
III. Tuna

Conclusion: Either kind of fishing can provide an exciting day on the water.

For one thing, *III. Tuna* is not coordinate with *I* and *II. Tuna* shouldn't get a Roman numeral in this outline. *Tuna* is really a supporting example subordinate to *I. Salt Water.* Another problem with this outline is the order in which the major points are presented. The topic sentence gives them in one arrangement, but the outline does not follow that pattern. Finally, coordinate points should be phrased in a similar way to emphasize their relatedness. So *Water that Is Fresh* should be *Fresh Water* to emphasize its coordination with *Salt Water* in I.

Here is a more accurate version of this outline:

Topic Sentence: Good fishing can be found in both fresh water and salt water.

I. Fresh Water
   A. Trout
   B. Carp
II. Salt Water
   A. Barracuda
   B. Tuna

Conclusion: Either kind of fishing can provide an exciting day on the water.

Outlining, then, can be a way to help you see the various levels of generalization in your writing and visualize the coordinate and subordinate relationships among your ideas.

EXERCISE E

Put the following lists of details into outline form. You may wish to do a rough grouping first, then a more formal outline.

1. a. Eskimos in the Arctic
   b. Build spacecraft
   c. Protect orphans
   d. Construct radio telescopes
   e. Tuaregs in the Sahara
   f. Live anywhere
   g. Make marvelous tools
   h. Computers
   i. Altruistic

j. Provide for the helpless

k. Mourn the dead

T.S. Human beings are amazing.

I.

    A.

    B.

    C.

II.

    A.

    B.

    C.

III.

    A.

    B.

Conclusion: Human beings are astonishingly complex.

2. a. *Typee* was a bestseller.

    b. He went to sea young.

    c. He lost his father.

    d. It was marred by tragedy.

    e. *Omoo* was popular.

    f. He lived with cannibals.

    g. It was full of adventure.

    h. His career failed.

    i. It was marked by success.

    j. His son committed suicide.

T.S. Adventure, tragedy, and success marked Herman Melville's life.

I.

    A.

    B.

II.

    A.

    B.

    C.

III.

    A.

    B.

Conclusion: Each of these aspects of his life left its mark on Melville.

In the remaining exercises, the topic sentence and the conclusion are part of the list of details.

3. a. The setting is beautiful.

    b. Everybody should try rafting.

    c. It is good exercise.

    d. The rocks are dangerous.

    e. A rafter paddles constantly.

    f. Rafting satisfies in several ways.

    g. A rafter occasionally swims.

    h. It is challenging.

    i. The valley is green.

    j. The rapids are tricky.

    k. The river sparkles.

T.S.

  I.

    A.

    B.

  II.

    A.

    B.

  III.

    A.

    B.

Conclusion:

4.   a. Winning teaches generosity.

    b. Athletics build character.

    c. Drama cultivates acting ability.

    d. Student officers learn procedure.

    e. Meeting people encourages tolerance.

    f. College offers many learning activities.

    g. Social activities teach.

    h. Conflict sharpens wits.

    i. College isn't just classrooms.

    j. Teamwork inculcates discipline.

    k. Responsibility fosters leadership.

    l. Politics can instruct.

    m. Dating teaches tact.

    n. Cultural activities encourage growth.

    o. Losing teaches self-control.

    p. Attending exhibits builds perception.

T.S.

  I.

    A.

    B.

II.
    A.
    B.
    C.

III.
    A.
    B.
    C.

IV.
    A.
    B.

Conclusion:

5. a. They can be used for games.
   b. A wide range of accounting programs are available.
   c. Personal computers have many uses.
   d. My personal favorite is Frogger.
   e. Several companies produce excellent word-processing packages.
   f. They have business applications.
   g. Some programs teach children to spell.
   h. All in all, personal computers are a good investment.
   i. My friends prefer Q-bert.
   j. Others teach adults geometry.
   k. They can educate.

T.S.

I.
    A.
    B.

II.
    A.
    B.

III.
    A.
    B.

Conclusion:

WRITING PRACTICE

1. Choose any one of the writing projects you worked on in Exercises A and C of this chapter and produce a finished version of it. If you wish, have someone else review a draft of your writing and make suggestions for revisions or corrections.

2.   You are a member of this year's commencement committee, working on the selection of a speaker for the event. Using whatever methods of exploring, focusing, and organizing you like, choose an appropriate candidate and write a report to the committee nominating your chosen speaker.

You may check with your instructor or a librarian for assistance in getting background information about possible speakers. Speakers may come from any field so long as you think they will have something interesting to say to those attending the commencement ceremony.

11

Revising for Unity

Since writing involves so many considerations—audience, purpose, organization, sentence structure, word choice—it is almost impossible for any
writer to keep all these factors in mind at once.

Because of this complexity, most writers will do some planning before
writing, then write a draft of the paper, then work on revising that draft.

Re-vision means *seeing again*. In revising a piece of writing, you go back to
it, perhaps several times, looking at it from different perspectives. One time,
you might be looking to make sure you have stayed with your main idea. On
another reading, you might be checking to see that connections have been
established between ideas. Looking a third time, you might concentrate on
whether the particular words you have chosen are suitable for your audience
and purpose.

During the revision process it is often helpful to have someone else read
your paper: your roommate, your teacher, your English lab instructor, a
friend, a classmate. Someone else may see problems in organization or
wording that you have overlooked because you are so familiar with the ideas
you are writing about.

A final version of your paper may come only after several revisions.
There is nothing out of the ordinary about this. No writer sits down and produces a perfect paragraph, essay, or report on the first try. It's important,
then, that you allow yourself plenty of time for revision. That way, your final
copy will present your idea as accurately and convincingly as possible. Time
spent in revising your writing is time well spent.

One way to begin the revision process is to evaluate the unity of your writing. How well does this piece stick to the main idea?

By the time you have finished your first draft, you should have pretty well committed yourself to dealing with a particular, limited subject in a particular, limited way.

RELATING SUPPORT TO TOPIC SENTENCE

The topic sentence of your paragraph is your written commitment to your audience of what you will do in a certain piece of writing. For instance, if your topic sentence has told the audience that you are going to write about the costs of opening a new dental practice, you can't turn around and discuss the rewards of dentistry as a profession. You must deliver to your reader what you promised in the topic sentence.

Look at this paragraph:

> Fictional detectives are frequently presented as smarter than ordinary human beings. For instance, Poe's classic hero, C. Auguste Dupin, in *The Purloined Letter*, quickly finds a stolen document that the police have spent months searching for in vain. Sir Arthur Conan Doyle's famous sleuth, Sherlock Holmes, baffles client after client by telling them what they have come for before they have said a word. In the twentieth century, Agatha Christie's Belgian detective, Hercule Poirot, prides himself on his ability to use his "little gray cells" more effectively than the police use theirs. No mere human villain can hope to outwit these superhumanly clever investigators.

What does this paragraph promise the reader? How does it keep that promise?

Well, the topic sentence limits the discussion to fictional detectives. The topic sentence also requires that the paragraph discuss only the intelligence of these characters, not their physical prowess or their social status. In addition, the topic sentence suggests that fictional detectives will be compared to ordinary people.

The topic sentence's promise is kept by the writer's giving three fictional detectives as examples and discussing the mental abilities of each one as compared to those of other people—the police or the client. So the paragraph does stick to the subject and focus set up in the topic sentence.

Because the focus part of the topic sentence exerts such control over what happens in the rest of the paragraph, it is frequently referred to as the controlling idea of the paragraph.

Now look at the paragraph below, which lacks a topic sentence. If the support and the conclusion are doing what the topic sentence promised, you should be able to figure out the subject and the controlling idea and construct a suitable topic sentence.

REVISING

At a minimum, all the rooms in the center should be well-lighted and clean. It should have fire extinguishers and clearly marked exits as well as smoke alarms. Windows on upper floors should be locked or made secure with screens or bars. Stairways should have handrails. All play equipment should be in good repair. Also the outside play area should be fenced and free of hazardous debris. Finally, a safe day-care center should provide enough staff supervision to keep childish exuberance or inexperience from causing a serious accident. The safety of the children is an important factor in choosing an acceptable child-care facility.

After reading this paragraph, you should see that the subject is a day-care center (references circled) and that the focus is on safety features (references underlined). Notice that every sentence in this paragraph makes some reference to either the subject or the controlling idea or both.

A suitable topic sentence for this paragraph might be:

Safety must be considered in choosing a day-care center.

or

In a good day-care center, parents should not have to worry about the safety of their children.

A paragraph in which the support fits the topic sentence is said to have *unity.* In a unified paragraph, all the supporting sentences relate directly to the subject and the controlling idea presented in the topic sentence.

EXERCISE A

For each of the following paragraphs, choose the topic sentence that best expresses the unifying idea of the paragraph. Be prepared to explain your choices.

1. *Topic Sentences:*
    A. The Olympic Games were held in Los Angeles in 1984.
    B. The Olympic Games include a wide variety of sports.
    Not only are there the traditional events like the marathon, the discus, swimming, diving, and track, but new events abound. Basketball has been in the Games only about twenty years. Volleyball is even newer. Synchronized swimming, or water ballet, was introduced in the '84 Olympics. Athletes compete on grass, cinder tracks, and horseback, in water and air. One can almost believe that if a human can do it, it's in the Games.

2. *Topic Sentences:*
   A. Marrakesh is a flourishing oasis.
   B. Marrakesh is the terminus for many caravan routes.

   From there, the roads lead west and south. In the west, they cut through the pass in the Atlas to reach out for the Algerian oases of Colomb-Béchar and Timimoun. To the south, the tracks run across the hard, rocky ground between the cinnamon-colored dunes. They spread out toward the copper and sulfate mines, down the Atlantic coast, and toward Timbuktu, cradled in a loop of the Niger. The goods of subSaharan Africa follow the trade routes to the oasis city of Marrakesh.

3. *Topic Sentences:*
   A. The Greek myths have many examples of startling cruelty.
   B. The Greeks told strange stories about their gods.

   Zeus had Prometheus chained to a mountain while a vulture gnawed at his liver for his crime of giving fire to the newly created humans. When Marsyas dared to challenge Apollo, god of the sun and music, to a contest and lost, he was flayed alive. Apollo and his sister killed all fourteen of Niobe's children after Niobe insulted the gods. Grieving Niobe turned to stone, but the stone still wept. The stories are as grim as the fairy tales children read or the prime-time movies they watch.

4. *Topic Sentences:*
   A. Soviet-bloc citizens sometimes have difficulty with their governments.
   B. Even Nobel Prize winners cannot always leave their countries freely.

   Lech Walesa, the Polish labor leader who recently won the Nobel Peace Prize, was not allowed to go to the award ceremonies. Only after much Western outcry was his wife permitted to go in his place. Likewise, when Boris Pasternak won the prize for literature in 1958 for his novel *Dr. Zhivago*, he could not get permission to go to Stockholm to receive his award. Communist governments do not like to let their famous citizens visit the West.

5. *Topic Sentences:*
   A. Banks act in the best interest of the consumers.
   B. Banks serve as financial intermediaries.

   Savers put their money into different kinds of accounts. The banks use this money to fund loans. The borrowers of these loans pay back the money along with a user's charge called interest. The banks take some of this interest as profit and return the rest to the savers. So banks provide the means for one person's savings to help other people get funds to improve their lives.

EXERCISE B

Here are several more paragraphs that are unified but lack topic sentences. Read the support and conclusion parts of the paragraphs and see if you can construct a topic sentence that will fit the subject and the focus of

REVISING

each paragraph. Circle all the references to the subject in each paragraph and underline all the references to the focus or controlling idea.

1. _____

_____

Many of Ellington's thousands of pieces were rhythmic songs like "Sophisticated Lady" or "I Let a Song Go Out of My Heart." He also wrote impressionistic mood music like "Azure" and "On a Turquoise Cloud." Social commentary was part of his repertoire in works like "Harlem Speaks." In addition he composed religious music, ballets, and film scores. Finally, and perhaps most significantly, he innovated new jazz concepts in works like "The Mooch" and "Ko-Ko." It is this kind of versatility that made Duke Ellington one of America's greatest composers.

2. _____

_____

For one thing, El Mirador is much larger than Tikal. Archeologists estimate that the newly uncovered city supported close to 80,000 people, twice the population of its neighbor to the south. El Mirador is also some 350 years earlier than Tikal, which was inhabited by the Mayans in the eighth century. The architecture and pottery of the two sites also show some significant differences. El Mirador's pyramids are much larger than those at other Mayan sites, and its houses don't have the triangular, arched roofs found at Tikal. The pottery at El Mirador lacks the painted scenes found on other Mayan pieces. Archeologists are hoping that the study of these differences may unlock the secret of the fall of the Mayan civilization in Central America.

3. _____

_____

One type of information furnished by an accounting system is that which shows whether an organization is performing well or badly over some period of time. Are its sales increasing? Is it reaching more people? These data can be used by the management to plan and control current operations. Stockholders and government agencies can use such data for investment, funding, or tax purposes. Another kind of information generated by an accounting system is that which calls attention to a problem in the organization. Is one department working less effectively than the others? Closely related to the performance data, this attention-directing information lets management focus quickly on areas of possible improvement. Finally, a good accounting system provides problem-solving information. It can quantify the relative merits of several courses of action. Can more money be saved by switching to new packaging or by moving the storage facility? If the company lowers the employees' medical benefits, can it afford to fund a dental plan? Thus, an effective accounting system has to be able to serve more than one purpose.

REVISING

4. _____

_____

Once a master builder had been hired and a design for the cathedral approved, the master carpenter could begin cutting the timber, and the master quarryman could begin cutting the stone. The laborers, meanwhile, would clear the site and dig the hole for the foundation, a process which could take up to a year. Another ten to fifteen years would be spent constructing the foundation and the main support piers and buttresses. It would take another five years or so to complete the main walls. Then work could start on the roof, which was made of a series of wooden trusses covered with lead sheets. In another five years, work might begin on the vaulted ceiling of the interior. After about fifty years of building, the cathedral would be ready for the glassmakers to prepare the stained glass windows. While the windows were being installed, sculptors would finish the decorative carving inside, and masons would lay the stone floor. Eighty years after the cathedral had been started, it might be ready for the finishing touches: a bell, doors, a spire. All told, a hundred years was not an unreasonable building time for a twelfth-century cathedral. And if the conditions were less than ideal, if there were financial or structural problems, the building might well take two hundred years from start to finish.

5. _____

_____

Behind me I was sure I heard relentless, ghostly footsteps, accompanied by a low, eerie laugh. Although the sounds seemed to be growing louder, I didn't dare turn around to see if *it* was catching up to me. Suddenly my chest felt too cramped to hold my heart, which was racing wildly. My palms were sweaty, but my mouth was dry, and when I tried to call out, no sound came except a faint croak. As the moaning laugh chased me down the hall, my bones seemed to turn to jelly. I stumbled and choked in the rising dust. Finally, after what seemed like hours, my groping hand found the door and pulled frantically at the knob. Slamming the heavy door behind me, I collapsed against the wall, a quivering lump of fear.

One way of ensuring unity in a paragraph is to eliminate, either in prewriting or in revision, any details which don't directly support the topic and controlling idea you have chosen.

EXERCISE C

In each of the following exercises, you are given a topic sentence and some possible supporting details. In each case decide which details would fit in a unified paragraph and be prepared to explain why.

REVISING

1. The reference books of the library can be a great help to a student.
   a. A good encyclopedia can give a student a general overview of a subject.
   b. The card catalog shows a student all the holdings the library has in any subject area.
   c. The card catalog is usually located near the main desk.
   d. The *Reader's Guide to Periodical Literature* can help a student find magazine articles on almost any topic.
   e. *Current Biography* can give a student background information on anyone who is in the news.
   f. This helpful reference tool is issued in monthly volumes.
   g. *Book Review Digest* tells the student the critics' views of major new books.
   h. The *Digest* covers only the twentieth century.
   i. The *Oxford English Dictionary* tells a student what a word means.
   j. It also can tell how the meaning of a word has changed over the years.
   k. The library has to spend a great deal of money to maintain a good reference collection.

2. British and American mystery writers emphasize different kinds of characters and settings in their stories.
   a. Mystery novels are one of the most popular kinds of fiction.
   b. Americans specialize in the hard-bitten detective novel.
   c. In these novels, a tough, but honest guy battles the forces of evil.
   d. A good example is *The Thin Man* by Dashiell Hammett, set in America's Jazz Age.
   e. Hammett was jailed during the McCarthy period.
   f. Ross MacDonald created another classic American detective.
   g. MacDonald was born in Canada.
   h. MacDonald's detective, Lew Archer, chases murderers in modern-day California.
   i. British writers thrive on murders occurring at a party at a lonely house.
   j. In British mysteries, an amateur detective often solves a mystery that baffles the professionals.
   k. Agatha Christie's *Then There Were None* is a superb example of this British form.
   l. Agatha Christie married a man many years her junior.
   m. More recently, English novelist P.D. James has triumphed in this genre with *The Skull Beneath the Skin.*
   n. She is one of my favorite authors.

REVISING

3. Genealogy, the study of family histories, should be done in an organized way.
   a. You should make or buy charts to record family information.
   b. The charts are usually inexpensive.
   c. You should keep systematic records of family births, deaths, and marriages.
   d. You should ask all your close relatives for information.
   e. Talking to your grandmother can be a very pleasant way to spend an afternoon.
   f. You should also check the family's written records like Bibles, diaries, and letters.
   g. Such records are frequently valuable to antique dealers.
   h. You also need to check public records like those in courthouses and churches.
   i. You can find additional information in historical or genealogical libraries.
   j. These libraries may cover one state or an entire region.

UNIFYING THROUGH SUBORDINATION

In the exercise you just worked on, you deleted any details that did not refer directly to the topic and controlling idea set up for the paragraph. There is, however, another way of dealing with such material. Some details that are interesting but not directly related to the controlling idea may be included in your writing through the use of subordination.

For example, suppose that you are writing to a friend to tell him or her about how you are doing in school. Perhaps your topic sentence is: *Last semester went well for me.* You have these three facts to report:

> I had trouble in English.
> My math grades were good.
> My history grades were the best I have ever earned.

If you just leave out all mention of English, you're not giving an entirely accurate picture of the semester. On the other hand, having trouble in English doesn't really support the impression of success you want to create.

One way of handling this difficulty is to emphasize your success in math and history by putting those ideas into the base sentence and to deemphasize your trouble in English by putting that in a subordinate word group.

> *Even though I had trouble in English, <u>my math grades were good, and my history grades were the best I have ever earned.</u>*

REVISING

Here is another situation that calls for the use of subordination. Suppose you are reviewing a new restaurant for the local paper. In your opening sentence, you want to convey your favorable impression of the place and also mention its location. Since the main purpose of the review is to give your opinion, you don't want to give too much emphasis to the location. However, the location is certainly important information to your readers. The solution is to subordinate the location.

> *Paul's Pizza Palace, located at 17 W. Tilman Street, offers good, but not elaborate, Italian food at reasonable prices.*

This version emphasizes your favorable attitude by putting it in the base sentence. You have not destroyed the unity of your article by having a base sentence with information that does not directly support the controlling idea.

The techniques of subordination are presented in Chapter 4; you may wish to review them before doing the exercises that follow.

EXERCISE D

Each topic sentence below suggests a unifying idea. Use subordination to make the supporting sentences fit that controlling idea.

EXAMPLES:

T.S. Walt Disney revolutionized animated cartoons.

Pre-Disney cartoons featured simple, two-dimensional pictures.

Disney insisted on rounded, humanized figures.

Earlier cartoons were based on slapstick comedy.

Disney wanted humor that developed out of personality.

While pre-Disney cartoons featured simple, two-dimensional pictures, Disney insisted on rounded, humanized figures. Disney wanted humor developed out of personality rather than the slapstick comedy of earlier cartoons.

1. *T.S.* Simplicity is the key to a good brand name.
The brand name should be easy to pronounce in all languages. "Coke" is a good example. "Coke" has been marketed in most foreign countries.

_____

_____

2. *T.S.* "Babe" Didrickson was the greatest female athlete in modern times.
She excelled in basketball. She excelled in track and field. She excelled in golf. Most athletes specialize in one sport.

_____

_____

3. *T.S.* My academic credentials qualify me for the position in the Modern Languages Department.
I attended Middle States University. I received my Bachelor of Arts degree in Spanish. My degree was awarded in 1982.

_____

_____

4. *T.S.* The American Indians have not fared well at the hands of white men.
The first settlers in the New World found a native population of almost 10 million people. By 1890, the Indian population had shrunk to 248,000.

_____

_____

5. *T.S.* Hours before a game, the ballpark bustles with activity.
The first arrivals are the ground crew. They assemble to "dump the tarp." This gets the rainwater and condensation off it. They begin this process by 7 A.M.

_____

_____

EXERCISE E

Combine each of the following sets of sentences to produce a unified paragraph. Subordinate or eliminate any details that do not relate directly to the paragraph's controlling idea.

TYPES OF STARS

T.S. The stars fall into categories.
There are three categories.
The categories are general.
You can see the stars.
This happens on a night.
The night is clear.

1. Star-gazing is a hobby.
   The hobby is inexpensive.
   The hobby is popular.
2. The first kind are dwarves.
   The dwarves are white.
3. These stars are dense.
   Their density is incredible.
   These stars are hot.
   Their heat is amazing.

4. There are also giants.
   The giants are red.

5. The word *giant* is derived.
   The derivation is from the Greek word.
   The Greek word is *gigas*.

6. One of these giants would engulf the system.
   The system is ours.
   The system is solar.
   The engulfing would reach out to the orbit.
   The orbit is of Pluto.

7. Other stars are in between.
   These stars are yellow.
   They are not giants.
   They are not dwarves.
   They are not wonderfully large.
   They are not wonderfully hot.

8. The sun is such a star.
   The sun is ours.
   The star is yellow.

9. All these stars die.
   The yellow die.
   The red die.
   The white die.
   This happens eventually.

10. Those spots may look pretty much the same.
    The spots are bright.
    They are in the sky.
    There are several kinds of stars.
    The kinds are different.
    This is actually the case.

LOS ANGELES

T.S. Los Angeles is a latecomer.
Its lateness is among cities.
The cities are American.

1. Los Angeles is old.
   It was founded by the Spanish.
   They founded it in the seventeenth century.
   Los Angeles was a village.
   The village was sleepy.
   This condition lasted for most of Los Angeles's long life.

REVISING

2. The Spanish founded.
   Other cities were founded.
   The other cities were many.
   The other cities were in California.

3. San Francisco was growing rapidly.
   The Gold Rush helped San Francisco grow.
   The Gold Rush was in 1849.

4. Los Angeles grew.
   The growth was slow.
   Los Angeles became a center.
   The center was agricultural.

5. The movies came.
   They were drawn by the climate.
   This happened early in the twentieth century.

6. Movie are the industry.
   The industry is associated with Los Angeles.
   The association is most close.

7. The aircraft industry came.
   It had reasons for coming.
   Its reasons were the same as those of the filmmakers.
   This happened a few years later.

8. War broke out in 1940.
   Los Angeles supplied planes.
   Los Angeles supplied movies.
   These supplies were for the war effort.
   Los Angeles's industries grew.
   The growth was enormous.

REVISION PRACTICE

Identify the controlling idea of each of the following paragraphs. Then revise the paragraphs for unity by eliminating any details not pertinent to the focus and by making sure that each base sentence relates directly to the controlling idea of the paragraph.

1. Wye Castle has a sinister reputation. The castle, which is featured in many legends of dark deeds, sits on a hill in Shropshire near the Welsh border. Of all the great mansions in the area, Wye Castle is the largest and grandest. According to one tale, moonlight shines where a bloodstain appears on the stone floor of the Duke's bedroom. Esmerelda, whose blood supposedly stains the floor, was a beautiful peasant whom the Duke set above his family. She was the youngest of five daughters. A mirror stands in the bedroom where one can allegedly see the Duke's sons stabbing Esmerelda while their mother looks on. The mirror has an elaborately carved

REVISING

mahogany frame that matches the other rich furnishings in the room. There is also the cellar door where, every New Year's Day, someone taps, asking to be let in. But although there is no one there, someone always opens the door. While no one lives there now because of its dark secrets, the castle is quite attractive by daylight.

2.   Homer celebrates cleverness and cunning in *The Odyssey*. The figures of Athena and Odysseus, who are extremely intelligent, dominate the poem. Odysseus, who is the cleverest man alive, is trying to get home to his wife and son. Odysseus is married to a patient and faithful woman named Penelope. While Odysseus, whom Homer calls "the man who is never at a loss," conquers Troy by using a clever stratagem, other heroes have fought for ten years without taking the city. The war over Troy begins with the kidnapping of the beautiful Helen. Although Odysseus finally manages to get home, on the way there his crew is disobedient, and several gods are against him. Athena is the courageous goddess of wisdom who is Homer's second example of cunning. Her father, whom she tricks, is the chief of gods, and her uncle, whom she outwits, is the sea-god. Many of the Greek gods seem as petty as the mortals whose lives they supposedly rule. Athena meets Odysseus and they argue in an unmatched battle of wits. Because of Odysseus' craftiness and Athena's cleverness, there is peace at last in the world of the poem. Homer admires honesty and respects courage, but he feels intelligence is greater. Other ancient writers put more value on courage than on cleverness.

WRITING PRACTICE

1.   Your speech class is preparing a debate on one of the issues listed below (or choose another issue that interests you). You have been placed on the A team, the team that will present the arguments in favor of the issue. A good debater should acknowledge the points on the other side, but emphasize the points on his own side. Prepare a summary of about 250 words that emphasizes the proponents' arguments while pointing out the opposing arguments in subordinate constructions.

Use the writing process strategies presented in earlier chapters to explore the issue and organize your presentation. In revision, be especially careful to check the unity of your summary. Be sure you have emphasized the favorable points of this issue.

2.   Prepare the same kind of summary for the negative side of the question.

ISSUES FOR DEBATE

Children's television programming harms children more than it benefits them.

REVISING

A used car is a better investment than a new car.

A literature course should be required for all college students.

All elementary school students should study a foreign language.

Our city/county should require licenses for handgun ownership.

Newspapers keep people better informed than television.

(Ask your teacher or librarian for suggestions if you need to find more information about the subject of your debate.)

12

Revising for Coherence

To communicate an idea clearly to an audience, it is certainly helpful to unify a paragraph around one central idea. But unity is not always enough to ensure clear communication. Research has shown that readers have very short memories and need constant reminders to help them keep the message in mind.

Therefore, your paragraph may be unified and well-organized but still be difficult to follow because you haven't provided the clues that will help your reader establish the connections between your ideas. In revising a piece of writing, you need to pay special attention to showing the relationships between and among your sentences. This quality of showing relationships is called *coherence*, making sure ideas stick together.

For instance, look at the two paragraphs below. Which one is easier to follow?

A. The fall of the Roman Empire has often been credited to very dramatic causes. A long, dull economic breakdown caused the collapse. A massive dose of lead poisoning has been claimed as the cause. Writers blame the persecution of Christians and Jews. A myth links the fall with moral decay. Wild parties led to a decline in strength. Nero and the other famous party-givers lived before the greatest days of Rome. Another cause can be found. Great

B. Although the fall of the Roman Empire has often been credited to very dramatic causes, it seems most likely that the actual cause was a long, dull economic breakdown. Some writers have attributed the fall to a massive dose of lead poisoning. Others have blamed the fall on the Roman persecution of Christians and Jews. The most widespread, but mythical, theory links the fall of Rome with moral decay, claiming that wild parties led to a

landholders gave up the business of foreign takeovers. Their estates at home gave them secure profits. The economies of Italy, France, and Spain stopped growing. The broken-up Western Empire was ripe for the coming of the Germanic invaders. The desire for a secure retirement felled the Roman Empire.

decline in Roman strength. This theory ignores the fact that Nero and the other famous party-givers actually lived before the greatest days of Rome. The real cause of the Empire's downfall, in fact, was probably much less dramatic than any of these theories suggest. The great Roman landholders simply gave up the risky business of foreign takeovers and went back to their estates, where the profits were secure. As a result, the economies of Italy, France, and Spain stopped growing, and the Western Empire broke up, ripe for the coming of the Germanic invaders. So it was not the drama of lead poisoning, or bloody persecutions, or hedonistic excesses that felled the Romans; it was the perfectly ordinary desire for a comfortable retirement.

Paragraph A is unnecessarily hard to read. To understand it, you may have to reread the paragraph several times, working to tie the ideas together. In Paragraph A, the relationships between one sentence and another and between one part of the paragraph and another are not clear. In this version, for instance, you may not have realized that the writer intends to emphasize one cause more than the others. Paragraph A lacks coherence—that is, the ideas do not stick together (cohere) well.

In Paragraph B, on the other hand, four specific writing techniques have been used to show the relationships between ideas. First, some sentences have been combined using methods familiar to you from exercises in previous chapters.

> *Although* the fall of the Roman Empire has often been credited to very dramatic causes, it seems most likely that the actual cause was a long, dull economic breakdown.
>
> The great Roman landholders simply gave up the risky business of foreign takeovers *and* went back to their estates. . . .

Second, some sentences have been tied into the paragraph by the addition of transition signals that explain their relationships either to the preceding sentence or to the topic sentence.

> The real cause of the Empire's downfall, *in fact,* was probably much less dramatic. . . .

REVISING

> *As a result,* the economies of Italy, France, and Spain stopped grow-
> ing. . . .

Third, some sentences have been rewritten to give them parallel structures emphasizing their parallel functions in the paragraph.

> *Some writers have attributed the fall* to a massive dose of lead poisoning.
> *Others have blamed the fall* on the Roman persecution of Christians and Jews.

Finally, the wording of some sentences has been changed so that key words and phrases are repeated to help the reader follow the discussion.

> Others have blamed the fall on the *Roman* persecution. . . . The great *Roman* landholders. . . .
> So it was not *the drama* of *lead poisoning,* or *bloody persecutions,* or *hedonistic excesses.* . . .

EXERCISE A

In each of the following paragraphs, identify the methods the writer has used to achieve coherence.

1. Like other rulers of the late eighteenth century, Empress Catherine the Great of Russia is often referred to as an "enlightened despot." On the one hand, she helped Russia by establishing closer diplomatic ties with European nations. She also founded hospitals, schools, and the St. Petersburg Public Library to benefit the Russian people. She even introduced some progressive legal ideas such as the abolition of torture. On the other hand, Catherine had no qualms about murdering her husband to gain his throne. In addition, she extended the appalling system of serfdom into vast areas of Russia when it suited her fiscal policies. Finally, in her foreign policy, she unscrupulously took advantage of neighboring countries' difficulties to seize their land. Poland, for example, was swallowed up during her reign. Because of the glaring contrasts in her actions, some historians find it hard to decide whether Catherine was more enlightened or more despotic as a ruler.

2. The link between intelligence and heredity has not been proved as important as some people have claimed. First, we have no solid definition of intelligence. Those who believe there is an important link base their claim on IQ tests, but these are intended only to predict an individual's success in school, and academic success is a poor definition of intelligence. Second, we have no good research on the inheritability of intelligence. The only sound evidence comes from studies of identical twins raised in different back-

grounds. These studies seem to show an important link between test scores and heredity, but they do not take into account the influence of the twins' shared age and sex, which are known to be important on the tests. By themselves, age and sex may account for the close scores achieved by twins. In addition, the most famous twin study now appears to have been faked to fit the researcher's prejudices. As a result of the lack of a solid definition and good research, we are not able to make a scientific generalization about intelligence and inheritance.

SENTENCE COMBINING

You have been learning this technique since you began speaking, and you have been working at it pointedly ever since you opened this book. It is one of the most useful tools in achieving coherence because it employs the most common devices in the language for bringing out the relationships between ideas. Every time you modify a word, coordinate two ideas, or subordinate one idea to another, you are creating and explaining relationships. So fundamental are these devices that you could say the invention of the conjunctions (*so, if, or,* and others) was one of humanity's giant steps forward.

Careful combining of sentences helps readers see precisely the connections you want them to see. For instance, compare these examples:

> The fall of the Roman Empire has often been credited to very dramatic causes. A long, dull economic breakdown caused the collapse.
>
> Although the fall of the Roman Empire has often been credited to very dramatic causes, it seems most likely that the actual cause was a long, dull economic breakdown.

In the first version, the dramatic theories and the nondramatic theory receive the same emphasis. In fact, a reader might almost think that the economic breakdown was an example of a dramatic cause for the fall of Rome. By using subordination, the second version helps the reader to see where the real emphasis of the paragraph falls and reduces confusion about the relationship between these two ideas. *Although* clearly suggests contrast, not example.

Sentence combining, then, is the basic stuff of coherence.

(If you need to review any of the techniques of sentence combining, refer to Chapters 2, 3, and 4.)

TRANSITION SIGNALS

This technique is closely related to sentence combining. You add a word or phrase to a sentence to make its connection to the preceding or following sentences clear. Words like *thus* or *in addition* serve as signs to your reader of

REVISING

the way in which one sentence relates to another. Transition signals can help your reader follow more easily the pattern of your thinking. For instance, in the paragraph shown at the beginning of this chapter, the last sentence begins with the word *so*, which lets the reader know that a conclusion is about to be drawn from what has been said before. Without that signal, the reader might be unprepared for a conclusion and might have to go back and reread the sentence.

Each transition signal sets up a different kind of relationship between ideas. Here are some of the most common transition signals, grouped according to the kind of connection they establish between ideas.

TRANSITION SIGNALS

Adding On:	also, besides, first, second, furthermore, in addition, moreover, next, then, after, finally, last, and
Comparing:	similarly, likewise, in the same way
Contrasting:	however, on the other hand, nevertheless, instead, otherwise, yet, but, on the contrary
Giving Examples:	for instance, for example, specifically, in fact, in particular
Showing Result:	thus, therefore, consequently, as a result, accordingly, so
Summing Up:	in conclusion, in short, on the whole, in general, in summary, in other words
Moving in Time:	then, shortly, afterward, in the meantime, soon, at last, now, later, meanwhile
Moving in Space:	nearby, overhead, opposite, on the left, on the right, there, here

REVISING

Transition signals usually require punctuation since they are interrupting or preceding the base sentence.

We met Sally and Dean at the movie. *Afterward,* we went to dinner.

Billman has cheated the city; *therefore,* I will not vote for her.

Their father leaves at 6 every morning. The children, *as a result,* rarely get a hot breakfast before school.

EXERCISE B

Use appropriate transition signals to show the relationship between the sentences in each of the following sets. Punctuate as needed.

1. Mr. Chanundra is a thoroughly traditional writer. Mr. Anderson has a reputation for eccentricity.

   _____

   _____

2. Computers are remarkable machines. Few people realize their ability to serve human needs.

   _____

   _____

3. Deanne and Lori are gourmet cooks. They invite interesting guests. Their party should be a great success.

   _____

   _____

4. Many of Ross MacDonald's novels deal with the search for a lost parent. *The Underground Man* uses this theme. *The Blue Hammer* uses it.

   _____

   _____

5. Captain Marvel is a lot like Superman. They are both invulnerable. They both have super strength. They are both on the side of truth and justice.

   _____

   _____

   _____

6. Dan would never go there. That school is too far away from home. It doesn't have an agricultural program. It is far too expensive.

   _____

   _____

   _____

REVISING

7. Martindale School has produced many successful women. Connie Newman became the vice-president of a major exporting company. Louraine Riser has published several widely acclaimed novels. Ann Terry is head of the State Association of PTAs.

_____

_____

_____

8. Tennis is very popular in Sewall County. The Women's Tennis League has 500 members this year. The children's program attracted 1,200 youngsters. Every school in the county offers tennis as a physical education option.

_____

_____

_____

9. Kenny's yard was our favorite place to play. A huge tree shaded it. The sandbox filled with toys was always ready for us. There was a swing set and a sliding board. It had a frontier fort complete with a lookout platform.

_____

_____

_____

10. Ms. Delaney never arrives on time for work. She makes at least one mistake with her cash count every day. Several customers have complained about her rudeness. I would recommend firing her.

_____

_____

_____

PARALLEL STRUCTURE

When you wish to show that two sentences do the same work or hold the same relationship to the topic sentence, arrange them in the same (or _parallel_) pattern.

For example, in the first version of the paragraph that opened this chapter, two of the theories about the fall of the Roman Empire were presented this way:

A massive dose of lead poisoning has been claimed as the cause.
Writers blame the persecution of Christians and Jews.

These two sentences are doing the same work, presenting theories about the same event, but their structure is not parallel, and the reader is not helped to see the similarity of their function.

REVISING

In the more coherent version, the same sentences read:

Some writers have attributed the fall to a massive dose of lead poisoning.

Others have blamed the fall on the Roman persecution of Christians and Jews.

Both these sentences follow the same pattern: they begin with the persons who hold the theory and end with the theory itself. Here the parallel structure signals the parallel function and helps the reader see the underlying sameness of the sentences.

In the combining exercises given earlier, you practiced all the major sentence patterns in English. You can apply your skill to create parallel structures when you want to give your reader a clearer sense of the underlying relationships within your paragraphs.

This device of parallelism can be used to stress the similarity of ideas within one sentence as well as between sentences.

For instance, in this sentence

In the evening, Jim likes *to read the newspaper*, to *drink a glass of wine*, and *to snooze before the fire*.

the three things that Jim likes are phrased in parallel ways—all using the *to* + *verb* construction.

EXERCISE C

Revise the sentences below using parallel structures to show the connection between related ideas.

1. Governor Von Mayer promised lower taxes, a legislature that is honest, and to make the state bureaucracy smaller.

_____

_____

2. Good photography depends on the skill of the photographer, having the best quality camera, and that you choose the proper film.

_____

_____

3. Franklin's success was due to his ability to work hard, the fact that he was curious, and because of his common sense.

_____

_____

REVISING

4. A hospice administers carefully controlled medication that does not cure illness or prolonging life, but is intended to relieve the pain of the dying person.

_____

_____

5. Buying government bonds yields a safe return. More risk and higher earnings come with investing in corporate stock.

_____

_____

6. Her lips were full and self-indulgent; large, limpid eyes sat in her face; smoothness and paleness characterized her forehead.

_____

_____

7. Sixty percent of the money goes to fundraising costs. The Association takes 30 percent for administration. The poor receive only ten cents out of every dollar contributed.

_____

_____

8. The first television sets were huge boxes with small, fuzzy images. Now tiny boxes that have images that are small and fuzzy are called televisions.

_____

_____

9. Paris has the Eiffel Tower. San Francisco is characterized by the Golden Gate. The Acropolis symbolizes Athens.

_____

_____

10. Pairs skating competition is characterized by showy lifts, spins that are elaborate, and jumps of an athletic nature. However, the skaters emphasize intricate footwork, precision in their movements, and the interpretation of music in the sport of ice dancing.

_____

_____

_____

REPETITION OF KEY WORDS

This important device consists of weaving the ideas of the paragraph together by repeating the words related to the topic and/or the controlling idea of the paragraph. Weaving is an appropriate image since this technique does not show relationships or organization; instead, it focuses the reader's attention on the "threads," the important ideas, as they move through the paragraph to make up the fabric of the discussion.

For example, in the paragraph that opens this chapter, the key words *Rome* and *fall* appear again and again, along with other significant words like *dramatic*. These repetitions help the reader to see the main ideas and look for important connections.

Part of the technique of repetition is the correct use of pronouns to help tie the paragraph together. For instance, proper use of *this* and *that* with words referring back to the key words helps the reader see the "threads" of your paragraph. Similarly, proper use of a pronoun like *it* to refer back to a key word creates coherence. However, using *this*, *that*, or other pronouns without clear reference back to the key word can destroy coherence.

> Connie is always late for work, and she cannot
> seem to be punctual for any appointment. This
> causes trouble.

In this example, the use of *this* hurts the coherence. What specifically does *this* refer back to? You can answer only with some awkward phrase like "her being late to work and for appointments." When you have this kind of situation in writing, pick a word that sums up what you are trying to say and use it with the *this* or *that* to make the meaning clear.

> *Connie is always late for work, and she cannot seem to be*
> *punctual for any appointment. This tardiness causes*
> *trouble.*

The same problem can exist with the use of any pronoun. When the pronoun does not refer back to any specific word before it, be careful! Replace the pronoun with a word or phrase that says exactly what you mean.

> We went to see *A Christmas Carol*, had a late supper, and dropped by some friends' place for eggnog. It was perfect.
> *We went to see* A Christmas Carol, *had a late supper, and dropped by some friends' place for eggnog. Our date was perfect.*

(Using pronouns is discussed in more detail in Chapter 6.)

EXERCISE D

Revise the following sets of sentences as appropriate to repeat key ideas. You may also use parallel structures or transition signals if you feel these would enhance the coherence of the sentences.

REVISING

EXAMPLE:

Simplicity characterizes Japanese art.

Lack of complexity rules their music.

Simplicity characterizes Japanese art. Simplicity rules their music, too.

1. My mother didn't allow us to play with guns. We couldn't even pretend we had any sort of firearms.

   _____

   _____

2. When in Rome, do as the people in that area do.

   _____

   _____

3. Ask not what your country can do for you. Inquire about what actions you can take for the benefit of the nation.

   _____

   _____

4. People who try to prove too much sometimes wind up giving a demonstration of nothing.

   _____

   _____

5. The gods help some people. Others have to come to their own assistance.

   _____

   _____

6. Money can't buy happiness. Contentment comes easier with a little wealth.

   _____

   _____

7. Peter was the original "organization man." His life was arranged so carefully that he drove the rest of us, who were slobs without any sense of order, crazy.

   _____

   _____

8. Spring has a special fascination for me. Everything seems full of potential. Nothing seems impossible.

   _____

   _____

9. No one is more laid back than a New Yorker. Cabbies don't look twice at a passenger in a mermaid costume. Shop clerks don't bat an eye when mink-wearing customers fight over a $1.50 tube of lipstick.

REVISING

_____

_____

_____

10. Smart buyers shop as carefully for the loan as they do for the car. People should not automatically let the dealer arrange the details. People should consider banks, credit unions, and life insurance policies as sources for money.

_____

_____

_____

REVISING TO HELP READERS SEE CONNECTIONS
Sentence Combining
Transition Signals
Parallel Structure
Repetition of Key Words

EXERCISE E

Using your knowledge of paragraph strategies and of coherence techniques, rearrange the following paragraphs so that they are presented in a coherent way.

1. (a) The Japanese also used color in a different way, modeling objects in solid blocks of color rather than with the shades and shadows favored by Western artists. (b) The two styles of art also presented their subjects in quite different ways. (c) When these Japanese woodcuts became known in the West, many European artists, especially the French Impressionists, began to experiment with Japanese-style subjects and techniques, so different from those produced in their own culture. (d) Unlike Western artists who used a proportional perspective, the Japanese presented a flat world where the size of an object was determined not by its distance from the viewer but by its importance in the picture. (e) Japanese woodcuts of the nineteenth century presented quite a contrast in subject matter and style to the Western paintings of the same period. (f) While much European painting glorified historical spectacle and myth, Japanese painting delighted in everyday activities.

REVISING

(g) First of all, the two traditions generally chose different subjects for their art.

2.   (a) To get the most from your harvest, be sure to pick your vegetables as they ripen. (b) Then, when you do move the seedlings outdoors, be sure to fertilize the soil before planting. (c) Also look for specially bred varieties that resist disease and adapt to climate changes. (d) You should also conserve garden space by training your vine crops on poles or trellises. (e) Plant the vegetables in wide, raised beds to get the most from your space. (f) Once you have picked the kind of vegetables you want to grow, you should start the seeds indoors to get a head start on the warm weather. (g) Likewise, put tomatoes and peppers in cages to keep them from spreading out over your garden. (h) First, choose your crops carefully. (i) Most vegetables taste best when they are harvested young. (j) You can easily increase your vegetable crop by knowing how to plan, plant, and harvest your garden most efficiently. (k) Choose high-yielding vegetables such as peas and onions and crops, like tomatoes, that taste best when they're fresh-picked. (l) By learning a few tricks about how and when to plant and harvest, you can almost certanly double your vegetable crop. (m) Finally, as soon as a crop is finished, you should either replant or mulch the row so the soil is always producing or improving itself. (n) Besides, production slows if you leave them on the plant.

EXERCISE F

From each set of details given below, compose a coherent paragraph. Combine sentences, add transition signals, or change wording and sentence patterns as you find appropriate.

1.   Antietam wasn't a victory.
Antietam was more of a stand-off.
The Civil War was to drag on.
It dragged on three more years.
Lincoln changed.
He changed his generals.
This happened three times.
He finally picked Grant.
The Army of the Potomac would fight.
The Army of Northern Virginia would fight.
They would fight at Chancellorsville.
They would fight at Gettysburg.
They would fight at the Wilderness.
They would fight in hundreds of skirmishes.
The skirmishes were little.
Thousands of boys would be killed.

Thousands of farms would be burnt.
Thousands of farms would be looted.
Valleys would be laid waste.
The valleys were in Maryland.
The valleys were in Virginia.
The valleys were in Pennsylvania.
The destruction was horrible.
The destruction was in the West.
The destruction was in the South.
Lincoln would test Lee.
Lee would test Lincoln.
The testing was to the extreme.
The road was long.
The road was ahead.
The road led to Appomatox.
The road was bloody.

2. Belinda didn't scare easily.
Belinda lay listening for a moment.
Belinda couldn't hear anything now.
Belinda was certain she had heard a hinge squeal.
Belinda threw back the covers.
Belinda got out of bed.
The floor was cold on her bare feet.
Belinda thought out her situation carefully.
Belinda groped for a candle and a match.
Belinda had some light.
Belinda made a slow circuit of the room.
Everything seemed normal.
Belinda came to the fireplace.
One of the hearth ornaments was crooked.
Belinda straightened the ornament.
There was the same squeal that had awakened Belinda.
A section of the chimney slid open.
There was an open section.
Inside there was a staircase.
Belinda didn't pause.
Belinda entered the secret passage.
Belinda started down the staircase.
Belinda held the flickering candle before her.

REVISION PRACTICE

Revise the following paragraphs so that they establish connections between ideas more clearly. Use any of the coherence techniques presented in this chapter.

REVISING

1.   America's attitude toward the handicapped has been undergoing a slow but definite change. There have been benefits from a general shift in peoples' expectation of government. Since the Depression, there has been an assumption that people in trouble should be helped with public funds. The handicapped have followed the lead of other minorities in demanding not just public assistance, but their full rights as citizens. Increased visibility is a reason for the different attitude. The population is growing older. More people are more subject to crippling diseases and injuries. Changes in medicine and technology have vastly increased the number of people, both young and old, who survive an accident or disease. The handicapped are moving out of hiding and into the mainstream of life.

2.   That two-minute interview with the expert on Soviet military planes that you saw on the network news last night probably took some associate producer weeks to line up. The "booker" has the job of finding interviewees. The booker has to maintain a long list of people who are knowledgeable in subjects ranging from Middle Eastern oil policies to urban soup kitchens. The booker needs phone numbers that will reach them at any hour. The booker may need a person on short notice. The booker interviews each person ahead of time. The booker must determine if the person has the right information and be sure the person will come across well in front of the camera. Some guests are invited to appear. Finding people for news shows is a demanding process.

WRITING PRACTICE

1.   Your campus organization has decided to raise money by writing and selling a student guide to local restaurants. Using whatever techniques of exploring, focusing, and organizing you like, choose one restaurant that might be included in such a guide and write a 300-word entry for it in the guide.

In a writing situation like this, the format of your entry can also be an important tool for coherence. Be sure you lay out the information on the page in such a way that it is easy to follow. Perhaps you and some classmates could design a standard format for restaurant-guide entries.

When you have written a draft of your entry, review it for its unity and coherence and make whatever revisions you feel are necessary. On your own, or with help from someone else, check your entry for problems with punctuation, spelling, or sentence structure and make whatever corrections are necessary before turning in your final version.

2.   In an effort to attract new listeners, the campus radio station, where you work, is planning a special celebration of one musician or one style of music. Prepare a proposal of 300 to 500 words for the station manager explaining which musician or style of music you would like to see featured. Use what-

REVISING

ever methods of exploring, focusing, and organizing you like as you prepare your proposal.

When you have a draft of your proposal, review it for unity and coherence and for any problems in punctuation, spelling, or sentence structure. Make whatever revisions or corrections are necessary before turning in your final version.

13

Revising for Word Choice

As you have seen in the previous chapters on revision, one way of writing a sentence does not have the same effect on a reader as another way. Different structures can convey different meanings. The same principle holds true with word choice. One word does not have exactly the same effect on a reader as another.

In drafting a piece of writing, you may not be too concerned about your individual word choices. As has been mentioned in earlier discussions of revising, you often need to get a feel for the shape of the whole piece of writing before you begin to focus on details of sentence structure and word choice. However, once you have a draft you feel comfortable with, you can look for ways to make your point more effectively by substituting a more exact word or eliminating some unnecessary words.

In revising your writing, you have to be as careful to choose the right words as you are to choose the right sentence structure, the right supporting examples, and the right pattern of arrangement for your subject, audience, and purpose. In evaluating the appropriateness of your language, you need to look at several different aspects: its level of generality, its connotative value, its degree of formality, and its degree of conciseness.

LEVEL OF GENERALITY

Earlier in the book, when you were looking at paragraph structure, you saw that paragraphs and longer pieces of writing often move among ideas on several levels of generality. That same scale of generality operates at the level of individual words and phrases. *Plants*, for example, is a more general word than *vegetables*, and *tomatoes* is still more specific, while *Early Girl tomatoes* is even more specific.

In revising your word choice, you want to make sure that your language is specific enough to suit your purpose and meet the needs of your audience.

For example, if you are trying to show your readers that your grandfather was a messy housekeeper, then a detail like "His dining room table was covered with books" may be specific enough to establish your point. But if you are trying to demonstrate your grandfather's intellectual curiosity, you may need to move to a more specific level of language and name the kinds of books that are on his table, or even give some specific titles.

"My grandfather read a lot of books" doesn't convey his curiosity as well as "My grandfather read everything from Aristotle's *Poetics* to Darwin's *Origin of Species*."

Similarly, "Mrs. Dulaney is big" doesn't describe the woman as exactly as "Mrs. Dulaney is obese" or "Mrs. Dulaney weighs 250 pounds." "Mr. Avery talked to me" doesn't give your readers as clear a picture as "Mr. Avery mumbled something to me."

Whether you choose *obese* rather than *big* or *talked* rather than *mumbled* might depend to some degree on who is going to read this piece and what purpose you want to achieve. As a rule, however, specific language is more effective than general language.

EXERCISE A

Arrange each group of words below in order from most general language to most specific language.

EXAMPLE:
to move, to walk, to sashay

1. area, Kansas City, the midwest, Hallmark Plaza

    _____

2. giggling, amused, laughing, entertained

    _____

3. baseball, shortstops, Cal Ripken, sports

    _____

4. to move fast, to scamper, to run

    _____

5. stingy, unpleasant, pinching every penny till it screams

    _____

REVISING

EXERCISE B

For each sentence below choose the appropriately specific word or phrase to fill in the blank. Be prepared to explain your choices.

EXAMPLE:

Audience: Members of the club

Purpose: Inform about club's financial status

Last year our club raised _____ for community projects. (a lot of money, hundreds of dollars, $675)

Explanation: Club members are entitled to exact figures; a report to the community-at-large might use the more general term "hundreds of dollars."

1. *Audience:* Mystery novel fans

   Purpose: Entertain by creating a feeling of suspense

   The man _____ from the door.

   (walked away, moved away, edged away)

2. *Audience:* Readers of *Seventeen Magazine*

   Purpose: Interpret Brooke Shields's style of beauty

   In her latest ad, Brooke Shields looks _____.

   (good, sensuous but innocent, pretty)

3. *Audience:* Home gardeners

   Purpose: Inform them about new varieties of vegetables

   _____ will do well in almost any kind of soil.

   (Early Prolific Straightneck, vine crops, summer squash)

4. *Audience:* High school history students

   Purpose: Inform them about life in the Depression

   Little children often wore _____.

   (old clothes, hand-me-downs, their father's cut-down shirts)

5. *Audience:* State senator

   Purpose: Persuade her to vote for a pending bill

   I urge you to support this bill because it _____.

   (is so important, will have long-term benefits for the state, can save the state $5 billion in pension costs)

REVISING

EXERCISE C

Revise each of the following sentences by making the underlined language more specific.

1. I didn't like his <u>looks</u>.

    _____

2. I have been in school <u>for a long time</u>.

    _____

3. The dogs <u>walked</u> across the yard.

    _____

4. A <u>vehicle</u> roared down the street.

    _____

5. The room looked <u>strange</u>.

    _____

6. The <u>event</u> was dull.

    _____

7. Someone <u>communicated with</u> the president.

    _____

8. Recently, <u>some people</u> were in Chicago on business.

    _____

9. During our vacation, <u>the weather was not good</u>.

    _____

10. The athlete <u>did well</u>.

    _____

CONNOTATIVE VALUE

The words in the list below are all related to the word *small*, and they are all at roughly the same level of generality. (You can find related words like this in a thesaurus.)

little	trivial
tiny	unimportant
short	petty
wee	puny
dwarfish	slight
undersized	weak
stunted	mean
minute	paltry
infinitesimal	pygmy
dainty	Lilliputian
petite	

REVISING

Now, because all these words are related to *small,* does that mean you can freely substitute one for the other? No.

How would you feel if someone described your brand new baby daughter as *undersized?* Would you feel different if she were described as *dainty?* What is the difference between the two words? The distinction lies mainly in the feelings that are associated with each word. These feelings are called *connotations. Undersized* has negative connotations while *dainty* has positive connotations.

Here are some other examples of differences in connotation.

NEUTRAL	POSITIVE	NEGATIVE
inexpensive	thrifty	cheap
worker	craftsman	drudge
slowly	leisurely	sluggishly

In choosing words, then, you need to be sure that a word carries the right feelings for the subject, audience, and purpose you have chosen. For instance, if you were trying to give an unbiased report, you would choose words that do not have strong favorable or unfavorable connotations:

Dr. Lucas has six months of teaching experience.

If you were trying to criticize, you would choose words that have an unfavorable connotation:

Dr. Lucas is a raw beginner in the field of teaching.

If you were trying to praise, you would choose words with favorable connotations:

Dr. Lucas brings a fresh, new approach to teaching.

EXERCISE D

Using your own knowledge and/or a thesaurus, for each word below list as many words of similar meaning as you can. Group the words as neutral, positive, or negative.

1. look (verb)

neutral   *positive*   *negative*

REVISING

2.   woman

neutral   *positive*   *negative*

3.   quickly

neutral   *positive*   *negative*

4.   careful

neutral   *positive*   *negative*

EXERCISE E

In each of the following paragraphs, you are given two controlling ideas in the topic sentence. You must choose one by underlining it. Then, in the supporting sentences, choose from each pair of words in parentheses the one whose connotations fit your controlling idea. Cross out the word whose connotations don't fit. Use a dictionary for unfamiliar words.

> EXAMPLE:
>
> It was a (pleasant, dull) winter afternoon. The sun
>   cast a (soft, feeble) glow on the (white, pale)
>   landscape.

While the dictionary definitions of *soft* and *feeble* are close in meaning, the connotations of *feeble* don't fit the controlling idea *pleasant*. Likewise, *pale*, which means whitish, has *unpleasant* connotations.

1.   Phillipa Marlow, private eye, glanced up to see a rather (sinister, appealing) figure enter her office. He was (obese, plump); his (graceless, awkward) body filled the doorway. He had tiny, (half-closed, squinty) eyes like a scared (rat's, fieldmouse's). Even at this distance, his skin appeared (creased, wrinkled), as though he had slept in it badly. Fittingly, his hair was (wild, mussed) and stood up in stiff (spikes, cowlicks). When he spoke, his voice was (high, shrill) and had a nasal (twang, whine). Phillipa shook his hand. The palm was (moist, clammy), his grip (hard, firm). Phillipa wanted to (help, get rid of) him.

REVISING

2.   Ms. Joan Bagley has asked me to recommend her for a place in your graduate program. I (can, cannot) do this wholeheartedly. Ms. Bagley is (intelligent, clever). She is (ambitious, driven). At the same time, there is about her a definite (inwardness, self-centeredness). She seems to (weigh seriously, brood over) the problems in her field of study. Though most of her work is (traditional, derivative), she can produce work of remarkable (originality, eccentricity). In short, I think she is one of the (most distinctive, oddest) graduates of this college in years.

DEGREE OF FORMALITY

In choosing language appropriate for your subject, audience, and purpose, you also need to consider how formal the diction should be. *Male progenitor, father, daddy,* and *my old man,* for example, could all refer to the same person. But these word choices would not be equally suitable for different writing situations. Which word would you choose if you were writing a safety pamphlet for young children? Which language would be appropriate for an academic paper in science or social science? Which language would you use in a satiric skit about family life for an audience of your friends?

Formal language often uses multisyllable words (*expeditiously* as opposed to *fast*), highly specialized terms (*regulated liability product* as opposed to *savings account*), or foreign words (*coiffure* as opposed to *hairdo*). Such formality may be appropriate for highly educated audiences, for experts in a particular field, or in important public situations such as a graduation speech or an inauguration address.

Informal language tends to be more conversational, more relaxed than formal language. In informal writing situations or in writing to young audiences or audiences without a great deal of education in your subject, you would choose more everyday words, shorter words, words that don't demand knowledge of a second language.

In a very informal writing situation, you might use slang words like *wheels* instead of *car,* or *put the pedal to the metal* instead of *do it quickly.*

Whatever level of language you choose, it should fit the subject, audience, and purpose of your writing, and it should stay consistent throughout a particular piece of writing. Shifts in the level of formality can destroy the unity of a paragraph.

EXERCISE F

Arrange each of the following lists of words in order from the most formal to the most informal language.

EXAMPLE:
inconsiderable, petty, small-time, dinky

REVISING

1. scare the pants off of, arouse trepidation, frighten
2. antithesis, a horse of a different color, opposite
3. car, passenger-carrying automotive vehicle, automobile, clunker
4. uncertain, fishy, questionable, dubitable
5. mistake, unintentional deviation, boo-boo, slip-up

EXERCISE G

From the following list of words and phrases, choose the ones appropriate to each audience or situation shown below. Some language may fit more than one situation. Use your dictionary to check the meaning of any unfamiliar words.

speak	articulate	verbalize	converse	chew the fat
jabber	talk	proclaim	sound off	say
flap your tongue	yak	state	affirm	tell
phonate		announce	run off at the mouth	

1. Which words would be appropriate for an audience of elementary school children?

2. Which words would be appropriate for a speech therapist's records of a client's progress?

3. Which language would be appropriate for a humorous description of a friend who likes to talk?

4. Which language would be appropriate for a newspaper account of the governor's speech?

5. Which language would be appropriate for a college speech teacher's instructions for a speaking assignment?

DEGREE OF CONCISENESS

Finally, in choosing appropriate language, you want to use your words efficiently. Every word should be necessary to convey your meaning. In revising a draft, then, you might look at it as though you had to pay a dollar for each word. Be sure each word is worth paying for. Wordiness may leave your readers feeling that you are not quite in control of your writing, or even worse, that you are wasting their time by not getting to the point.

REVISING

Look at these sentences. Which version is more concise?

A. Food technologists have radically altered the diet of the average American. In fact, they have almost done away with *real* food. Milk shakes may have no milk. Hamburgers may have no meat.

B. People who work in food technology have radically and drastically altered or changed the dietary habits of the average member of the American public. As a matter of hard fact, these food scientists have almost completely more or less done away with anything that might resemble *real, true, natural, honest-to-goodness* food that people can eat. Milk shakes don't often deserve the name because they aren't made with milk anymore. Also hamburgers have been designed to be made without meat.

Paragraph B shows several of the problems that can lead to wordiness. For one thing, the writer has frequently used a phrase where one word would have conveyed exactly the same information: *people who work in technology* instead of *technologists*, *dietary habits* instead of *diet*. Second, the writer here has repeated herself in several places: *radically* **and** *drastically*; *altered* **or** *changed*; *real, true, natural, honest-to-goodness*. Nothing is gained by this unnecessary repetition.

In writing, more words are not necessarily better than fewer words. What matters is not so much the number of words as the fact that each word does its fair share of work in the sentence or paragraph.

You can often spot wordiness in your writing by looking closely at your verbs. For example, what do you notice about the verbs in the following paragraph?

College students who (are) involved in cheating do so for many reasons. One reason they may cheat (is) that they may not realize that what they (are) doing (is) cheating. Getting help from a friend on a term paper, for example, may not seem (to be) something that (is) seriously wrong. Other students who (are) cheating and know that they (are) cheating do it because it (is) their feeling that tuition (is) too expensive for them to risk failing a course. Another reason for cheating (is) that students may feel tremendous pressure (is) on them from their parents (to be) successful. If one (is) looking at the situation objectively, none of these reasons (is) enough to justify cheating, but to some students, no further reason (is) needed than their own feelings of fear or helplessness.

The verb *to be* occurs sixteen times in six sentences. The *to be* verbs (am, is, are, was, were, be, been) carry little meaning of their own. When you use them, therefore, you often have to add a few extra words to get the meaning across.

If you find your writing leaning too heavily on these verbs, look for other words in the sentence that you can make into verbs. For example, "college students *who are involved in cheating*," can become "college students *who cheat.*"

Here is the same paragraph revised to use fewer *to be* verbs.

> College students who cheat do so for many reasons. For one thing, they may cheat because they do not realize that their actions ⟨are⟩ dishonest. Getting help on a term paper from a friend doesn't seem seriously wrong to them. Other students, who cheat knowingly, do it because they feel tuition⟨is⟩too expensive for them to risk failing a course. Other students cheat because they feel tremendous parental pressure to succeed. When someone looks at the situation objectively, none of these reasons justifies cheating, but some students don't need any justification except their own feelings of fear or helplessness.

By eliminating most of the *to be* verbs and the extra words they dragged along with them, the revision covers in 98 words what it took the original 135 words to say. (If you were paying for this paragraph, you would now be $37 richer.)

Besides getting rid of *to be* verbs, you can also make your writing more concise and more forceful by building your sentences with the most *meaningful* words, that is, with words that convey your meaning most directly.

For example, look at the base sentence buried here:

> In order for a television network to be able to engage in the coverage of the Olympic Games in an effective way, *it is required* for the network to make a commitment that is truly Olympian: of dollars, of equipment that is specialized, and of people who are knowledgeable.

This whole forty-nine-word structure rests on a vague pronoun and a weak verb. To revise a sentence like this, you first need to mark the words that carry the main ideas. If the sentence is long, you may need to break it into smaller units and find the meaning-bearing words in each section of the sentence:

> In order for a <u>television</u> network/ to be able to engage in the <u>coverage</u> of the <u>Olympic</u> Games,/ in an <u>effective</u> way,/ it is <u>required</u> for the network/ to

REVISING

make a <u>commitment</u> that is truly <u>Olympian</u>:/ of <u>dollars</u>,/ of <u>equipment</u> that is

<u>specialized</u>,/ and of <u>people</u> who are <u>knowledgeable</u>.

Then you can rebuild the sentence to emphasize the *meaning*-ful words:

> *Effective television coverage of the Olympics requires a truly Olympian commitment of dollars, specialized equipment, and knowledgeable people.*

This sentence now weighs in at a trim eighteen words—a mere one-third of its former flabby self, and virtually every word carries its share of the weight of the sentence.

EXERCISE H

Using one or more of the revision techniques discussed above, rewrite each of the following sentences to make it more concise. Note the number of words in your revision.

1. In the movie it shows how the two little young children who are twins were affected by a divorce their parents got. (22 words)

   _____

2. The driver of the car, which was a rusty Pinto, neatly executed an escape only seconds before the car started burning with flames. (23 words)

   _____

3. There are two rules that I always follow when I am on a date. (13 words)

   _____

4. Whatever the course I am taking, it always seems necessary for me to involve myself in a considerably large amount of writing. (22 words)

   _____

5. Long-range forecasts trying to predict the weather in advance of when it happens are always risky and uncertain things to try to do. (23 words)

   _____

6. Several ideas that were innovative were taken out or deleted by my boss from the report that I wrote. (19 words)

7. Many students who have graduated with a Ph.D. from a graduate school will find it very difficult or discouraging to find a job in the field of teaching. (27 words)

8. The "Big Band" sound associated with the music of the '30s and '40s is making a return to a comeback in popularity among some of the musicians who are young in today's society. (33 words)

9. The very first electoral vote in the history of the United States for the last 200 years ever cast for a woman of the female sex was given to Theodora Nathan, a candidate representing the Libertarian Party, in the year 1976, during the Bicentennial. (44 words)

10. Many people who live in American society at the present time and age do not look with favor on the practice of censoring books that students in schools can read from libraries operated by public school systems. (37 words)

EXERCISE I

The following paragraphs contain many examples of wordiness. Rewrite the paragraphs using the fewest possible words. Be ruthless.

I am writing this letter to answer your letter written on the 25th of January. You made a request for information concerning the dimensions in size of our newest unit most recently produced for sale. The unit we are speaking of is 5 feet in length, 2 feet in width, and 4 feet tall in height. It should be observed that this unit under discussion will fit into most storage areas in most places. It was our purpose when we designed the unit that it should fit in these areas. It is the smallest of the units offered for sale at the present point in time, and it is our opinion that we can be proud, and justifiably so, of this product of ours. It is our hope and expectation that you will find it likable. (136 words)

The purpose of this handbook is to give you guidance through the days, which are difficult, of your first time on the campus of a college like ours. Most

REVISING

people who are entering freshmen have the experience of a nervous state during this time period. One of the reasons why this is so is because they have not developed familiarity with the design and layout of the campus. It is to help them develop this familiarity that in this handbook it contains maps of the campus. Another of the reasons is the one that exists because they lack sureness concerning the procedures to be followed for registration. The handbook contains a list of the procedures to be followed for registration, as well as a list of offices of the administration, and a list of the groups on campus which exist to be of use. (144 words)

REVISION PRACTICE

Revise the following paragraph so that its language is appropriate in its level of generality, its connotative value, its degree of formality, and its degree of conciseness.

Those of us who live in America have a tendency to undervalue the idea of friendship. We are often guilty of the use of the term in such a loose way that we don't give much real thought to what behaving in an amicable way means. We call other members of the human species our good buddies when we have been introduced to them on only a few social occasions. Such free and easy utilization of this verbal utterance makes it seem trivial instead of a description of one of the greatest things that can happen to us. The word *friend* should be reserved for someone with whom our hard work has been shared and perhaps even our hard times, someone who is aware of what is going on in our noggins or is able to bring to his recollection the same events we do, a childhood chum or a colleague from the time of our service in the armed forces of our country. We may be acquainted with lots of people, but we really have only a couple of friends.

WRITING PRACTICE

1. You have just moved into your neighborhood/apartment/dorm, and you want to describe it to a friend back home. Since you are feeling a bit lonely this particular evening, everything about the place seems unappealing. Using the techniques you have learned for the various stages of the writing process, compose a description of about 200 words that will convey your negative impression. When you are revising, be sure to check the connotations of the descriptive words you have chosen.

2. A few weeks later, your outlook has brightened as you have gotten involved in more activities. Write another description that makes the place seem more attractive. If possible, use some of the same details that previously seemed unappealing, but describe them in positive language this time.

REVISING

14

Editing for Spelling

In the revision process, you are looking for ways to clarify your ideas through improved unity, coherence, and word choice.

In the editing process, which should be the last step before preparing a final copy, you are looking for errors that may distract your reader from your idea.

Misspelled words, sentence construction errors, or improper punctuation can give your reader a negative impression of a piece of writing. These errors may be so annoying to a reader that he or she will not really pay attention to your carefully organized, well-supported, beautifully worded paper.

So, teach yourself to recognize the errors you know you are prone to, and check your writing very carefully for those kinds of mistakes.

In writing, one of the most important impressions you want to create for your reader is the feeling that you are in control. No matter how exact or how concise your word choices, the impression of being in control of your material can be destroyed by a series of misspelled words. One spelling error might be overlooked, but a pattern of poor spelling can make even a sympathetic reader doubt the value of your ideas. Therefore, you need not only to choose the correct word for each writing situation but also to edit carefully for correct spelling.

USING THE DICTIONARY

The most useful, all-around tool in editing is the dictionary. It helps with spelling, pronunciation, grammar, word choice, defining, and understanding.

lim·o·nene (lim′ə nēn′) *n.* [< ModL. *Limonum* (< Fr. *limon*, LEMON) + -ENE] any of three isomeric terpenes, C₁₀H₁₆, present in many plant products such as lemon peel, orange oil, pine needles, peppermint, etc.

li·mo·nite (lī′mə nīt′) *n.* [< Gr. *leimōn*, meadow, orig., low ground (for IE. base see LIMB¹) + -ITE¹] a brownish, hydrous ferric oxide consisting of several minerals: an important ore of iron —**li′mo·nit′ic** (-nit′ik) *adj.*

Li·mou·sin (lē mōō zan′) region & former province of WC France: chief city, Limoges

lim·ou·sine (lim′ə zēn′, lim′ə zēn′) *n.* [Fr., lit., a hood: from the costume worn in LIMOUSIN] **1.** a former kind of automobile with a closed compartment seating three or more passengers and the top extended forward over the driver's seat **2.** any large, luxurious sedan, esp. one driven by a chauffeur ☆3. a buslike sedan used to carry passengers to or from an airport, train station, etc.

limp¹ (limp) *vi.* [ME. *lympen* < OE. *limpan*, to befall, occur (in a specialized sense, to walk lamely), akin to MHG. *limpfen*, to walk with a limp, OHG. *limfan*, to befall, happen < IE. *lemb-* < base *leb-*, to hang down, be limp, whence L. *labor*, *limbus*] **1.** to walk with or as with a lame or partially disabled leg **2.** to move or proceed unevenly, jerkily, or laboriously, as because of being impaired, defective, damaged, etc. —*n.* a halt or lameness in walking —**limp′er** *n.* —**limp′ing·ly** *adv.*

limp² (limp) *adj.* [< base of prec., akin to MHG. *lampen*, to hang limply] **1.** lacking or having lost stiffness or body; flaccid, drooping, wilted, etc. **2.** lacking firmness, energy, or vigor **3.** flexible, as the binding of some books — **limp′ly** *adv.* —**limp′ness** *n.*

limp·et (lim′pit) *n.* [ME. *lempet* < OE. *lempedu* < ML. *lempreda*, limpet, lamprey: cf. LAMPREY] any of several varieties of mostly marine, gastropod mollusks, with a single, low, cone-shaped shell and a thick, fleshy foot, by means of which it clings to rocks, timbers, etc.

lim·pid (lim′pid) *adj.* [Fr. *limpide* < L. *limpidus* < OL. *limpa*, *lumpa*, water: see LYMPH] **1.** perfectly clear; transparent; not cloudy or turbid [*limpid* waters] **2.** clear and simple [*limpid* prose] —**lim·pid′i·ty**, **lim′pid·ness** *n.* —**lim′pid·ly** *adv.*

☆**limp·kin** (limp′kin) *n.* [LIMP¹ + -KIN: from its walk] a raillike wading bird (*Aramus vociferus*), found in Florida, Central America, and the West Indies

Lim·po·po River (lim pō′pō) river in SE Africa, flowing from South Africa into the Indian Ocean: c. 1,000 mi.

limp·sy, **limp·sey** (limp′sē) *adj.* -si·er, -si·est [Dial.] limp, as from exhaustion or weakness

lim·u·lus (lim′yoo ləs) *n.*, *pl.* -li′ (-lī′) [ModL., name of the genus < L. *limulus*, dim. of *limus*, sidelong (see LIMES) + -OID] *same as* HORSESHOE CRAB

lim·y (lī′mē) *adj.* **lim′i·er**, **lim′i·est** **1.** covered with, consisting of, or like birdlime; sticky **2.** of, like, or containing lime —**lim′i·ness** *n.*

lin. **1.** lineal **2.** linear

lin·ac (lī′nak) *n.* *shortened form of* LINEAR ACCELERATOR

lin·age (lī′nij) *n.* **1.** the number of written or printed lines on a page or in an article, advertisement, etc. **2.** payment based on the number of lines produced by a writer

lin·al·o·ol (li nal′ə ōl′, -ōl′; lin′ə lōōl′) *n.* [< MexSp. *linaloa*, an aromatic Mexican wood (< Sp. *lináloe* < L. *lignum aloēs:* cf. LIGNALOES) + -OL¹] a terpene alcohol, C₁₀H₁₇OH, in several essential oils, used in perfumery

linch·pin (linch′pin′) *n.* [ME. *lynspin* < *lyns* (< OE. *lynis*, linchpin, akin to G. *lünse* < IE. base *elei-*, to bend, whence ELL, Sans. *āṇíḥ*, linchpin) + *pin*, PIN] a pin that goes through the end of an axle outside the wheel to keep the wheel from coming off

Lin·coln (liŋ′kən) **1.** [after Pres. LINCOLN] capital of Nebr., in the SE part: pop. 150,000 **2.** *same as* LINCOLNSHIRE **3.** city in Lincolnshire, England: pop. 73,000 —*n.* a breed of sheep with long wool: orig. from Lincolnshire

Lin·coln (liŋ′kən), **Abraham** 1809–65; 16th president of the U.S. (1861–65): assassinated —☆**Lin·coln·esque** (liŋ′kə nesk′) *adj.* —☆**Lin·coln·i·an** (liŋ kō′nē ən) *adj.*

Lin·coln·i·an·a (liŋ kō′nē an′ə, -än′ə) *n.pl.* [LINCOLN + -IANA] books, papers, objects, etc. having to do with Abraham Lincoln

Lincoln Park city in SE Mich.: suburb of Detroit: pop. 53,000

Lin·coln·shire (liŋ′kən shir) county in NE England, on the North Sea: 2,272 sq. mi.; pop. 513,000

Lincoln's Inn *see* INN OF COURT

☆**lin·co·my·cin** (liŋ′kō mī′sin) *n.* [(*Streptomyces*) *lincoln-* (*ensis*), the bacteria from which derived (isolated from a soil sample collected near Lincoln, Nebr.) + MYC- + -IN¹] an antibiotic drug, C₁₈H₃₄N₂O₆S, used in the treatment of various bacterial diseases, esp. those resistant to penicillin or those involving an allergy to penicillin

Lind (lind), **Jenny** (born *Johanna Maria Lind; Mme. Otto Goldschmidt*) 1820–87; Swed. soprano: called the *Swedish Nightingale*

Lin·da (lin′də) a feminine name: see BELINDA

lin·dane (lin′dān′) *n.* [after T. van der *Linden*, Du. chemist (20th c.) who isolated the isomer + -ANE] an iso-

meric form of benzene hexachloride, used as an insecticide

Lind·bergh (lind′bərg, lin′-), **Charles Augustus** 1902–74; U.S. aviator: made first nonstop solo flight from New York to Paris (1927)

Lin·den (lin′dən) [from its *linden* trees, brought from Germany] city in NE N.J.: pop. 41,000

lin·den (lin′dən) *n.* [ME., *adj.* < OE. < *lind*, linden, akin to G. *linde:* popularized as *n.* via G. *linden*, pl. of *linde:* prob. < IE. base *lento-*, flexible, yielding, whence LITHE] any of a genus (*Tilia*) of trees of the linden family, with dense, heart-shaped leaves, widely cultivated throughout the North Temperate Zone: the American variety is also called BASSWOOD —*adj.* designating a family (Tiliaceae) of chiefly tropical trees including the lindens and jutes

Lind·say (lin′zē, lind′-), **(Nicholas) Va·chel** (vā′chəl) 1879–1931; U.S. poet

☆**Lin·dy (Hop)** (lin′dē) [after C. A. LINDBERGH'S ("*Lindy's*") transatlantic "*hop*"] [also **l- h-**] a lively dance for couples, popular in the early 1930's

line¹ (līn) *n.* [ME. *lino*, merging OE. *line*, a cord, with OFr. *ligne* (both < L. *linea*, lit., linen thread, n. use of fem. of *lineus*, of flax < *linum*, flax)] **1.** *a)* a cord, rope, wire, string, or the like *b)* a long, fine, strong cord with a hook, sinker, leader, etc. used in fishing *c)* a clothesline *d)* a cord, steel tape, etc. used in measuring or leveling *e)* a rope, hawser, or cable used on a ship *f)* a rein: *usually used in pl.* ☆2. *a)* a wire or wires connecting stations in a telephone or telegraph system *b)* the whole system of such wires *c)* effective contact between stations [hold the *line*, please] **3.** any wire, pipe, system of pipes or wires, etc. for conducting water, gas, electricity, etc. **4.** a very thin, threadlike mark; specif., *a)* a long, thin mark made by a pencil, pen, chalk, etc. *b)* a similar mark cut in a hard surface, as by engraving *c)* a thin crease in the palm or on the face **5.** a mark made on the ground in certain sports; specif., *a)* any of the straight, narrow marks dividing or bounding a football field, tennis court, etc.: often used in combination [*sideline*] *b)* a mark indicating a starting point, a limit not to be crossed, or a point which must be reached or passed ☆6. a border or boundary [the State *line*] **7.** a division between conditions, qualities, classes, etc.; limit; demarcation **8.** outline; contour; lineament **9.** [Archaic] [*pl.*] lot in life; one's fate **10.** [*usually pl.*] a plan of construction; plan of making or doing **11.** *a* row or series of persons or things of a particular kind; specif., *a)* a row of written or printed characters extending across or part way across a page ☆*b)* a row of persons waiting in turn to buy something, enter a theater, etc.; queue *c)* an assembly line or a similar arrangement for the packing, shipping, etc. of merchandise **12.** a connected series of persons or things following each other in time or place; succession [a *line* of Democratic presidents] **13.** *same as* LINEAGE¹ **14.** the descendants of a common ancestor or of a particular breed **15.** ☆*a)* a transportation system or service consisting of regular trips by buses, ships, etc. between two or more points ☆*b)* a company operating such a system *c)* one branch or division of such a system [the main *line* of a railroad] *d)* a single track of a railroad **16.** the course or direction anything moving takes; path [the *line* of fire] **17.** *a)* a course of conduct, action, explanation, etc. [the *line* of an argument] *b)* a course of movement **18.** a person's trade or occupation, or the things he deals in [what's his *line*?] ☆19. a stock of goods of a particular type considered with reference to quality, quantity, variety, etc. **20.** *a)* the field of one's special knowledge, interest, or ability *b)* a source or piece of information [a *line* on a bargain] **21.** a short letter, note, or card [drop me a *line*] **22.** a single metrical unit consisting of a specified number of feet; verse of poetry **23.** [*pl.*] all the speeches in a play; esp., the speeches of any single character **24.** [Colloq.] persuasive or flattering talk that is insincere **25.** [*pl.*] [Chiefly Brit.] a marriage certificate: in full, **marriage lines 26.** *Bridge* the horizontal line dividing trick scores from honor scores ☆27. *Football a) short for* LINE OF SCRIMMAGE *b)* the players arranged in a row on either side of the line of scrimmage at the start of each play **28.** *Geog.* an imaginary circle of the earth or of the celestial sphere, as the equator or the equinoctial circle **29.** *Math. a)* the path of a moving point, thought of as having length but not breadth, whether straight or curved *b)* such a path when considered perfectly straight **30.** *Mil. a)* a formation of ships, troops, etc. in which elements are abreast of each other *b)* the area or position in closest contact with the enemy during combat *c)* the troops in this area *d)* the officers in immediate command of fighting ships or combat troops ☆*e)* the combatant branches of the army as distinguished from the supporting branches and the staff **31.** *Music* any of the long parallel marks forming the staff **32.** *TV* a scanning line —*vt.* **lined, lin′ing 1.** to mark with lines **2.** to draw or trace with or as with lines **3.** to bring or cause to come into a straight row or into conformity; bring into alignment (often with *up*) **4.** to form a line along [elms *line* the streets] **5.** to place objects along the edge of [*line* the walk with flowers] ☆6. *Baseball* to hit (a pitched ball) in a line drive —*vi.*

To get the most use out of any tool, you have to know how to handle it. In the case of the dictionary, you must first be able to find the word you want and then understand the information the dictionary is giving you.

Finding the Word

When you use a dictionary to look up a word in a book you are reading, you have no problem finding the word. However, when you are writing, you often use the dictionary to find words you have seen or heard but do not know how to spell. You can do two things: (1) get yourself a "bad speller's dictionary" listing many of the common misspellings in alphabetical order with the correct spelling after, and (2) learn the commonly confused letters and sounds.

The same sound can be produced by different combinations of letters. For instance, suppose that you are looking up the spelling of a word that means "a severe inflammation of the lungs" and sounds like *newmonya*. If you look under *n* in the dictionary, you won't find the word. But what other letter combinations also have the sound of *n*? *kn*, *gn*, and *pn*. Therefore you should look under each of these combinations until you find the word you want: *pneu mó nia.*

Here are some of the most common sound combinations. You can use these to help you look up words in the dictionary.

ā (long *a*, says its own name)	*a*–consonant–silent *e*	name
	ai	laid
	au	gauge
	ay	play
	ea	steak
	ei	veil
	ey	grey
ē (long *e*, says its own name)	*e*	she
	e–consonant–silent *e*	Pete
	ea	team
	ee	feed
	ie	believe
	(c) *ei*	receive
	ey	key
	eo	people
	oe	amoeba
	y	city
ī (long ī, says its own name)	*i*–consonant–silent *e*	fire
	y	cry
	ie	tie
	ei	height
	ai	aisle
	igh	high
	uy	buy

EDITING

ō (long ō, says its own name)	*o*	no
	o–consonant–silent *e*	note
	oa	boat
	ow	flow
	oe	foe
	ough	dough
	eau	beau
ōō	*oo*	cool
	ew	blew
	ue	clue
	eu	maneuver
	u–consonant–silent *e*	rule
	ui	suit
	o	move
	oe	canoe
ū (long ū, says its own name)	*u*–consonant–silent *e*	mule
	ou	you
	ew	few
	eau	beauty
	eu	feud
	iew	view
	yu	yule
ə(uh) schwa—used in unaccented syllables	*a*	above
	e	agent
	i	busily
	o	bottom
	u	circus
	ou	curious
k	*k*	kill
	c	car
	cc	account
	ch	character
	ck	back
	qu	liquor
s	*s*	see
	c	city
	ps	psychology
	sc	scene
sh	*sh*	shine
	ci	special
	sci	conscious
	ch	machine
	ce	ocean
	ti	nation

EXERCISE A

Using the sound lists above and your own knowledge of letter combinations, find the correct spelling of each of the following words in a dictionary.

1. sī kō′ sis
   a severe mental disorder _____

2. bə sil′ əs
   a rod-shaped bacteria _____

3. plak
   a tablet used to commemorate an event _____

4. ə rān′
   to bring before a law court _____

5. kon′ shē en′ shəs
   scrupulous; honest _____

6. nok
   to strike with the fist _____

7. mor′ fēn
   a medicine used to dull pain _____

8. hā′ dā
   the period of greatest success _____

9. byoo′ rō
   an office or department _____

10. fō′ bē a
    a fear with no basis in reality _____

Spelling Variations

Obviously, when your dictionary search has been successful, the spelling of the word is in front of you in dark type. Sometimes you will find the dictionary giving you more information than you expected: a word may be given with several spellings. For example, the sample dictionary page shows two spellings for a word meaning limp or tired out: *limpsy* and *limpsey.* Either spelling is correct. In most dictionaries, the first spelling given is the more commonly used.

EXERCISE B

What are the other accepted spellings of these words?

1. chiseled _____

2. catalog _____

EDITING

3. theater   _____

4. judgment   _____

5. Parcheesi   _____

Syllables

When you find a word in a dictionary, it is usually broken up by dots. These dots show where the word may be divided when the whole word won't fit on the end of a line. For example, if you had to split the word *linchpin,* you could do it only between the *h* and the *p: linch-pin.* These divisions can be a help in learning to spell the word.

EXERCISE C

Where can you divide the following words? Show how you think each word should be divided. Then check yourself with a dictionary.

EXAMPLE:

Lincolniana *Lin-coln-i-an-a*

1. recommend   _____

2. prophet   _____

3. California   _____

4. Roosevelt   _____

5. continental   _____

Pronunciation

After the word has been given in dark type, most dictionaries give the pronunciation in parentheses. For example, look at the word *limy* on the sample dictionary page. In parentheses, you are told the pronunciation is *lī′ mē.*

The accent (′) shows you which syllable receives more force in saying the word. The symbols above the *i* and *e* indicate specific sounds. The key to the pronunciation symbols is at the bottom of the sample dictionary page. There you are shown the symbol in a common word in which the sound appears. For instance, the sound indicated by *ē* is the sound of the first *ē* in *even.*

EXERCISE D

Use the pronunciation key at the bottom of the sample dictionary page. For each symbol, write in the word the dictionary uses to give you the sound.

EXAMPLE:

ô horn

1. zh   _____
2. u   _____
3. ä   _____
4. ī   _____
5. ō   _____

When you check the pronunciation of some words, you will find several pronunciations given. All are correct. For example, there are three correct ways given on the sample dictionary page for the pronunciation of the unusual word *linalool.*

EXERCISE E

Look up the following words in the dictionary and give the pronunciations listed.

EXAMPLE:
calm   *käm källm*

1. futurity   _____   _____   _____
2. harass   _____   _____
3. tomato   _____   _____
4. nauseous   _____   _____
5. pecan   _____   _____   _____

Parts of Speech

The dictionary also tells you whether the word is a noun, a verb, an adjective, or some other part of speech. For example, the *n.* placed after the pronunciation of the word *linden* on the sample dictionary page means *linden* is a noun. Recognizing these abbreviations is useful because many words can play several parts. Finding the precise form of the word you are looking for often means checking for the abbreviations. The word *line* on the sample page, for

EDITING

instance, is used both as a noun (*n.*) and as a verb (*vt.* and *vi.*). The definitions for each form are grouped after each abbreviation.

EXERCISE F

Using your own dictionary, give the full term represented by the following abbreviations.

EXAMPLE:

n. noun

1. *adj.*   _____
2. *prep.*   _____
3. *pron.*   _____
4. *interj.*   _____
5. *adv.*   _____

EXERCISE G

List the parts of speech given in the dictionary for each of the following words.

EXAMPLE:

line   *n., vt., vi., adj.*

1. round   _____

2. in   _____

3. clean   _____

4. model   _____

5. yesterday _____

Meanings

Finding the meanings of words is the basic use of the dictionary. Most words have several meanings, all closely related, but with shades of difference. It is important to check all the meanings until you find the one that explains the word in the context you are reading. For instance, if you were looking for the meaning of *line* in the sentence "She came from a great line of champions," you would have to look under the meanings until you came to number 14: *the descendants of a common ancestor or of a particular breed.*

EXERCISE H

Look up the italicized word in each sentence and give the definition that best fits the context.

EXAMPLE:
It was a *limp,* dog-eared copy of "Hamlet."
flexible, as in the binding of some books

1. He wanted his coffee *black.*

   _____

2. The committee finally got down to the *core* of the issue.

   _____

3. The horse was *scratched* before the first race.

   _____

4. The police were in *hot* pursuit.

   _____

5. My challenge did not *draw* a reply.

   _____

Usage Labels

Dictionaries also label certain meanings of words if they are specialized or particular to a certain dialect of English. For example, on the sample dictionary page, definition number 24 for *line*—as it would be used in the sentence "She handed him a *line* about her last job"—is labeled [Colloq.], meaning *colloquial* or informal. These labels may help you choose your words with greater precision.

EXERCISE I

Using your own dictionary, find the meanings of the following terms.

1. Colloquial [Colloq.] _____

   _____

2. Slang _____

   _____

3. Archaic [Arch.] _____

   _____

EDITING

4.   Obsolete [Obs.] _____

_____

5.   Dialect [Dial.] _____

_____

EXERCISE J

Find the meaning given for the italicized words in the following sentences. Put the usage label accompanying that meaning in the blank.

EXAMPLE:

He had a smooth *line. Colloquial*

1.   He got some more *ammo* and continued firing. _____

2.   I have a *boon* to ask of you. _____

3.   Anne decided to *perk* some more coffee. _____

4.   Then she *rustled* up some pancakes. _____

5.   He was drowned in the *crick.* _____

Word History

Dictionaries also give the history of the word: they tell you what it meant in the past and what languages it came from. (You will find a section in the front of most dictionaries explaining the symbols used in the word histories.) For example, the sample dictionary page gives the history of *line* in brackets after the pronunciation. The word came from a merging of the Middle English *line* with the Old French *ligne.* Both these words came from the Latin *linea,* which meant "linen thread" and derived from *linum,* which meant "flax," the plant which gives us linen.

Learning the history of a word often makes the word easier to remember. Paying attention to word histories will gradually deepen your knowledge of the language you speak and write.

EXERCISE K

What unusual meanings did the words below have in the past?

EXAMPLE:

line   *linen thread*

1.   sacrifice   _____

2.   hazard   _____

EDITING

3. window   _____

4. marshal   _____

5. baron   _____

EXERCISE L

What languages produced the following words?

EXAMPLE:

linalool   *Mexican Spanish*

1. dandelion   _____

2. coleslaw   _____

3. horoscope   _____

4. rouge   _____

5. pajama   _____

WHAT'S IN THE DICTIONARY

Spelling
Syllabication
Pronunciation
Parts of Speech
Meanings
Usage Labels
Word History

IMPROVING YOUR SPELLING

If you are a poor speller, you may get very discouraged sometimes because you think you can't spell *anything.* But that's not the case. Most people have definite patterns to their misspelling. They miss the same words over and over, or they make the same kinds of mistakes.

EDITING

The way to overcome this spelling problem is to recognize what words or what spelling patterns give you trouble by keeping a list of words that you misspell. When you get a paper back from your teacher, write down any words that are marked for spelling. In one column, put down the word the way you spelled it. In another column, write the correct spelling. When you have a dozen or so words, study your list to see if there are any patterns of spelling that regularly give you trouble. For instance, look at this list:

INCORRECT SPELLING	CORRECT SPELLING
terrable	terrible
refussing	refusing
planed	planned
evidince	evidence
occured	occurred
hopping	hoping
returnible	returnable
dependibility	dependability
acceptence	acceptance
riden	ridden
terreble	terrible
ocurred	occurred

What spelling problems seem to give this student trouble? She misses the *i, e,* or *a* at the end of several words: return*a*ble, terr*i*ble, evid*e*nce, accept*a*nce, depend*a*bility. She also isn't sure when to double the consonant: ri*dd*en, re-fusing, pla*nn*ed, ho*p*ing, o*cc*urred.

Here is another list. Can you spot any problem areas for this student?

INCORRECTLY SPELLED	CORRECTLY SPELLED
aventure	adventure
strat	straight
almos	almost
moshun	motion
minature	miniature
piture	picture
suppose	supposed
Wensday	Wednesday
there	their
sucseed	succeed
recieve	receive

This student seems to spell by pronunciation. He leaves letters out because he doesn't hear those letters when he says the word: *a*dventure, straight, pic-ture. Sometimes, he doesn't choose correctly between two possible spellings for the same sound: mo*ti*on, rec*ei*ve, th*ei*r.

If you're lucky, you will notice some patterns in the words you have trouble spelling, and then you can train yourself to watch out for those trouble areas or those specific words that always give you problems.

IMPROVING YOUR SPELLING

1. **Keep a spelling list.**
2. **Break words into syllables.**
3. **Memorize the four spelling rules.**

However, even if you don't discover a pattern, there are some ways you can improve your spelling.

Spelling Cards

First, make a 3 × 5 card for each word whose spelling gives you trouble. Tape these cards to your bathroom mirror or on the cover of a notebook or on the bulletin board next to your phone, anywhere that you will see them every day. Practice a few words as you brush your teeth, or wait for class to start, or talk on the phone. Just seeing the words correctly spelled will help them to stay in your memory, but spelling them out loud or copying them a few times will help even more. Every three weeks or so take down some old cards and put up some new ones.

Syllables

Second, get into the habit of breaking words down into syllables. The dictionary will show you the syllables in a word. Every word is a combination of vowel sounds (*a, e, i, o, u,* and sometimes *y*) and consonant sounds (all the other letters). Each syllable in a word contains one vowel sound and usually one or more consonant sounds. It is easier to spell a word if you break it into syllables and can hear more easily the separate sounds of each part of the word. The words below are divided into syllables:

    sep a rate
    Feb ru ar y
    ad ven ture
    min i a ture

EDITING

ter ri ble

ac cept ance

oc curred

Seeing and hearing the syllables of words can help you spot the part of the word that's giving you trouble. Many people, for example, have trouble remembering the first *a* in sep*a*rate. You can handle a trouble spot like this by thinking of some memory trick such as, "There's *a rat* in the middle of separate," or by making a card with *sep a rate* written on it and studying it for a few weeks until you have mastered that word, or by using a dictionary to check your spelling of that word whenever you use it.

Breaking a word into syllables can also help you see if there is a root part of the word to which some prefix or suffix has simply been added. In the box are some examples of words that are generally in the same family.

RELATED WORDS

Prefix	*Root*	*Suffix*
pro	**ceed**	**ing**
ex	**ceed**	
suc	**ceed**	**ed**
pro	**claim**	
re	**cla(i)m**	**ation**
dis	**claim**	**er**
in	**duc(t)**	**tion**
pro	**duc(t)**	**tiv ity**
pro	**duc(e)**	**er**
con	**duct**	

Recognizing a familiar part in an unfamiliar word may help you to spell the unfamiliar word correctly.

Studying the syllables in a word can also help you overcome the problem of leaving out letters. You can train yourself to see and/or hear all the letters. For example, if you had made a study card for *Feb ru ar y,* you could probably spell the word easily by concentrating on the sound that is frequently lost in pronunciation: Feb *ru* ar y.

Spelling Rules

Third, there are some fairly reliable spelling rules. Memorizing these rules can cut down on the number of individual words whose spelling you have to memorize.

1. Use *i* before *e*
Except after *c*,
Or when sounded as *a*,
As in *neighbor* and *weigh*.
EXAMPLES:

re ceive	re lief
con ceive	be lieve
de ceive	be siege

Exceptions (No rule is perfect!)
leisure, neither, weird, height

2. Words ending in silent *e* usually drop the *e* before adding a vowel suffix. The *e* remains with a consonant suffix.
EXAMPLES:

hide	+	-ing	=	hiding
name	+	-ed	=	named
desire	+	-able	=	desirable
drive	+	-er	=	driver
name	+	-less	=	nameless
care	+	-ful	=	careful
sincere	+	-ly	=	sincerely
amaze	+	-ment	=	amazement
Exceptions				
judge	+	-ment	=	judgment
argue	+	-ment	=	argument
true	+	-ly	=	truly
peace	+	-able	=	peaceable
courage	+	-ous	=	courageous

and other
soft *c* and
g words
with *a*, *o* or
u suffixes

3. In a word ending with consonant -*y*, change the *y* to *i* before adding any suffix that doesn't begin with *i*.
EXAMPLES:

worry	+	-ed	=	worried
worry	+	-ing	=	worrying
lonely	+	-ness	=	loneliness
try	+	-ed	=	tried

EDITING

try	+	-ing	=	trying	
study	+	-ous	=	studious	
silly	+	-ness	=	silliness	

4. Words of one syllable or accented on the last syllable that end in a vowel-consonant pattern double the final consonant before adding vowel suffixes. The doubled consonant keeps the vowel sound short.

EXAMPLES:

slip	+	-ed	=	slipped
plan	+	-ing	=	planning
occur	+	-ence	=	occurrence
hid	+	-en	=	hidden
jam	+	-ed	=	jammed
permit	+	-ing	=	permitting

EXERCISE M

Suffixes

-ed

-ing

-ous

-able

-ible

-ness

-ance

-ence

-ment

-ly

-less

-ful

To each word given below, add as many of the suffixes in the box as you can. What spelling rules can you use for each word? Check the dictionary for each.

EXAMPLE:

manage	+	-ed	=	managed	Rule 2
manage	+	-ing	=	managing	Rule 2
manage	+	-able	=	manageable	Rule 2 (Excep.)
manage	+	-ment	=	management	Rule2

1. grace
2. happy
3. grieve
4. prefer
5. equip
6. commit
7. pity
8. fit
9. transfer
10. state

EDITING

EASILY CONFUSED WORDS

In some cases, what looks like a misspelling is really a confusion between two similar words. Look at the following list. If any of these pairs of words give you trouble, make study cards for them or try to find some memory trick to help you remember the difference between them.

1. ac CEPT   ex CEPT
    (to receive)   (to exclude)

    He accepted the reward.
    No one except his mother came.

2. af FECT   ef FECT
    (to influence)   (a result; to bring about)

    Her life affected us all.
    The effect was tremendous.
    The doctor effected her recovery.

3. cite   site   sight
    (to summon or quote)   (place)   (the power to see;
                                               something seen)

    She cited the line from the play to prove her point.
    The site for the new bank is on the corner.
    The sight of the accident victim made me sick.

4. DES ert   des SERT
    (a hot, dry place)   (a sweet served after a meal)

    Camels live easily in the desert.
    I rarely eat desserts.

5. here   hear
    (in this place)   (to sense with the ears)

    I have lived here for forty years.
    You hear with your ears.

6. it's   its
    (it is)   (belonging to it)

    It's a shame you didn't win.
    Our team has lost its standing.

EDITING

7. new   knew
     (not old)   (to know in the past)

Her new car got better mileage.
I knew him before he was famous.

8. passed   past
     (went by)   (a time before the present)

I passed the house several times.
In the past, women were not allowed at this school.

9. PRIN ci pal   PRIN ci ple
     (most important;   (a fundamental law)
     head of a school)

His principal reason for becoming a principal was to make more money.
Religion gives us an ethical principle to guide our actions.

10. right   rite   write
     (just; correct;   (a ceremony)   (to make letters)
     that which is due to
     anyone)

You're right; it is your right to have an attorney present.
Funeral rites help us to deal with death.
He could write a very effective letter.

11. scene   seen
     (a sight; part of a play)   (observed)

I have never seen such a beautiful scene.

12. their   there   they're
     (belonging to them)   (in that place)   (they are)

Their houses all looked alike there.
They're conformists.

13. two   too   to
     (2)   (also; excessive)   (toward; for)

Too has too many o's.
Zoo too has too many o's.
The two words sound alike to many people.

14. your   you're
     (belonging to you)   (you are)

You're very possessive of your belongings.

15. whose   who's
     (belonging to whom)   (who is)

Who's to say whose way is best?

EXERCISE N

Choose the correct word for the blanks in each sentence below.

(two, too, to)   1. I ordered _____ boxes _____ be sent _____ my

                         house _____ .

(affect, effect)   2. What _____ will this test have on my class grade? It will not

                         _____ your grade too much.

(here, hear)   3. Can you _____ me in _____?

(new, knew)   4. He _____ this group when their act was _____.

(scene, seen)   5. That _____ was the clumsiest one I have _____ in some

                         time.

(your, you're)   6. If _____ a police officer, let me see _____ identifica-

                         tion.

(principal,   7. A basic _____ of good writing is to emphasize the
principle)
                         _____ idea.

(their, there,   8. _____ the children learn to read _____ letters before
they're)
                         _____ five years old.

(accept,   9. Everyone _____ Don will be there to _____ the
except)
                         award.

(its, it's)   10. _____ very difficult to hold _____ keel steady in a

                         heavy wind.

EXERCISE O

Edit the following sentences by circling any misspelled words. Using your dictionary as necessary, write the correct spelling of the circled words on the line beneath each sentence.

1. Our high school principal recieved a community award.

   _____

2. It's been hard, but I past English.

   _____

3. The riseing sun lit the mountaintops and filled the vallies with shadow.

   _____

4. We're going skiing this weekend, whether permitting.

   _____

5. I never even concieved of anyone making that argument.

   _____

6. My boss doesn't have the liesure for swiming or boating.

   _____

7. Hank tore up the receipt carfully.

   _____

8. Suzanne sliped on the ice and jammed her foot into a pole.

   _____

9. Ms. Smith, I promise you truely this will be the last occurence of this sort.

   _____

10. Our team played an amazingly courageous fourth quarter.

   _____

EDITING PRACTICE

Circle any misspelled words in the following paragraphs. Then rewrite them, correcting any spelling errors. Use your dictionary to check yourself.

1.   You're environment as a riter can be a principle ingrediant of your sucess. Too write, you should chose an amosfere of quite, away from the distracshuns of telvision and children. You should have the rite tools, two. Your sure to need plenty of stationary, pens or pensils, and a good diction-ery. You shoud have a comftable chair, a large, flat writting surfice, and a good lite. If you have the write conditions, you can help yourself achieve ex-cellance as a writer.

2.   Its know suprise to me that you one the gold metal. After seeing what occured during the figir skatting competision, I new you wood win. Beleive me, I was so proud of you're preformance. Your rhythm and controll couldn't help but effect the judges. Their can be no arguement that youre the best in your catagory. The other too skaters don't posess half your lovlyness on the ice. I relize you had to work long hours to succede. So please except a personnel word of congradulations from me on this happyest of occassions. Its a privledge to know you and be your freind.

15

Editing for Problems in Sentence Construction

In the editing process, you should be checking for errors in sentence construction that may confuse or distract your reader. In this chapter you can review some of the most common sentence problems and their solutions.

SENTENCE FRAGMENTS

(*See also page 12*).

A base sentence expresses a complete idea by showing a subject involved in some action set in a time frame and not introduced by a subordination signal. A fragment is an incomplete idea that has been punctuated as if it were a base sentence.

FRAGMENT	For instance, if the tulips die.
FRAGMENT	To the moon.
FRAGMENT	Backing up slowly.

A fragment can be corrected either by attaching it to an existing base sentence or by rewriting the fragment so that it has its own subject and its own verb that shows time.

FRAGMENT	When I am near Orlando. I will visit Jodie.
EDITED	When I am near Orlando, I will visit Jodie.
EDITED	I am near Orlando. I will visit Jodie.
FRAGMENT	Smiling broadly, Bruce walking down the aisle.
EDITED	Smiling broadly, Bruce walked down the aisle.
EDITED	Bruce smiled broadly. He walked down the aisle.

EXERCISE A

Edit the following groups of words so that there are no sentence fragments.

1. When José has opened the city's first Spanish restaurant. Near the old market. Another new eating place also opening this week. An English-style pub.

   _____

   _____

   _____

2. Letter writing, which is a lost art. In today's society. Everyone uses the telephone. Being faster. But not as permanent. As a letter.

   _____

   _____

   _____

3. In a recession. Because people have less money to spend. Forcing them to watch every penny carefully.

   _____

   _____

   _____

4. Huge theme parks in many areas of the country. To provide a family with varied entertainment. Reasonably priced.

   _____

   _____

   _____

5. After studying Greek for three semesters. When Liz attempted to read Aristotle in the original language. Not succeeding very well.

   _____

   _____

   _____

6. Advertisers who don't always sell a product. On its own merits. Appealing instead to people's vanity.

   _____

   _____

   _____

7. Alan spends a lot of time with his children. Helping them with their homework. And who plays games with them.

_____

_____

8. Martha's car being an ancient blue Dodge. Its chrome pitted and rusty. Its upholstery torn and stained.

_____

_____

9. Since penguins are a wingless birds. Who are awkward on land. But to be graceful in the water.

_____

_____

10. Since it opened. The Katherine House to shelter over 300 women. And their children. Providing them with temporary housing and counseling.

_____

_____

_____

SUBJECT-VERB AGREEMENT

(See also pages 48–53.)

In order to avoid confusing your reader, you have to be sure that the subjects and verbs in your sentences match. A singular subject needs a singular verb, and a plural subject needs a plural verb.

Most of the time, agreement is no problem since the form of the verb is usually exactly the same whether it is singular or plural.

Problems with agreement can occur only when the verb is in the present form or the has-or-have-plus-participle form. These verb forms have two endings, one with an *-s* (for *he, she,* or *it* subjects) and one without (for all other subjects). For instance:

Jane writes. *(singular)*
Jane and Bill *write. (plural)*
Jane *has* written. *(singular)*
Jane and Bill *have* written. *(plural)*

When the subject is obviously singular or plural, and it occurs in its usual position at the beginning of the sentence, you should have no trouble using the correct singular or plural verb.

EXERCISE B

In each sentence below, label the subject as singular or plural, then make the verb agree with the subject by choosing the appropriate present tense verb form.

EXAMPLES:

(develop)   McDonnell Douglas Corporation *has developed* a new insulation system for tankers carrying liquefied natural gas.

(find)   Readers *find* our coverage thorough.

(prosper)   1.   Mr. Knoll _____ since his defeat.

(hire)   2.   The new chairperson _____ the administrative staff.

(make)   3.   Aluminum _____ new cars lighter.

(cost)   4.   Two new stereos _____ over $1,000.

(refuse)   5.   Morris and Chester _____ to eat canned cat food.

(guarantee)   6.   Banks _____ a steady rate of interest.

(blame)   7.   Lucy _____ Charlie Brown for her trouble.

(give)   8.   This hotel _____ fine service.

(save)   9.   Our experts _____ you money.

(sing)   10.   Blaise _____ the tenor solo.

There are a few situations where you may have trouble recognizing the subject or recognizing whether it is singular or plural. These are the situations you need to watch out for in editing your writing.

1.   Subjects joined by *and* are plural. However, singular subjects followed by *as well as, together with,* or *in addition to* do *not* become plural.

The necklace *and* the bracelet (*plural*)
The necklace *as well as* the bracelet (*singular*)

The knight *and* his lady (*plural*)
The knight *together with* his lady (*singular*)
Tennis *and* soccer (*plural*)
Tennis *in addition to* soccer (*singular*)

2. Subjects joined by *or* and *nor* are considered separately. The subject closer to the verb determines whether the verb should be singular or plural.

Mr. Owens or his *sons* (*plural*)
The sons or *Mr. Owens* (*singular*)
A horse or *two cows* (*plural*)
Two cows or *a horse* (*singular*)
The Chase Building nor the *Merritt Building* (*singular*)
The Merritt Building nor the *Chase Building* (*singular*)

3. Prepositional phrases after the subject do not change the subject.

The *son* of the immigrants (*singular*)
Some *presents* for his daughter (*plural*)
A *painting* with over a hundred colors (*singular*)
The *ringing* of the bells (*singular*)
Twelve *airlines* in our region (*plural*)

4. *Here* and *there* are not subjects. These words signal a delayed subject with which the verb must agree.

There is a *wealth* of information (*singular*)
There are a dozen *ways* (*plural*)
Here comes the *bride* (*singular*)
Here come the *bridesmaids* (*plural*)

5. These subject pronouns are always singular:

another	everybody	no one
anybody	everyone	nothing
anyone	everything	one
anything	much	somebody
each	neither	someone
either	nobody	something

Everything is wonderful (*singular*)
Neither fights as well (*singular*)
Anyone gets a refund (*singular*)

6. These subject pronouns are always plural:

both   few

many   several

Few claim victory (*plural*)

Several agree (*plural*)

Many know (*plural*)

Both cry (*plural*)

7. These subject pronouns may be either singular or plural, depending on what is being discussed:

all   any   enough

most   none   some

All of his writing is (*singular*)

All of the eggs are (*plural*)

Some of the dress has (*singular*)

Some of the trains arrive (*plural*)

None of the cake remains (*singular*)

None of the cakes remain (*plural*)

8. Some subjects, called *collectives*, may appear to be plural but are considered singular in most cases. Collective nouns are nouns like *team, herd, troop, audience, group,* and *jury,* in which a number of individuals are considered as one unit. These nouns require a plural verb only when the members of the unit act as individuals rather than as part of the unit. (This happens rarely.)

The jury disagree on the verdict (*plural*)

The jury agrees on the verdict (*singular*)

The herd stampedes across the prairie (*singular*)

The team have their uniforms cleaned (*plural*)

The audience cheers that scene (*singular*)

EXERCISE C

Edit the following sentences so that the verbs agree with the subjects. Cross out any incorrect forms; write correct forms above them.

1. Everybody need love.
2. Grace Kelly and James Stewart makes that film successful.

EDITING

3. Michael, as well as his brother, attend Middle States University.
4. Several bottles of expensive perfume stands on the counter.
5. The big peach pie or the two lemon tarts costs the same.
6. Neither my car nor my husband's car start in cold weather.
7. Here lie the body of the Unknown Soldier.
8. Nothing grows in that barren soil.
9. The deans or the president welcome the incoming freshmen.
10. The audience stamps its feet and whistle whenever Julia comes on stage.
11. There lurks dragons.
12. Smith, together with James, represent the 33rd District.
13. A dancer in elegant clothes glide majestically around the floor.
14. Either the ski team or the skaters win a gold medal every winter.
15. Few realizes the value of antique dolls.
16. Full-sized cars and compact cars fights for the consumer's dollars.
17. The pleasures of the scholar's life offers great satisfaction.
18. The troop spend the income from the candy sale on community service projects.
19. The managers and the clerical staff receives a cost-of-living increase every year.
20. Some of the ornaments is broken.
21. Neither newspapers nor radio dominate the entertainment field any more.
22. Coffee, along with a light dessert, complement a fine dinner.
23. Here goes our finest gourmet chefs.
24. All of the turkey was eaten in 15 minutes flat.
25. The dictionary, with its thousands of entries, explain the meaning of every word in the language.

PRONOUN REFERENCE

(See also pages 126–29.)

A pronoun is a word that stands for a noun. For example:

> Mary Lou bought a car, and she paid for it in cash.

In this sentence, *she* stands for *Mary Lou,* and *it* stands for *car.*

Confusion arises for your reader when it is not clear what word the pronoun refers to, as in this sentence:

UNCLEAR   REFERENCE   When Mike saw the thieves shoot at the policemen, he ran toward them.

Does *them* mean *thieves* or *policemen?*
In editing this sentence, you might write:

EDITED   When Mike saw the thieves shoot, he ran toward the police.

or

EDITED   Mike ran toward the thieves when they shot at the policemen.

PRONOUN AGREEMENT

(See also pages 122–126.)

If a pronoun refers to a specific person, place, or thing, it must match the noun that it refers to. A singular noun (*chair*) requires a singular pronoun (*it*). A plural noun (*chairs*) requires a plural pronoun (*they, them*). A feminine noun (*Rachel*) requires a feminine pronoun (*she, her*). A masculine noun (*Grover*) requires a masculine pronoun (*he, him*). Nouns of indefinite gender (*the producer, the owner*) can use masculine or feminine pronouns (*he, him, she, her*).

EXERCISE D

Using the list of pronouns below, show which ones would match each of the following nouns or groups of nouns.

SINGULAR	PLURAL
I, me	we, us
you	you
he, she, it, him, her	they, them

1. Professor Alden _____
2. two dozen cookies _____
3. a counterfeit diamond _____
4. St. Elizabeth Ann Seton _____

EDITING

5. the Brownies _____

6. Rob and I _____

7. a bottle of ink _____

8. my mother _____

9. you and the captain _____

10. the bantam rooster _____

11. Dr. Chin _____

12. Rachel and John _____

13. the Navaho chief _____

14. a new pair of curtains _____

15. you and Marlene _____

16. the neighbors and I _____

17. a gang of thieves _____

18. Rupert _____

19. his adopted family _____

20. the dancer _____

EXERCISE E

Edit the following sentences to correct any errors in the use of pronouns.

1. Neither the Joneses nor the Smiths liked his trip to Mexico.

_____

_____

2. Celia gave her mother her favorite quilt.

_____

_____

3. No one wanted their picture taken.

_____

_____

4. The electric company and the water service raised its rates this year.

_____

_____

5. The saleswoman offered us an unbelievable discount. We immediately accepted their proposal.

_____

_____

6. The company moved their office to Maclean. Ms. Campbell told Denise she would have better research facilities there.

_____

_____

7. His closet was a mess. They were falling off the hangers and lying on the floor.

_____

_____

8. If an accused person needs a lawyer, they can get them from the Public Defender's Office.

_____

_____

9. All the girls must pay her deposits before leaving on her trip.

_____

_____

10. Gloria asked Meg if she could visit her.

_____

_____

EXERCISE F

Rewrite the following paragraphs to correct any errors in subject–verb agreement or pronoun agreement.

1. Membership in the State Consolidated Drivers' Clubs now offer unbelievable benefits. First of all, the entire family are covered by one low fee of $12.50. And that's just the beginning. The club reimburses drivers up to $50 if them have to call a tow truck. The club pay for emergency travel expenses, and they offer a reward for information on cars stolen from members. A member also get discounts on car rentals, hotel accommodations, and meals if they travel within the state. Most of these benefits is available only to Consolidated members. Smart drivers belongs to Consolidated.

2. My new Camaro with their streamlined body is the sharpest-looking car on the block. Its glossy, metallic paint and gleaming chrome makes them sparkle when the sun hit it. Another feature that sets off the car are his mag-

EDITING

nificent spoilers. Then there is her classy mag wheels. Inside, the camel-colored upholstery, as well as the sleek console panel, looks luxurious. All of these features shows why my car is the star of the neighborhood.

ADJECTIVE AND ADVERB FORMS

Adjectives

You use adjectives to describe a subject or other noun more precisely. In editing, you should be sure you have used the correct form of the adjective.

The basic form of the adjective is called the simple form, but adjectives can take more than one form to show different degrees of the quality they describe. For instance, to show that one test is more difficult than another, you might say:

This test was *harder* than the first one.

Or, to show that one bicycle was more recently acquired than another, you might say:

My bike is *newer* than yours.

This form of the adjective is called the *comparative* because it is used to compare two people or objects. The word *than* appears after the comparative form.

There is also a *superlative* form of the adjective for use when you want to compare more than two people or objects. For example:

This story is the *hardest* one in the book.
or
My bike is the *newest* one on the block.

Notice that the word *the* usually appears in front of the superlative form of the adjective.

Here is how you construct the comparative and superlative forms of adjectives.

Adjectives of one syllable
or
Adjectives of two syllables ending in -ow or -y → add *-er* or *-est*

SIMPLE		COMPARATIVE		SUPERLATIVE
tall	$\longrightarrow$	taller	$\longrightarrow$	tallest
*fit	$\longrightarrow$	fitter	$\longrightarrow$	fittest
long	$\longrightarrow$	longer	$\longrightarrow$	longest
*big	$\longrightarrow$	bigger	$\longrightarrow$	biggest
†funny	$\longrightarrow$	funnier	$\longrightarrow$	funniest
yellow	$\longrightarrow$	yellower	$\longrightarrow$	yellowest

* Most adjectives that end in a single consonant double the consonant before adding -er or -est.

† Change the -y to -i before adding -er or -est.

Other adjectives of two syllables
or
Adjectives of three or more syllables
> take *more* or *most*

SIMPLE		COMPARATIVE		SUPERLATIVE
exciting	$\longrightarrow$	more exciting	$\longrightarrow$	most exciting
villainous	$\longrightarrow$	more villainous	$\longrightarrow$	most villainous
isolated	$\longrightarrow$	more isolated	$\longrightarrow$	most isolated
awful	$\longrightarrow$	more awful	$\longrightarrow$	most awful
remarkable	$\longrightarrow$	more remarkable	$\longrightarrow$	most remarkable

A few adjectives have their own unique comparative and superlative forms:

SIMPLE		COMPARATIVE		SUPERLATIVE
good	$\longrightarrow$	better	$\longrightarrow$	best
bad	$\longrightarrow$	worse	$\longrightarrow$	worst
little	$\longrightarrow$	less	$\longrightarrow$	least

EXERCISE G

For each sentence below, supply the correct form of the adjective: simple, comparative, or superlative.

(sturdy)   **1.** This oak tree looks _____ than the one in back.

(early)   **2.** Please reply at the _____ possible date.

(perceptive)   **3.** His papers were the _____ in the class.

EDITING

(elaborate)   **4.** The company is planning a _____ retirement
party this year than last.

(hot)   **5.** Cleo's curry is the _____ dish I have ever tasted.

(serious)   **6.** The Jaffe case will be the _____ one the committee has had this year.

(complicated)   **7.** Calculations on compound interest are _____
than those on simple interest.

(big)   **8.** The _____ health care problem today is cost.

(good)   **9.** Clark's offers _____ tractor service facilities than
any other dealer in town.

(disturbing)   **10.** Drug use by preteenagers has become a _____
problem.

EXERCISE H

Edit the following paragraphs for any errors in adjective form.

1.   Senta is one of the abler managers in our company. She asks questions
that are best than anyone's. And she is the attentivest listener I've met. She
not only gives the more penetrating criticism, but couples it with some of the
most sound advice one can get. Our company is certainly luckier to have
managerial talent like Senta's.

2.   Peter thought things would get gooder after the first of the year, but they
seemed to go from bad to badder. His fiancee found someone more good. He
had had only a little money; now he had more little. He had hoped for a
gooder job; instead, he lost his old one. If things didn't take a turn for the
more good by June, he was moving to California. This was certainly the most
baddest year of his life.

Adverbs

Like adjectives, adverbs may take different forms to show the degree of the
quality involved. For instance, if you want to say that one student worked
with more care than another, you could say:

> Jennifer did the assignment *more carefully* than
> Judi.

If you want to say that Jennifer used more care than anyone else, you could
say:

> Jennifer did the assignment the *most carefully* of
> anyone.

In general, *-ly* adverbs form the comparative and superlative by using *more* and *most*.

SIMPLE		COMPARATIVE		SUPERLATIVE
commonly	⟶	more commonly	⟶	most commonly
slowly	⟶	more slowly	⟶	most slowly
deeply	⟶	more deeply	⟶	most deeply

A few adverbs use *-er* and *-est* to form the comparative and the superlative.

SIMPLE		COMPARATIVE		SUPERLATIVE
fast	⟶	faster	⟶	fastest
late	⟶	later	⟶	latest
near	⟶	nearer	⟶	nearest

Some adverbs have special forms for the comparative and superlative.

SIMPLE		COMPARATIVE		SUPERLATIVE
well	⟶	better	⟶	best
badly	⟶	worse	⟶	worst

EXERCISE I

In each sentence below, supply the appropriate form of the adverb: simple, comparative, or superlative.

(frequently)   **1.** According to the police, murders occur _____ during the early morning than at any other time.

(suspiciously)   **2.** The man who acted _____ of all was Col. Mustard.

EDITING

(enthusiastically)   3. Peggy applauded _____ than anyone else in the auditorium.

(artistically)   4. However, the poster designed _____ of the whole group was Sheri's.

(accurately)   5. This map shows the soil conditions _____ than the one put out by the Department of Agriculture.

(badly)   6. No man has ever behaved _____ to a woman than Hamlet behaved toward Ophelia.

(pedantically)   7. Dr. Hermann droned on _____ about the development of laser technology.

(dangerously)   8. The _____ underfunded area of the budget is repairs and maintenance.

(fast)   9. The new train covered the distance 2 hours _____ than the old one.

(well)   10. Allen loved Cissie _____ of all his sisters.

EXERCISE J

Edit the following paragraph for any errors in adverb form.

The trip ended more badly than it had begun. The raft moved toward the opening in the rocks rapidlier than they had thought it would. The guide standing on the large rock near the shore motioned to them to paddle strenuousliest on the left side. They tried to. But the current was carrying them definitelier to the right. The guide gestured franticlier. It was too late. They were caught most completely in the current and their raft capsized more fast than anyone could yell, "Person overboard!"

Confusion of Adjectives and Adverbs

Many times, you can't tell whether a word is an adjective or an adverb just by looking at it. While it is true that many adverbs end in -ly, the word *early* can be an adjective as well as an adverb. And words like *better, fast,* and *worst* can also be either adjectives or adverbs.

When you are editing, you need to look at how the word is used in the sentence in order to choose between the adjective form and the adverb form. For instance, look at these two sentences:

EDITING

The Sioux are *independent*.
The tribe responded *independently*.

Independent in the first sentence describes *Sioux*. *Independent* functions as an adjective telling *what kind* of people the Sioux are. In the second sentence, *independently* tells *how* the action of responding took place.

Which of the following two sentences contains an adverb?

Erica sang weakly.
She seemed weak.

In the first sentence *weakly* tells *how* she sang. *Weakly* is an adverb. *Weak,* in the second sentence, describes *she*. *Weak* is an adjective.

You also use adverbs to modify adjectives or other adverbs as the following examples show.

Jeff looked especially handsome.

Handsome describes Jeff; *handsome* is an adjective. *Especially* tells *how* handsome; *especially* is an adverb.

The paramedics arrived unbelievably quickly.

Quickly is an adverb telling *how* the paramedics arrived. *Unbelievably* is an adverb telling *how* *quickly* they arrived.

EXERCISE K

Supply the correct adjective or adverb form for each of the following sentences.

(loud)   1. The radio is playing too _____.

(quiet)   2. This dishwasher is guaranteed to run _____.

(bad)   3. Bill has very _____ handwriting.

(agile)   4. Charlie is an _____ skier.

(bitter)   5. The coffee tasted _____.

(devastating) 6. Marlene certainly looked _____ last night.

(impish)   7. She smiled _____ at her friend.

(strange)   8. The room seemed _____ empty.

(diligent) **9.** A dozen soldiers searched the area _____ for the missing keys.

(clear) **10.** The sky looked _____ this morning for the first time in weeks.

(complete) **11.** At the trial, Murray was _____ exonerated.

(practical) **12.** When solar energy becomes _____, it will change our lives.

(real) **13.** Many supermarkets offer _____ inexpensive store brands.

(noisy) **14.** The fly buzzed _____ by my ear.

(noisy) **15.** The fly's buzzing was too _____ for me to sleep.

EXERCISE L

Edit the following paragraph for correct use of adjective and adverb forms.

Brian arrived at the gym prompt at 5:30, feeling tiredly. He quick changed clothes, putting on a workout suit that was fresh washed and a pair of newly sneakers. Then, he went upstairs and did a strenuously workout. Thursdays, he always worked his chest and arms. He did several sets of bench presses, raising and lowering the bar careful with completely concentration. After several other chest exercises, he blasted his biceps with super sets of curls. These helped his growth tremendous. Incredible, he had gone from a 16-inch to a 19-inch arm in just two months of real intensely exercises. Finished, he took a warmly shower and was on his way home by 7:30. After his workout, he felt total well.

MISPLACED MODIFIERS

(*See also pages 35–37.*)

You choose modifiers to clarify or describe a particular word in a sentence. In order to avoid confusing your reader, you should be sure that the modifier is as close as possible to the word it describes.

MISPLACED Look for problems in every sentence with spelling.
EDITED Look for spelling problems in every sentence.
EDITED Look for problems with spelling in every sentence.

MISPLACED Covered with onions and mushrooms, Ron makes the best hamburger in town.

EDITED	Ron makes the best hamburger in town, covered with onions and mushrooms.
EDITED	Ron's hamburger, covered with onions and mushrooms, is the best in town.

DANGLING MODIFIERS

(See also pages 92–94)

Your reader will get very confused if your sentence has a modifier that has nothing to describe.

DANGLING	Many community colleges offer on-the-job training while taking regular classes. (Who is taking classes?)
EDITED	Many community colleges offer on-the-job training to *students* who are taking regular classes.
EDITED	Many community colleges offer *students* on-the-job training as well as regular classes.
DANGLING	In order to be a doctor, long years of training are necessary. (Who wants to be a doctor?)
EDITED	If *someone* wants to be a doctor, long years of training are necessary.
EDITED	In order to be a doctor, a *person* needs long years of training.

EXERCISE M

Edit the following sentences so that all modifiers are clearly related to the words they describe.

1. Filling out the application, my head began to ache.

2. The museum is presenting an exhibit for students in the main gallery on French Impressionism.

3. We got through the meeting that was called because of John's attitude.

4. Diane admired the lush flowers strolling through the garden.

5. Scattered by the sudden wind, we watched the flock of sparrows flash across the twilight.

6. Singing in the shower, the glass became fogged up.

7. To open the package, the side of the box had to be ripped off.

EDITING

8. The man decided to take another bus with the umbrella and briefcase.

_____

9. Sitting on the beach, several dolphins leaped from the water.

_____

10. Freshly painted, the sailor admired the deck of the ship.

_____

SHIFTS IN VERB TENSE

(*See also pages 129–33.*)

You can confuse your reader if you set up a certain time frame in your sentence and then don't follow it. In editing, check your verbs for consistency.

SHIFT	Ellen *left* for St. Louis, but suddenly the car *breaks* down.
EDITED	Ellen *left* for St. Louis, but suddenly the car *broke* down.
SHIFT	The new advertising campaign *will cost* half a million dollars. However, it *was* worth the money.
EDITED	The new advertising campaign *will cost* half a million dollars. However, it *will be* worth the money.

SHIFTS IN POINT OF VIEW

(*See also page 133–36.*)

Your reader can easily become confused if you keep moving the focus from *I* to *you* to *he* in your sentences. In editing, make sure your sentences keep the same point of view.

SHIFT	*I* like going to a school where *you* have small classes.
EDITED	*I* like going to a school where *I* have small classes.
SHIFT	A *student* preparing for the test should realize that *you* will be graded on *your* punctuation and spelling.
EDITED	A *student* preparing for the test should realize that *she* will be graded on *her* punctuation and spelling.

EXERCISE N

Edit the following sentences for shifts in verb tense or point of view.

1. We start when we were infants to shape your adult personality.

_____

_____

EDITING

2. Peterson owned the only car dealership in town until Ryan opens one in the fall.

   _____

3. If you buy a wood-burning stove, a family can usually lower its heating costs.

   _____

4. Eisenhower wants to review the treaty before the delegates signed it.

   _____

5. Credit cards allowed people to make purchases when you don't have the cash available.

   _____

6. Sprays that are intended to kill weeds were dangerous to children and pets too.

   _____

7. We have ordered the most advanced computer system a person can afford.

   _____

8. The county road crews will work day and night so the roads were cleared.

   _____

9. There was no reason why anyone has to buy "blind." You found expert consumer advice written every year.

   _____

10. The best history teacher I ever had was Mrs. Donaldson. You can always count on her for unusual facts.

    _____

PASSIVE VERBS

A sentence can be written so that it emphasizes action being done (*active*) or action being received (*passive*).

ACTIVE	Henry baked a cake.
PASSIVE	A cake was baked by Henry.

EDITING

(For the formation of the passive verb, see pages 383–86.)

In most sentences, the active verb is more effective than the passive. Sentences with an active verb tend to be shorter and more direct. However, there are some times when you will want to use the passive verb. In editing, check any use of the passive verb to be sure it is appropriate.

Suppose, for instance, that you do not know who performed a certain action. You could write an active sentence such as:

> Someone stole the diamonds.

But that sentence would just emphasize your lack of knowledge. A passive sentence like

> The diamonds were stolen.

would probably be more effective since it puts emphasis on what you do know.

Or, suppose that you know who performed an action, but you do not want your reader to know. For instance,

> Bathing suits are not permitted in this restaurant.

If you are the owner of the restaurant, this use of the passive may keep you from having to deal with complaints. However, readers may be suspicious of the passive that is used to conceal. Such use of the passive is frequent in bureaucratic and governmental writing where no one wants to assume responsibility for an action.

Finally, the passive verb can help you put emphasis on a certain idea. This sentence, for instance,

> The teacher distributed the grades.

puts emphasis on the teacher by making her the subject. This passive sentence,

> Grades were distributed by the teacher.

puts emphasis on the grades by making them the subject. Which sentence you would use would depend on whether you were writing primarily about the teacher or primarily about grades.

EXERCISE O

Rewrite each of the following sentences, changing active verbs to passive and passive verbs to active. In some sentences, you must supply a doer for the action. Be prepared to explain when you might choose one sentence or the other as more appropriate.

EDITING

1. That bill will be introduced by Senator Cade next week.

    _____

    _____

2. The children were lined up on the parking lot.

    _____

    _____

3. I will hand out the souvenirs after the ceremony.

    _____

    _____

4. You must turn in an expense voucher.

    _____

    _____

5. The opening hymn is sung by the congregation.

    _____

    _____

6. My brother has broken the vase.

    _____

    _____

7. Seventeen rooms have been prepared.

    _____

    _____

8. A family of beavers dammed the creek.

    _____

    _____

9. The school paper was closed down.

    _____

    _____

10. A lifeguard needs at least 40 hours of training.

    _____

    _____

EXERCISE P

> The following sentences contain a mix of all the problems discussed in this chapter. Edit them. Some sentences have more than one problem.

EDITING

1. After the play has finished, everyone stayed rooted in their seats.
2. While the group of mammals are warm-blooded and furry.
3. The old elm was cut down by the road crew, growing in the front yard.
4. Luke smelled well after his bath.
5. The factory floods whenever it rained.
6. Anybody can float, if they just try.
7. Quitting after his fourth enchilada.
8. The sum of the calculations were phenomenal.
9. Benjamin looked healthily even though he'd been sick.
10. Trapped in a tree, Rosemary saw the mewling kitten.
11. My father told my uncle sometimes he would catch lots of fish in the surf.
12. After a full day driving slow home, a pleasantly exhaustion is felt by everyone.
13. Recovering from the first week of classes, the whole weekend went by too fastly.
14. I don't like cooking always because you makes such a mess in the kitchen.
15. That book, written by two psychologists, have gooder advice than most books usually for newlyweds.

EDITING PRACTICE

Edit the following paragraphs to correct any problems in sentence construction that may confuse or distract a reader from the ideas being presented.

1.   Ranging from the tiny to the oversized, nature contain many unusually adaptations. One tiny species of insect, for example, adapts by eating its mother called gall midges. The young usually hatches from eggs, but when the food supply is more abundanter, the midges reproduce as faster as possible sometimes. As they rushing to make use of the abundant food. The female midges incubate the eggs in their bodies, and the newborn fed on their mothers. Irish elk, on the other hand, to adapt in a big way by growing enormous antlers. These antlers were part of a display for mating which reached a span of twelve feet. Natural adaptations could be fascinatingly in its variety and subtlety.

2.   Although some people resents writing for a grade, saying it is unfairly. You are wrong. Writing is the efficiently way to test only a person's independence. Other ways of testing does exist, such as objective tests and oral exams. However, while objective tests are efficient, always someone else

making up the questions; someone else making up the answers. Therefore, the student get no practice in independence. Oral exams, on the other hand, does test independent thought. But it is incredible inefficient. They took enormous amounts of time, and since they leave no records. For fairness they cannot be reviewed. Writing allows for independence and for records only. In a written test, students answering questions in their own way or formulating even their own questions. The papers themselves provides proof of grading fairness when my teacher comments on it. Writing is definitely a useful tool for students which you needed to learn for your own advantage.

16

Editing for Punctuation

Punctuation is an important way that you help your readers keep their focus on your main ideas. In editing, check to see that your punctuation clarifies rather than confuses.

DEFINITION OF A BASE SENTENCE

A group of words that expresses a complete idea with a SUBJECT
and a VERB showing past, present, or future time > not introduced by a SUBORDINATION SIGNAL

BASIC SENTENCE PATTERNS

Following is a list of the common sentence patterns and their punctuation. These will each be discussed individually.

Sentence.
1. Sentence?
   Sentence!
2. Sentence; sentence.

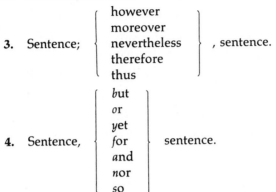

3. Sentence;
   - however
   - moreover
   - nevertheless
   - therefore
   - thus
   , sentence.

4. Sentence,
   - but
   - or
   - yet
   - for
   - and
   - nor
   - so
   sentence.

5. Subordinate word group, BASE SENTENCE.
6. BASE SENTENCE subordinate word group.
7. BASE, subordinate word group, SENTENCE.

Pattern 1

A sentence by itself begins with a capital letter and ends with a period, a question mark, or an exclamation point. In all of the basic patterns, a question mark or an exclamation point could be substituted for the period.

She can make it.
Can she make it?
She made it!

IMPORTANT: A subordinate word group (that is, any word group that does not fit the definition of a sentence) by itself should not be punctuated like a sentence. (See Chapter 1.)

CONFUSING	CORRECTED
If I had a dime.	She asked if I had a dime.
Running swiftly.	Running swiftly, I caught the train.

Pattern 2

Two or more sentences joined without any coordination signal must be linked by a semicolon (;). Never use a comma in this pattern. (See Chapter 3.)

EDITING

Lois brought the sandwiches; Herb picked up the beer.

Bees produce honey; wasps produce nothing.

NEVER: Bees produce honey, wasps produce nothing.

Pattern 3

Two sentences joined by a linking adverb (*however*, *thus*, etc.) are punctuated with a semicolon placed after the first sentence and a comma placed after the adverb. This is simply a variation of pattern 2, except for the comma after the adverb. (See Chapter 3.)

I enjoy hot weather; however, I dislike the humidity.

She missed half the semester; consequently, she must repeat the course.

Pattern 4

Two sentences joined with a coordination signal should be linked with a comma. An easy way to remember the coordination signals is by the first letters, which spell *boy fans*: *but*, *or*, *yet*, *for*, *and*, *nor*, *so*. (See Chapter 3.)

Greg was tired of small-town life, so he moved to Chicago.

Harry must buy back the check, or the store will prosecute him.

Pattern 5

When a sentence starts with a subordinate word group, a comma is a useful way of marking the end of the subordinate word group and the beginning of the base sentence. The marker helps signal the reader that the central idea in the sentence is coming. (See Chapter 4.)

If you will have a seat, the doctor will see you soon.

Even though wages stayed low, prices continued to climb.

Pattern 6

On the other hand, no punctuation is required when the subordinate word group follows the base sentence since the subordination signal by itself tells the reader the base sentence is finished. (See Chapter 4.)

He had his first accident when he was sixteen.

Casey would waltz while the band played on.

Pattern 7

When a subordinate word group interrupts the flow of the sentence, you should set it off with commas. (See Chapter 4.)

EDITING

Agnes, who was nobody's fool, called the police immediately.

The Rams, even without their first-string quarterback, won easily.

EXERCISE A

Edit the following sentences for correct punctuation. Use the list of sentence patterns to help identify the appropriate pattern, and write the number of the pattern in the space provided.

EXAMPLE:

_____ Is Mary driving or will Ted bring her?

___4___ *Is Mary driving, or will Ted bring her?*

_____ 1. Since it was April we expected some mild weather.

_____ 2. Montreal is a beautiful city but the winters are too cold for me.

_____ 3. The Everglades kite is dying out because its habitat is being destroyed.

_____ 4. Anna married Karenin however she loved Vronsky.

_____ 5. Small-town life has its pleasures it also has serious drawbacks.

_____ 6. Your car once it passes 100,000 miles will probably need more frequent oil changes.

_____ 7. Carlisle wants that report by Thursday and you had better get it to him on time.

_____ 8. Bobby had no talent nevertheless he became a TV star.

_____ 9. As he was dying the great poet asked for more light.

_____ 10. Detroit the auto capital of the United States is also an important cultural center.

COMMA SPLICES AND RUN-ON SENTENCES

If you fail to show with your punctuation where one idea ends and another begins, you run a great risk of confusing your reader. Sentences are the basic units of thought in writing, so sentences must be clearly marked.

COMMA SPLICE   The woods were filled with snow, the snow was filled with children.

EDITING

RUN-ON	The woods were filled with snow the snow was filled with children.
EDITED	The woods were filled with snow. The snow was filled with children.
EDITED	The woods were filled with snow, and the snow was filled with children.
EDITED	The woods were filled with snow; the snow was filled with children.
COMMA SPLICE	Dying of cancer is often lonely and painful, hospices can help.
RUN-ON	Dying of cancer is often lonely and painful hospices can help.
EDITED	Dying of cancer is often lonely and painful. Hospices can help.
EDITED	Dying of cancer is often lonely and painful, but hospices can help.
EDITED	Dying of cancer is often lonely and painful; hospices can help.

EXERCISE B

Edit the following sentences so that one sentence is correctly separated from another.

1. Margaret tasted the prime rib, it was flavorless and dry.
2. The Congo flows into the Atlantic the Nile empties into the Mediterranean.
3. Arthur could have played pro football but he signed with a baseball team instead.
4. The going gets tough, the tough get going.
5. Myra enjoys back packing. She says it relaxes her.
6. Rhett loved Scarlett, she thought she loved Ashley.
7. India plowed into the Asian continent the Himalayas were formed.
8. The Industrial Revolution enriched Europe, it created huge social problems too.
9. Timbuktu is on the Niger River it was once the greatest city in Africa.
10. Frank raises Irish setters, he has bred several champions.

COMMAS

The basic function of the comma is to separate. As you can see from the sentence patterns shown at the beginning of this chapter, commas may separate two or more equally important ideas, or they may separate a more important idea from a less important one used as an introduction or an interrupter.

Commas with Coordinate Ideas

A series of coordinate (equally important) adjectives should be separated by commas:

> The room was small, stuffy, and crowded.
> The stuffy, crowded room made me feel sick.

You can tell adjectives are coordinate if you can reverse their order:

> Joe was an ambitious, hard-working, and honest businessman.
> Ellen was an honest, hard-working, and ambitious businesswoman.

In a sentence where you cannot reverse the order, no commas are used:

> Four tall trees / tall four trees

Tall and *four* are not really coordinate adjectives here. They do not modify the same word. *Tall* modifies *trees*, but *four* modifies *tall trees*.

Commas are used only where the adjectives are coordinate. Here are other examples of commas with a series of coordinate ideas:

coordinate subjects
Ronda, Margo, and June made the team.

coordinate verbs
Fred *dusted, straightened, and vacuumed* the living room.

coordinate complements
My favorite cities are *Boston, Atlanta, and Denver.*

coordinate modifiers
Jim hunted ducks *in the fields, by the pond, and on the river.*

coordinate sentences
The Prince owed everyone money, and he had no way to pay his debts.

Although the comma before the *and* in a series is sometimes omitted, that comma can make a significant difference in the meaning of a sentence.

> Warren ordered a green sweater, a case of champagne, a car with cut-velvet upholstery, and a radio.

Without the last comma, it is not clear whether Warren ordered a car and a radio separately, or a car with a radio in it.

Sometimes, as the examples following show, the comma may be even more significant, a matter of millions of dollars in investments, or even of life and death.

EDITING

Renegade comma stirs
legal debate in county

By KATHERINE WHITE

*Baltimore County Bureau
of The Sun*

What's in a name, or a comma? In Baltimore county government circles, quite a bit.

The fate of a controversial shopping center, the proposed Franklin Mall in Reisterstown, has teeter-tottered for the past several weeks on either side of a comma in a local law. Everyone involved, from the Planning Board to the County Council to the county solicitor, has had a different view of what a single sentence really means—and what various people intended it to mean at various times.

The county leaders are not alone in their confusion, however. A survey by *The Sun* of local language experts and nationally known authorities on English usage resulted in only one clear conclusion: If words could kill, the poorly written sentence in question might have taken its revenge on public officials in Towson.

Leading off the consultants in *The Sun*'s informal survey was Edwin Newman, an NBC correspondent and the author of "Strictly Speaking" and "A Civil Tongue." He said the sentence in question "is so incompetently written, I can't tell what they mean, but they have managed to be fairly confusing."

Richard Mitchell, an English professor at Glassboro State College in New Jersey, the editor of "the Underground Grammarian," as well as the author of "Less Than Words Can Say," was aghast.

"Good God!" was all he could say at first. He paused a moment and then summoned his courage to comment, "The sentence is terrible! Either it has too many commas or not enough. . . . The person who wrote it should be castigated."

The troublesome section of the law establishes exemptions to new development rules contained in the county's growth management ordinance. A subparagraph of the law outlines those rules, but concludes with a sentence that is supposed to enlighten the reader about which properties are exempt from the rules. That sentence reads as follows:

"This subparagraph does not apply . . . to any development in a CCC [community core commercial] district, CSA [commercial support area] district or RAE [residential apartment-elevator] zone in a town center. . . ."

Does that mean properties in all three districts are exempt? Or only if those zones—or just the last two of them—are also located in a town center? Or does it only exempt the last zone if it is in a town center? Such is the stuff of which legal—and language—debates are made.

Dr. Mitchell said the sentence "is as much a problem in logic as a problem in grammar. . . . Why there isn't a comma after CSA I can't imagine."

He called the situation an interesting example of what "those damn teachers" tell their students today: "That little things like punctuation don't matter. Go with what makes you feel better."

Baltimore *Sun*, January 20, 1980.

Death penalty ambiguous
Parker fate tied to comma

By SCOTT LEBAR

Staff Writer

William Joseph Parker's life may be hanging by a comma.

After all the arguments on the constitutionality of the death penalty are voiced, Prince George's County Circuit Court Judge Howard S. Chasanow will be left with the new Maryland statute and its punctuation in deciding the fate of 28-year-old Parker.

A critical phrase in the law has drawn careful examination since Parker's conviction last week of the first-degree felony murder and second-degree rape of 13-year-old Elizabeth Archard.

That phrase may be missing the comma that could send Parker to jail instead of the gas chamber.

Under the new law, a person convicted of first-degree murder committed with any of 10 so-called "aggravating circumstances" is eligible for the death penalty.

Parker's conviction falls under the 10th circumstance: "The defendant committed the murder while committing or attempting to commit robbery, arson, or rape or sexual offense in the first degree."

Parker's attorney, Fred W. Bennett, said he will file his arguments next week claiming the death penalty is not only a disproportionate punishment for Parker's conviction, but that the conviction does not fall in this category because Parker was found innocent of first-degree rape. If the law was to apply to all rapes, Bennett argues, a comma would have followed the phrase "or rape." And according to several defense attorneys, the confusion caused by a missing comma is enough to prevent a man's being put to death.

That decision rests with Chasanow, who has not yet scheduled a sentencing hearing for Parker. By law, the judge's decision is automatically reviewed by the Court of Appeals.

But the St. Mary's County jury's verdict has already generated concern about the wording of the law.

"We're curious ourselves," said Assistant Attorney General Deborah Handel, who heads the criminal appeals division. "We're aware the question has been raised . . . and we'll be checking that."

Chasanow, who is regarded as scholarly and sensitive judge, has not contacted her office. But her interest was aroused when she heard the verdict and became aware of the possible ambiguity of the law.

"That's the $64 question," she said. "It's up to the Court of Appeals to make that determination."

Annapolis *Evening Capital,* May 16, 1979.

EXERCISE C

Edit the following sentences to make the coordination of parts clear to the reader.

1. The sophomores juniors and seniors attended the assembly.
2. Hans served California dip chips and Velveeta on Triscuits.
3. Rising from behind the hill glinting through the trees illuminating the world, the sun appeared.
4. Cautiously precisely and patiently, Sergeant Godovsky disarmed the bomb.
5. Their civilization appeared flourished and vanished in little more than a century.

EDITING

6. None of the children wanted to go to a movie visit a museum or have dinner with their grandmother.
7. Dorothy the scarecrow and the tin woodman were afraid of lions tigers and bears.
8. California is famous for movies beaches and blondes.
9. We had scrambled eggs buttered toast and bacon.
10. The receiver picked the pass out of the air avoided three tacklers and scrambled into the end zone.

Commas with Subordinate Ideas

Subordinate ideas need to be separated from the main idea in two situations. The first is when the subordinate idea precedes the main idea.

Jim, Marian called.
After the show, we had dinner.
Marching down the street, the circus was a child's dream come true.
To win the contest, Joel spent hours rehearsing his speech.
Filled with anger, the prisoners refused to speak to the warden.
When the ballots were counted, Teresa won.

The second situation calling for a comma is when the subordinate idea interrupts the main idea.

I think, *Dorothy,* that you should go home.
Mei Ling, *the hostess,* told us to be seated.
Joshua, *despite his quick temper,* is generous.
The answers, *however,* may not be the same.
Their faces, *scrubbed and shining,* were angelic.
The prisoners, *filled with anger,* refused to talk to the warden.
That book, *if you want my opinion,* is dull.

In both situations, you use the commas to be sure that your reader is aware of what is the most important idea in your sentence—the base sentence. In a case where you begin with the base sentence and follow it with a less important idea, it is not usually necessary to separate the ideas with a comma.

Theda will return your call *when she gets home.*
Money is not that important *anyway.*

Note that sometimes a subordinate idea in the middle of a sentence is *not* an interrupter; it is an important part of the main idea. For instance:

Any student *who doesn't study* deserves to fail.

Here, the idea *who doesn't study* is necessary to the meaning of the sentence and should not be cut off from the main idea by commas.

USES OF THE COMMA

To separate coordinate ideas:
> Baltimore is Maryland's biggest city, but Annapolis is the state capital.
> Kateri Tekawitha was a Mohawk, a martyr, and possibly a saint.

To separate subordinate ideas from the base sentence:
> A native of the Northeast, Georgia O'Keeffe is the unrivaled painter of the Western landscape.
> Georgia O'Keeffe, a native of the Northeast, is the unrivaled painter of the Western landscape.

EXERCISE D

Edit the following sentences, using commas to keep the reader's attention focused on the main idea.

1. Whenever Cruz gets a hit there's no one on base.
2. "Let's eat Granma" said the children.
3. You may find however that this budget is too restrictive.
4. My sister Louise who was married yesterday went to Bermuda for her honeymoon.
5. With only seconds to go in the fourth quarter Jabbar shot from down court and hit.
6. I believe your honor that my client is innocent.
7. David Sterling my best friend in high school married Karen my old girlfriend.
8. Once I started the paper was easy to write.
9. The New Kingdom which lasted from 1567 to 1085 B.C. inspired a golden age of architecture in Egypt.

EDITING

10. From playing monopoly my favorite game I learned how to become a business tycoon.

EXERCISE E

Edit the following sentences for appropriate use of commas.

1. The ladies of the Elk prepared a magnificent feast which included spinach salad quiche roast beef potatoes and ice cream with chocolate sauce.
2. You were hired to cook Miss Genderson not to dispense advice to the lovelorn.
3. *Meetings and Conventions* a trade publication estimates that American corporations and organizations held over 757,000 meetings last year.
4. As new car prices escalate more people are learning to repair their old cars.
5. The coach's disposition except during hockey games was cool quiet and even.
6. The lake was filled with fish and deer roamed the nearby woods.
7. The Board will consider a tuition increase limitation of enrollment and state funding for new buildings.
8. Kitty received our assignments evaluated our individual performances and decided on our raises.
9. General Murchison ordered jeeps amphibious vehicles and tanks into the war zone.
10. My preference Dr. Fernando is to postpone the surgery.
11. Clyde spent months getting ready for the exams which were given in March.
12. Lynn who was my roommate for four years is now the sales manager.
13. Oliver remained loyal to the team even though it finished last.
14. The queen sent for her clever mischievous court jester.
15. Hayden's service was prompt but his merchandise was inferior.
16. The car which is parked in the driveway has just been repaired.
17. The car which is parked in the driveway has just been repaired. The other one still needs a new battery.
18. Overcome with emotion Tess hugged everyone in the room.
19. Under the bed piles of unwashed socks moldered undisturbed.
20. My daughters hot and sweaty lounged on the porch after the game.
21. I really think ladies and gentlemen that a taste for Mozart is easily acquired.

22. Having carefully prepared the slides in advance Greg completed the demonstration in less than 10 minutes.

23. The chairmen who agreed with the Speaker sat on one side of the aisle.

24. Jackson's new album was a sentimental romantic departure from his usual style.

25. In some elementary schools teachers spend less than half of each classroom hour actually teaching.

APOSTROPHES

The apostrophe is used mainly in two situations: to show possession and to show that a letter has been left out of a word.

In this sentence,

> Carla's decision was irrevocable.

the apostrophe and the *s* show that the decision belongs to Carla. Singular nouns of more than one syllable that end in an *s* and plural nouns that end in *s* show the possessive with the apostrophe alone.

Dickens' book	*Keats's* book
students' tests	*student's* test
critics' reviews	*children's* gifts
buses' turn signals	*bus's* turn signal
girls' drawings	*girl's* drawing

Apostrophes also show that a letter has been left out when two words have been combined into one. For instance, instead of writing *do not*, you frequently use the less formal version, *don't*. The apostrophe shows that the letter between *n* and *t* has been omitted.

EXERCISE F

What words do each of the following contractions stand for?

> EXAMPLE:
> haven't = have not

1. I'll =
*2. it's =
*3. you're =
4. didn't =
5. she's =

* Watch out for these words. They are easily confused with the possessive forms, which do not have apostrophes.
Its means belonging to it. (*its cave*)
Your means belonging to you. (*your sweater*)
Their means belonging to them. (*their house*)

EDITING

6. wouldn't =
7. we're =
8. you've =
9. they'll =
10. hadn't =
11. I'm =
12. he'd =
*13. they're =
14. I've =
15. can't =

EXERCISE G

Edit the following sentences for appropriate use of apostrophes.

1. I have never met Jeans mother, but I cant' help feeling I know her since Jean hasnt stopped talking about her all year.
2. The Mitchells house couldnt go another winter without it's exterior being painted.
3. Medusas ugly face turned people to stone.
4. Although she is tiny, its amazing how much energy she packs into that routine of hers.
5. Its a shame that they wouldnt spend an hour with their daughters teacher.
6. Samuel didnt even hesitate in his' passage from the Torah; he followed the Rabbis directions perfectly.
7. Solomons temple, with its rich furnishings, took years to build.
8. In the game of checkers, Aunt Frances cant be beat; shes brilliant.
9. When you have arthritis, you can usually tell when its going to snow; youre warned by a certain feeling in your bones.
10. Its not hard to predict what Darnley will do in a crisis; hell hide behind his brothers reputations.

EDITING PRACTICE

Edit the following paragraphs for appropriate punctuation.

1. Roberta Turner
    Superintendent of Schools

    Dear Ms. Turner,

    Discipline problems on the countys school buses are getting out of hand. When students shout run and throw books the drivers cant maintain safe conditions. As a driver I dont feel that the school system supports the drivers. Were expected to maintain order yet we have no power to suspend disruptive students from the bus. If we fill out the school systems report forms on such students its often three or four week's before we get any response. Ms Turner Im afraid that well have a major accident on one of our buses unless your office begins to take the discipline problem seriously. Your the only one who can help.

Sincerely,
Frank Borden
Driver

2.   Square dancing which many people associate with the West requires a quick mind as well as quick feet. First of all there are 150 basic moves in the square dancers repertory and these moves can be combined into many patterns like "load the boat" "peel the top" and "relay the deucy." Once the steps have been learned its practice perseverance and concentration that dancers need to respond to the callers voice without missing a beat. Even advanced dancers cant follow without hour's of practice and memorization. So square dancing isnt just good physical exercise its also good mental exercise.

REVIEW OF EDITING SKILLS

Edit the following letter to correct any errors in spelling, sentence structure, or punctuation.

Dear Freind,

The Special Olympics an organization which provides atheletic compitition for the mentally retarded continue to develope expand and improve it's programs. Approximately 10,000 atheleets in our state now participating in some phase of this program.

We are currently involved in planing for our Winter Games in January. Because of last years overwhelmingly sucess 130 special athletes have been invited to particapate this year.

As with any activity of this nature the winter program involve considerable expence. A partisapents lodging meals equipment and transportation requires an allocation of $175.

The Special Olympics Comittee would like to invite your group to except the challinge of supporting our program. Your contribution to help our Special Olympians reaching the finish line.

The sucess of our programs have been so large dependant on the involvement of individual's and community groups and it is only threw these cooperative efforts that we have been able to grow.

Thank you for your consederation of this request.

EDITING

17

Case Studies
in the Writing Process

Throughout Part 3 of this book, you have seen various stages of the writing process. Here are two case studies that follow students through the whole process. These case studies may give you a feel for how the various stages fit together.

CASE STUDY 1: DEBATE ON CAPITAL PUNISHMENT

A student is preparing for a debate on capital punishment in her speech class. Each student is to prepare a brief statement on some aspect of the subject.

Here is how one student does her assignment:

Exploring

AUDIENCE	PURPOSE/STRATEGY	VOICE
speech class, debate hostile to death penalty?	explain position arouse interest	serious not emotional

mostly 18 year olds
middle class
no involvement
  with crime
uninformed
no legal background
possibly some
  religious attitudes
conservative ?

share knowledge
impress teacher
help debate
strategy – examples?

knowledgeable.

SUBJECT (before research)

deterrent ?
Supreme Court decision
cruel
cheaper to tax payer
  than jail
Speck
guy in California
atlanta
ok to stop murder
"an eye for an eye"

SUBJECT (after some research)

Old/New Testament
Eye for an eye
Thou shalt not kill
does it stop crime ?
mercy
Supreme Court decision
cruel and unusual
punishment
  (Bill of Rights)
discrimination in
  death penalty
Black/white rich/poor
  (cf. _Time_)
mass murderers
Richard Speck –
  Chicago nurses –
  early 60's
Juan Corona – Calif.
  migrant workers
black children: atlanta

Focusing and Organizing

Possible topics
—Supreme Court decision
—religious aspects of capital punishment
—punishment for mass murderers

The writer chooses to go with the topic of the 1972 Supreme Court decision on "cruel and unusual punishment." She could, of course, have made other choices, but this was a sound one. After exploring her audience, she felt that its outstanding characteristic was its lack of information ("uninformed"). By choosing to discuss the Court decision, she has decided to give her readers information that will interest them and that they will need in order to carry on an informed debate.

Her choice also satisfies several of the purposes she listed. She is sharing information central to the debate, showing her knowledge, stirring up the group, creating a good impression on teacher and students, and helping the debate. Her other main choices would not have suited the audience and purposes so well. The discussion of mass murder may have been more sensational, but would not have been as central to the debate and would have led the discussion off into a side issue. Likewise, her analysis shows no particular interest in the religious aspects of the question, and a repetition of the familiar Ten Commandments and other Biblical quotations would probably not have given new, useful information to many members of the class.

Next, the student comes up with the following list of possible focusing ideas related to her audience's lack of information.

The decision was wrong.
The decision has been misunderstood.
The decision caused a rise in crime.
The decision has caused a lot of confusion.
The decision went against the people's opinion.

Topic Sentence #1:

The Supreme Court confused everybody with its
decision on capital punishment.

Thinking about this sentence, the student decides that it is not quite accurate. She, after all, understood the decision as soon as she took the trouble to read about it.

Topic Sentence #2:

People have not taken the trouble to find out
what the Supreme Court's decision on capital
punishment was all about.

The student doesn't want to attack her audience, so she tries again. Topic Sentence #3:

> Many people do not understand the real basis of the Supreme Court's decision on capital punishment.

Looking at her topic sentence, the writer on capital punishment checks her subject exploration list to see which items pertain to the topic she has chosen—understanding the Supreme Court's decision. She comes up with this list:

Cruel and unusual punishment — (Bill of Rights)

discrimination in death penalty
    black/white   rich/poor   (Time)

morality
mercy
does it stop crime? (deterrent)

All these things represent different ways in which the decision has been understood by different people.

Studying the list a little further, she sees that some of these ideas can be grouped together.

Morality
Mercy   ⟩ Misunderstandings
Deterrent

Real Reasons ⟨ Cruel and unusual punishment
              Discrimination
              Black/white, rich/poor

Constructing an Outline

T.S: *Many people do not understand the real basis of the Supreme Court decision on capital punishment.*

I. Misunderstandings
   A. Morality
   B. Mercy
   C. Deterrent
II. Real Basis—Discrimination
   A. "Unusual punishment"
   B. Black/white
   C. Rich/poor

Conclusion: Understanding the reason for the Court's decision will help make discussions of capital punishment clearer.

Drafting, Revising, and Editing

After constructing a draft of her paper, the student reviews it for unity, coherence, and word choice. She also edits her draft for errors in spelling, punctuation, and sentence construction.

> Many people do not understand the real basis for the Supreme Court's decision on capital punishment. ~~You~~ *Some* might think the Court ~~thought~~ *found* the death penalty ~~was bad. I might say that~~ *immoral. Others believe* the Court stopped capital punishment because it violated ~~our~~ *an* ideal of mercy. *Still* ~~Others~~ ~~say~~ *argue* that the Court believe*d* the death penalty ~~was not a useful tool in the deterence of~~ *did not deter* murder. ~~and other violent crimes. Supreme Court decisions have often had more than one reason behind them.~~ *Actually,* The Court ~~finding~~ *ruled against capital punishment because it found* this penalty being applied in discriminatory ways. It was*, therefore,* unconstitutional since the Bill of Rights forbids "unusual" punishments, and the Court felt that ~~because of~~ discrimination ~~it was making~~ *made* the death penalty ~~be handled~~ unusually severe*ly* on certain groups. *For example,* ~~According to~~ TIME magazine, ~~someone presented~~ *presented* statistics to the Court show~~ing~~*ed* that for the same kind of ~~crime~~ *murder,* a black American would be ~~done away with~~ *executed* while ~~an~~ *a white killer* ~~American who was Cawcasion~~ would get life in prison. Studies *also* indicated that ~~people with big bucks~~ *rich murderers* did not go to the gas chamber, ~~the way those who were~~ *but* ~~short of bread~~ *poor ones* did. Understanding the reason for the Court's decision will help make discussions of capital punishment clearer.

Revised and Edited Version

Many people do not understand the real basis for the Supreme Court's decision on capital punishment. Some think the Court found the death penalty immoral. Others believe the Court stopped capital punishment because it violated an ideal of mercy. Still others argue that the Court believed the death penalty did not deter murder. Actually, the Court ruled against capital punishment because it found this penalty being applied in discriminatory ways. It was, therefore, unconstitutional since the Bill of Rights forbids "unusual" punishments, and the Court felt that discrimination made the death penalty unusually severe on certain groups. For example, according to TIME magazine, statistics presented to the Court showed that for the same kind of murder, a black American would be executed while a white killer would get life in prison. Studies also indicated that rich murderers did not go to the gas chamber, but poor ones did. Understanding the reason for the Court's decision will help make discussions of capital punishment clearer.

CASE STUDY 2: HISTORY EXAM

A student is taking a final exam in American history. The class has spent the last three weeks studying the Civil War. Now the major essay question is on the causes of the War. The student has about 60 minutes to answer this question.

Exploring

He puts down his first thoughts:

Slavery

Western expansion—free soil/slavery

Abolitionism

Industry/ Agriculture

Lincoln's election

Audience: Teacher, knowledgeable

Purpose: demonstrate my knowledge

Voice: impersonal, serious

Focusing and Organizing

After looking at this quickly drafted list, he makes two headings:

DEEP, UNDERLYING	IMMEDIATE
Slavery	Lincoln's election
Industry/ Agriculture	Abolitionism
Western expansion—free soil/slavery	

And the new division spurs him to add to the lists:

DEEP, UNDERLYING	IMMEDIATE
Slavery	Lincoln's election
Industry/ Agriculture	Abolitionism
Western expansion—free soil/slavery	Cotton markets
Belief in the Union	Regional loyalties

It occurs to him as he looks at the left-hand list that most of his reasons are economic (slavery, industrial/agriculture, Western expansion—free soil/slavery), but that the last one is a cultural or political belief; a principle. He casts his preliminary topic sentence:

> *The Civil War was a conflict of economics and great principles.*

Of course, he had other choices. He could have used any pair of the deep causes, merely mentioning the others. Or he could have used an immediate cause (Lincoln's election would be an excellent one), as a focus and discussed the deeper causes behind it. But the choice he made is a good one. It gives the paragraph a shape by dividing it into two major points: economics and principles. It also lets him use all of the items he has thought of.

Since he has got a good, inclusive topic sentence, he can use most of his two lists. He doesn't have too much time, but he still might add some specifics to his lists.

DEEP, UNDERLYING	IMMEDIATE
Slavery	Lincoln's election
• Constitution (⅔ person)	• Douglass debates
• Dred Scott decision	• Illinois' background
Industry/Agriculture	• 1860
• Northern mills	Abolitionism
• Cotton/tobacco	• "Uncle Tom's Cabin"
• Railroads	Cotton markets
Western expansion—free soil/slavery	Regional loyalties
• Kansas	• Lee's decision
• Missouri Compromise	
Belief in the Union	
• vs. states' rights	
• Copperheads	
• Lincoln	

Constructing an Outline:

In this kind of exam situation, it is often useful simply to number the items already written down in an order that seems logical. For example, he could mark Industry/Agriculture with a (1), Slavery with (2), and so on.

DEEP, UNDERLYING	IMMEDIATE
(2) Slavery	(EX) Lincoln's election
• Constitution (⅔ person)	• Douglass debates
• Dred Scott decision	• Illinois' background
(1) Industry/Agriculture	• 1860
• Northern mills	Abolitionism
• Cotton/tobacco	• "Uncle Tom's Cabin"
• Railroads	Cotton markets
(3) Western Expansion—free soil/slavery	Regional loyalties
• Kansas	Lee's decision
• Missouri Compromise	
(4) Belief in the Union	
• vs. states' rights	
• Copperheads	
• Lincoln	

He has also decided to use Lincoln's election as an example of all the main points.

Draft

The Civil War was a conflict of economics and great principles. Since the founding of the U.S., the North and South developed very different economics. The South was nearly all an agriculture society specializing in cotton and tobaco. To make it worse, the South's fields were worked by slaves, and the holdings could be huge. Free-soil Westerners worked mostly small farms and are unwilling to compete with the slave system. The leaders of both regions wanted the Great Plains and many battles were battled in Congress that resulted in Bloody Kansas and the Missouri Compromise. The interests of Northern industrialists and the morality of the Abolitionists united with the Western feeling to push the North towards War. The Republicans were the party of the Westerners, Abolitionists and industrialists, when they elected Lincoln under the rules of the Constitution, the South rebelled; and the Northern cause became holding the Union together.

Although this draft is rough in some places and contains minor spelling and punctuation errors, it does answer the question adequately and demonstrate the student's knowledge. If he has time before the end of the exam, he may try to polish this draft through revision and editing.

WRITING PRACTICE

Take each of these assignments through the various stages of the writing process—exploring, focusing, organizing, drafting, revising, and editing—as you feel appropriate.

1. To help him plan the writing course more carefully, your teacher has asked you and your classmates to describe yourselves as writers. Your description might include such things as your past experience as a writer, your strong points as a writer, your weak points as a writer, the kinds of writing you most enjoy or least enjoy, or any other information that would help your teacher plan the course to suit your needs. (If you are writing this at the end of a semester, assume that your audience is the instructor of your next writing course.)

2. To help you and your teacher evaluate your progress through this writing course, compare yourself as a writer now with the way you felt about yourself as a writer at the beginning of the semester. How have you changed as a writer? How have you stayed the same as a writer?

3. In order to understand yourself better as a writer, use a current or recently completed writing project to analyze the stages you went through to produce a finished draft. What steps did you follow? How much time did you spend at each stage? How did the writing change at each stage? Which stage did you find most difficult? Were you satisfied with the process you went through?

Special Study: A Closer Look at Verbs

Verbs are the heart of language. They show people or objects involved in action: physical (running, singing), mental (thinking, observing), or just the action of existence (being, feeling).

Using verbs well can add a great deal to your flexibility as a writer. Verbs can do tremendous work for you if you know how to use them skillfully.

VERB FORMS

To use verbs effectively, you first need to understand that they have several different forms. Every verb, in fact, has three basic forms: the *present* form, the *past* form, and the *past participle* form, each used to indicate a different time for the verb.

For instance, here are three forms of the verb *walk:*

PRESENT	PAST	PAST PARTICIPLE
(Today I) walk	(Yesterday I) walked	(For years I have) walked

Notice that the past is formed by adding *-ed* to the present and that the past participle looks like the past.

EXERCISE A

Using the pattern shown above, write out the three forms of these verbs.

PRESENT	PAST	PAST PARTICIPLE
1. deliver		
2. hypnotize		
3. plant		
4. rub*		
5. try*		
6. cook		
7. play		
8. open		
9. start		
10. watch		

* Watch out for spelling change.

Most English verbs are regular in the way they form their basic parts. All you have to watch out for with these regular verbs is an occasional spelling change like doubling the final consonant (as in *ru**bb**ed*) or changing *y* to *i* (as in *tri**ed***).

IRREGULAR VERB FORMS

There are some verbs that do not follow the *-ed* rule. For instance, the verb *sing* has as its three forms:

PRESENT	PAST	PAST PARTICIPLE
sing	sang	sung

Look at these other irregular verb forms:

PRESENT	PAST	PAST PARTICIPLE
think	thought	thought
come	came	come
go	went	gone
write	wrote	written

As you may have suspected already, there is really no substitute for just plain memorizing the irregular verb forms. However, you are probably already familiar with a number of those forms, especially if you are a native speaker of English. Test yourself with the list below by covering up the second and third columns. Check off the ones you know and then concentrate on memorizing the rest. It is often helpful to say the three parts out loud while you are memorizing them.

PRESENT (Today I—)	PAST (Yesterday I—)	PAST PARTICIPLE (For years I have—)
(be) is, are, am	was, were	been
beat	beat	beaten
begin	began	begun
bite	bit	bitten
blow	blew	blown
break	broke	broken
bring	brought	brought
burst	burst	burst
buy	bought	bought
choose	chose	chosen
come	came	come
do	did	done
draw	drew	drawn
drink	drank	drunk
drive	drove	driven
eat	ate	eaten
fall	fell	fallen
fight	fought	fought
find	found	found
fly	flew	flown
forget	forgot	forgotten
freeze	froze	frozen
give	gave	given
go	went	gone
grow	grew	grown
hang (suspend)	hung	hung
have	had	had
hide	hid	hidden
hold	held	held
know	knew	known
lay	laid	laid
lie	lay	lain
lose	lost	lost
ride	rode	ridden
ring	rang	rung
rise	rose	risen
run	ran	run
see	saw	seen
send	sent	sent
set	set	set
shake	shook	shaken
shine	shone	shone
show	showed	shown
shrink	shrank	shrunk
sing	sang	sung
sink	sank	sunk
sit	sat	sat
slide	slid	slid

PRESENT (Today I—)	PAST (Yesterday I—)	PAST PARTICIPLE (For years I have—)
speak	spoke	spoken
spend	spent	spent
spin	spun	spun
stand	stood	stood
steal	stole	stolen
stick	stuck	stuck
strike	struck	struck
swear	swore	sworn
swim	swam	swum
swing	swung	swung
take	took	taken
teach	taught	taught
tear	tore	torn
think	thought	thought
throw	threw	thrown
wear	wore	worn
weave	wove	woven
win	won	won
write	wrote	written

Whenever you are doubtful about the form of a verb, look up the word in the dictionary. It will show you all the forms of an irregular verb. If the dictionary shows only one form of the verb, that means the verb is regular and forms the past and past participle parts in the regular way, by adding *-ed.*

VERB TENSE

One of the most important uses of the three different verb forms is the formation of different tenses. *Tense* is the quality of a verb that shows *when* an action takes place. English has six main verb tenses: *present, past, future* (the simple tenses) and *present perfect, past perfect, future perfect* (the perfect tenses).

There are some verb forms that do not show time—for instance, *to cry* or *crying.* When you are constructing a sentence, you must include a verb that shows time. A verb that has tense is one of the requirements for a complete sentence.

Present Tense

You use the present tense when you want to talk about action that is going on now or when you are talking about things that are always true. For example:

One hundred centimeters *equal* one meter.

The present tense is formed by using the first, or present, form of the verb. For instance, the verb *write,* with all its possible subjects in the present tense, looks like this:

I write	we write
you write	you (pl.) write
he, she, it writes	they write

Notice that there is a change in the verb when its subject is a *he*, a *she*, or an *it*. In that case, the present tense verb adds an *-s*.

EXERCISE B

Try writing out all the present tense forms of the verb *show*:

I_____   we_____

you _____   you (pl.) _____

he, she, it _____   they _____

The verb *fall*:

I _____   we _____

you _____   you (pl.) _____

he, she, it _____   they _____

The verb *talk:*

I _____   we _____

you _____   you (pl.) _____

he, she, it _____   they _____

EXERCISE C

Fill in a present tense verb for each subject below. Remember to add an *s* to the verb if the subject is a *he*, a *she*, or an *it*.

1. Robert _____.

2. The horses _____.

3. You and Sharon _____.

4. Laurie and I _____.

5. The light _____.

6. Two men _____.

7. Stella _____.

8. That station wagon _____.

9. The choir director _____.

10. Dr. McKenna _____.

EXERCISE D

Write a summary of the plot of a TV show you have seen recently. Tell the story in the present tense. Circle all the present tense verbs in your story.

Past Tense

You use the past tense of the verb to show that an action was completed at some time before now.

The past tense uses the second form of the verb. For instance, the verb *write* looks like this in the past tense:

I wrote	we wrote
you wrote	you wrote
he, she, it wrote	they wrote

The verb *look:*

I looked	we looked
you looked	you looked
he, she, it looked	they looked

Notice that all the forms of the verb are the same in the past tense.

EXERCISE E

Write out the past tense for each of these verbs:

1. *show*

I _____	we _____
you _____	you _____
he, she, it _____	they _____

2. *fall*

I _____	we _____
you _____	you _____
he, she, it _____	they _____

3. *begin*

I _____   we _____

you _____   you_____

he, she, it _____   they _____

4. *lie* (to recline)

I _____   we _____

you _____   you_____

he, she, it _____   they _____

5. *go*

I _____   we _____

you _____   you _____

he, she, it _____   they _____

EXERCISE F

Underline all the verbs in the following paragraph; then rewrite the paragraph, changing the verbs from the present tense to the past tense.

Steve is determined to become a professional singer. He gets up early every morning and jogs because he wants to increase his lung capacity. Exercise helps him with breath control. Then he attends voice and music classes for 4 hours. In the afternoon, he practices in his studio. He warms up by singing scales. Then he rehearses some songs he already knows. Finally, he works on a new piece. While he eats dinner, he listens to recordings of famous singers. Almost every night, he either performs somewhere himself or goes to listen to another singer perform. Steve spends every minute of the day working toward his goal.

Your new paragraph should begin: When he was younger, Steve . . .

EXERCISE G

Underline all the verbs in the following paragraph; then rewrite the paragraph, changing the verbs from the past tense to the present tense. (Watch out for the *-s* on the verb if the subject is a *he*, a *she* or an *it*.)

Twenty years ago, Frenchman's Point was an inexpensive place to live. Houses sold for under $10,000, and interest rates on mortgages were low. A family of four could easily eat for $50 a month. Food cost even less if the family had a garden, which most families did. Since the weather rarely became cold, people spent very little on heat. The simple life there demanded only simple clothes, so not much money had to be spent on finery. The most expensive entertainment was a 50-cent movie and a 10-cent soda. The people of Frenchman's Point lived well without much money.

Your new paragraph should begin: Even today, Frenchman's Point . . .

EXERCISE H

Choose any ten irregular verbs from the list on pages 358–59. List the present forms here:

1. _____   6. _____

2. _____   7. _____

3. _____   8. _____

4. _____   9. _____

5. _____   10. _____

Now write a short story in which you use each of these verbs at least once in the past tense. Circle each past tense verb in your story.

Future Tense

You use the future form of the verb to show that an action is going to take place at some time after the present moment: next hour, next day, next week, next year, and so on. For example:

I *will bring* the dessert.
Mark *will report* you to the dean.

The future tense uses the present form of the verb with the helping verb *will*. Here is the verb *write* in the future tense:

I will write	we will write
you will write	you will write
he, she, it will write	they will write

Here is the verb *begin* in the future tense:

I will begin	we will begin
you will begin	you will begin
he, she, it will begin	they will begin

Notice that the form of the verb is exactly the same no matter what the subject is.

EXERCISE I

Using the verbs above as models, write out the future tense of the following verbs.

want

I _____   we _____

you _____   you _____

he, she, it _____   they _____

show

I _____   we _____

you _____   you _____

he, she, it _____   they _____

talk

I _____   we _____

you _____   you _____

he, she, it _____   they _____

EXERCISE J

Underline all the verbs in the following paragraph. Then rewrite the paragraph, changing the verbs to the future tense.

Two years ago, I began at the bottom of the field of journalism. I started out selling advertisements for a small weekly paper. At the same time, I asked the sports editor to let me cover some high school games. Gradually, I worked my way up to college games. Then a job as a reporter opened up at a paper in the next town. I grabbed it. Soon, I wrote half the stories in the paper. However, I wanted more money. So I moved to a daily paper as the police reporter. I did such good work that I quickly received a raise. Finally, I made the big time: The *Washington Post* offered me a job!

Your new paragraph should begin: Two years from now, I . . .

Review: The Three Simple Tenses

	I called before now	I call now	I will call after now
TIME	past tense	present tense	future tense

The three simple tenses place action in three broad categories of time. Action that is happening now is shown by the present tense. Action that happened before now is shown by the past tense. Action that will happen at some time after now is shown by the future tense.

EXERCISE K

Identify the tense of the verb in each of the following sentences. Then rewrite the sentence using the verb tense indicated in parentheses. How does the meaning of the sentence change when you change the tense of the verb?

1. Pat satisfied the requirements. (future)

   _____

2. The contractor prepared his bid. (present)

   _____

3. Those children will require some assistance. (past)

   _____

4. Everyone watches the conductor. (past)

   _____

5. Margie will graduate in December. (present)

   _____

6. Walter reported the news. (future)

   _____

7. Bob grows huge tomato plants. (past)

   _____

8. How many students take that course? (past)

   _____

9. She struck the chord loudly. (future)

   _____

10. The committee sends monthly reports. (past)

    _____

11. Our convention was held in New York. (future)

_____

12. That man ran for governor in every election. (present)

_____

13. We will swim for an hour a day. (past)

_____

14. The council resolved several issues. (present)

_____

15. Pepe feels uncomfortable in his uniform. (past)

_____

16. The Board passed the resolution. (future)

_____

17. Four scouts will achieve the rank of Eagle. (past)

_____

18. Only 40 percent of the voters came to the polls. (present)

_____

19. I expect to stay healthy. (past)

_____

20. Jorge will exercise during his lunch hour. (present)

_____

21. The Puritan writers use much symbolism. (past)

_____

22. The oak tree shaded the back porch. (future)

_____

23. Skateboarding will require protective equipment. (present)

_____

24. Rita finds the matching sock. (future)

_____

25. My sons will smile angelically into the camera. (past)

_____

Present Perfect Tense

What is the difference between these two sentences?

> I *sang* for ten years.
> I *have sung* for ten years.

The first sentence uses a past tense verb to tell the reader that although you had a singing career at some time in the past, your singing career is now over.

The second sentence tells the reader that your singing career began ten years ago and still continues now.

What is the difference between these two sentences?

The Pirates *won* the pennant.

The Pirates *have won* the pennnant.

The first sentence tells the reader that the winning took place sometime in the past. The second sentence, using the present perfect tense, indicates that the winning has just taken place, in the very recent past.

The *present perfect* tense, then, is used to show actions that are not going on simply in the present; such actions have some relationship to the past too. Either the action began in the past and is still going on, or it has been completed so recently that it might almost be considered as a present action. The present perfect tense is formed by combining the past participle form of the verb with the present form of the verb *have*.

Here is the verb *write* in the present perfect tense:

I have written	we have written
you have written	you have written
he, she, it *has* written	they have written

The verb *look:*

I have looked	we have looked
you have looked	you have looked
he, she, it *has* looked	they have looked

EXERCISE L

Using these two verbs as models, write out the present perfect tense of the verbs below. (Notice the change in the helping verb (*has*) when the subject is *he, she,* or *it.*)

begin

I _____   we _____

you _____   you _____

he, she, it _____   they _____

talk

I _____   we _____

you _____   you _____

he, she, it _____   they _____

show

I _____   we _____

you _____   you _____

he, she, it _____   they _____

fall

I _____   we _____

you _____   you _____

he, she, it _____   they _____

go

I _____   we _____

you _____   you _____

he, she, it _____   they _____

EXERCISE M

In each of the following sentences, supply the appropriate form of the verb, past tense or present perfect tense. Be prepared to explain your choice.

(throw)   **1.** Since last April, he _____ 1179 strikes and only 230 balls.

(build)   **2.** Mr. Crosby _____ our house two years ago.

(swallow)   **3.** Rover _____ a bone. We must get him to the vet's.

(go)   **4.** You just missed Rene. She _____ to work.

(speak)   **5.** Ms. Jordan _____ for an hour. I am getting bored.

(hate)   **6.** When we moved to Chicago, we _____ living in the city.

(love)   **7.** Ever since we moved to San Francisco, we _____ living in the city.

(spend)   **8.** Before entering medical school, my sister _____ three years in the Navy.

(grow)   **9.** For the last twelve years, the farmers around here _____ only one kind of corn, Silver Queen.

(teach)   **10.** Professor Dalton _____ mathematics here for so long that he is practically a legend.

(teach)   **11.** Professor Abbott _____ history here for so long that she was practically a living history book.

(submit)   **12.** The contractor _____ an estimate. But his bid is far more than we can afford.

(draw)   **13.** The architect _____ a plan. But last year's committee found her design much too elaborate.

(eat)   **14.** Ever since they were children, Sarah and Michael _____ nothing but oatmeal for breakfast.

(drink)   **15.** When we were young, we never _____ coffee.

(cover)   **16.** So far, our insurance policy _____ all our losses. But the repairs aren't finished yet.

(evaluate)   **17.** The supervisor _____ all the library employees just this week.

(win)   **18.** My father's pickles _____ the first prize at the county fair every year except last year.

(increase)   **19.** Since the new sales campaign began in July, our orders _____ by 20 percent.

(increase)   **20.** During the last sales campaign, our orders _____ by 20 percent.

EXERCISE N

Underline all the verbs in the following paragraph; then rewrite the paragraph, changing the verbs to the present perfect tense.

Jennings dedicated his life to peacemaking. After years of study, he published several major works on the psychology of violence. He lectured on peacemaking before hundreds of audiences. He developed innovative means of conflict resolution. World leaders consulted him about negotiating for peace. At home, he organized nonviolent demonstrations in Washington. He also endowed a National Institute for Peace. For his service to the cause of peace, we selected Emile Jennings as this year's Fordham Award winner.

Your new paragraph should begin: For fifteen years, Jennings . . .

Past Perfect Tense

Look at the verbs in these two sentences:

1   2

Margaret *left* the office and *returned* an hour later.

2   1

Margaret *returned* an hour after she *had left*.

In each sentence there are two actions. In the first sentence, the actions are mentioned in the order in which they occurred. First she left; then she returned. Therefore, both verbs are in the past tense. However, the second sentence presents the second action first and then the first. In order to make the time sequence perfectly clear, the second sentence uses the past perfect tense, *had left*.

Here is another example:

1   2

The children *picked* two quarts of strawberries and *ate* them for dessert.

2   1

For dessert, the children *ate* the two quarts of strawberries they *had picked*.

The past perfect tense is also used to emphasize that one action was completely finished before another action started. For instance:

As the electrician *repaired* the washing machine, sparks *shot* out.
After the electrician *had repaired* the washing machine, sparks *shot* out.

These two sentences present different sequences of action. In the first, the repairing and the shooting are going on at the same time. In the second, the repairs are finished before the sparks start shooting out. This second case is where the past perfect tense is needed.

Here is another example of that use:

Cinderella *had scrubbed* the kitchen floor when her fairy godmother arrived.
Cinderella *scrubbed* the kitchen floor when her fairy godmother *arrived*.

Which sentence indicates that Cinderella finished her work before her fairy godmother got there?

The past perfect tense is formed by using the past tense of the helping verb (*had*) with the past participle form of the main verb. The verb *write* looks like this in the past perfect tense:

I had written   we had written
you had written   you had written
he, she, it had written   they had written

The verb *show:*

I had shown   we had shown
you had shown   you had shown
he, she, it had shown   they had shown

EXERCISE O

Using the above verbs as models, write out the past perfect tense of the verbs below:

fall

I _____   we _____

you _____   you _____

he, she, it _____   they _____

talk

I _____   we _____

you _____   you _____

he, she, it _____   they _____

begin

I _____   we _____

you _____   you _____

he, she, it _____   they _____

go

I _____   we _____

you _____   you _____

he, she, it _____   they _____

lay

I _____	we _____
you _____	you _____
he, she, it _____	they _____

EXERCISE P

In each of the following sentences fill in the appropriate form of the verb. Be prepared to explain your choices.

(say)   1. Suddenly I remembered what the coach _____ about bunting.

(close)   2. Lupé _____ her briefcase and left the room.

(close)   3. Lupé left the room after she _____ her briefcase.

(paint)   4. Jeff _____ the whole porch by the time Vance arrived.

(call)   5. After they _____ us, we picked them up at the train station.

(call)   6. They _____ us earlier, so we picked them up at the train station.

(read)   7. Tom _____ the chapter and made some notes on it.

(read)   8. Because Tom _____ the chapter, he passed the test.

(read)   9. This morning Tom made notes on the chapter that he _____ last night.

(pack)   10. Celia _____ the suitcase almost two weeks before we left.

(undergo) 11. When the salesman left, Mr. and Mrs. Murphy _____ two solid hours of high-pressure tactics.

(spot)   12. When someone _____ the burglary in progress, the police were summoned immediately.

(bake)   **13.** I _____ the cake, and my sister frosted it.

(bake)   **14.** My sister frosted the cake that I _____.

(pass)   **15.** The lead car _____ the halfway mark before the

last car started.

(forget)   **16.** After Sheila had mailed all her Christmas cards, she realized

that she _____ zip codes on the envelopes.

(snow)   **17.** Even though it _____, we finished the match.

(buy)   **18.** My wife made me return the golf clubs that I

_____ the day before.

(receive)   **19.** Since the patient _____ two units of morphine

already, I did not prescribe any further medication.

(hang)   **20.** Doris _____ the picture in the den, but later she

moved it to the living room.

EXERCISE Q

Underline all the verbs in the following paragraph; then rewrite the paragraph, changing the verbs to the past perfect tense.

Fred prepared the house for his guests. He picked up all the old newspapers and dirty clothes in the TV room. Then he vacuumed the whole downstairs. In the kitchen, he put all the dirty dishes in the dishwasher and wiped down the counters, the stove, and the table. He swept the floor; he even scrubbed and waxed it. He cleaned up the bathroom; he wiped all the fixtures with soapy water, polished the mirror, and scrubbed the floor. He laid out fresh towels. Finally, he set vases of flowers throughout the house. The house had never looked so nice.

Your new paragraph should begin: By the time we arrived, Fred . . .

Future Perfect Tense

Look at these two sentences:

I *will save* a thousand dollars.
By the end of the summer, I *will have saved* a thousand dollars.

In the first sentence, the future tense indicates that the saving will be done at some indefinite time in the future. In the second sentence, there is a definite time in the future by which the saving will have been done. You use the *future perfect tense* in a case like this where an action will be completed at some specific time in the future.

Here is another example of that use:

I *will accumulate* forty days of sick leave.

Before I retire, I *will have accumulated* forty days of sick leave.

The future perfect tense is formed by using the future tense of the helping verb (*will have*) with the past participle of the main verb. Here is the verb *write* in the future perfect tense:

I will have written	we will have written
you will have written	you will have written
he, she, it will have written	they will have written

The verb *show:*

I will have shown	we will have shown
you will have shown	you will have shown
he, she, it will have shown	they will have shown

EXERCISE R

Using the verbs above as models, write out the future perfect tense for the following verbs.

buy

I _____   we _____

you _____   you _____

he, she, it _____   they _____

lay

I _____   we _____

you _____   you _____

he, she, it _____   they _____

begin

I _____   we _____

you _____   you _____

he, she, it _____   they _____

fall

I _____	we _____
you _____	you _____
he, she, it _____	they _____

go

I _____	we _____
you _____	you _____
he, she, it _____	they _____

EXERCISE S

Underline all the verbs in the following paragraph; then rewrite the paragraph, changing the verbs, if appropriate, to the future perfect tense.

I will live through that Civil Service Exam. I will get up early, and I will eat a good breakfast. I will spend at least 2 hours reviewing the chapter on postal regulations. I will remember to put an extra pencil in my pocket. I will leave the house by 12:30. I will arrive in plenty of time. I will read each question carefully. I will follow all instructions to the letter. I know* I will pass. I think* I will score high. I hope* I will be chosen for the job.

* This verb stays in the present tense.

Your new paragraph should begin: By this time next month, I . . .

EXERCISE T

In each of the following sentences, supply an appropriate form of the verb, future tense or future perfect tense. Be prepared to explain your choice.

(drive)   **1.** By the time I get to Evanston, I _____ 2,000 miles.

(receive)   **2.** She _____ not _____ your letter before Tuesday.

(buy)   **3.** Everyone in the class _____ his or her own subscription to *Newsweek*.

(give)   4.   When I agree to marry him, he _____ me a huge
                diamond ring.

(dress)   5.   The children _____ in their costumes when the
                principal arrives.

(make)   6.   Harry _____ his second million on the sales of
                that record.

(lose)   7.   The library _____ over 2,000 books by the end
                of the semester.

(pay)   8.   Since no one will volunteer for the extra duty, the home office
                _____ someone to attend the meeting.

(apply)   9.   We expect that several women _____ for this job
                by the time the deadline arrives.

(see)   10.   On graduation day this year, our college _____
                23 classes leave its campus.

Review: Simple Tenses and Perfect Tenses

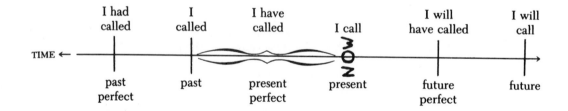

While the simple tenses show broad categories of time, the perfect tenses
help to place actions more specifically within those time periods of past,
present, and future. The past perfect shows a definite time in relation to the
past. The present perfect shows a definite time in relation to the present. The
future perfect shows a definite time in relation to the future.

EXERCISE U

Identify the tenses of the verbs in the following sentences. Rewrite the
sentences, changing the verb tense as indicated. How does the meaning of
the sentence change when the tense of the verb is changed?

1.   Sandra moved to St. Paul. (future)

2. I prepared an estimate. (past perfect)

_____

3. Tina dances more expertly than Yolanda. (past)

_____

4. We will advertise the sale. (past perfect)

_____

5. You have received several promotions. (past)

_____

6. The general signs all the recommendations. (future perfect)

_____

7. They will have elected the president by then. (past perfect)

_____

8. Henry reported on the marina project. (present)

_____

9. The committee has announced its choice. (present)

_____

10. We had not discussed the matter. (present perfect)

_____

11. The auditor made an error. (past perfect)

_____

12. Mr. Lopez became the advisor. (future)

_____

13. Such drastic action seems unnecessary. (past)

_____

14. Where will you find a sounder investment? (present perfect)

_____

15. I tried again. (future perfect)

_____

16. His new novel, *Sirens,* appeared in February. (future)

_____

17. Many secretaries will prefer computers for word processing. (present)

_____

18. You have been helpful. (past perfect)

_____

19. Our office was on Rowe Boulevard. (future)

_____

20. More than 300 people had worked on the campaign. (past)

_____

21. At first, the injury seemed minor. (past perfect)

_____

22. Many dealers arrange financing. (future)

_____

23. Letter writing has become a lost art. (past)

_____

24. Historic Centerville restored the house. (future perfect)

_____

25. Cable television expanded its service by 70 percent. (present perfect)

_____

THE VERB "TO BE"

One verb in English deserves special attention, the verb _to be_. Not only is it used very frequently, but it is extremely irregular in the way it forms tenses.

Look at the following table, which shows the verb _to be_ written out in six tenses.

PRESENT		PRESENT PERFECT	
I am	we are	I have been	we have been
you are	you are	you have been	you have been
he, she, it is	they are	he, she, it has been	they have been

PAST		PAST PERFECT	
I was	we were	I had been	we had been
you were	you were	you had been	you had been
he, she, it was	they were	he, she, it had been	they had been

FUTURE		FUTURE PERFECT	
I will be	we will be	I will have been	we will have been
you will be	you will be	you will have been	you will have been
he, she, it will be	they will be	he, she, it will have been	they will have been

Because this verb is used so much and because it has so many different forms, it would be a good idea to memorize this table so you will always know the form you need.

Linking Verbs

One important use of the verb *to be* is as a link between ideas. In this use, the verb *to be* is the main verb in the sentence. For example,

> Margie *is* our representative.
> *or*
> Rich *was* angry last night.

There is a certain identity between *Margie* and *representative* and between *Rich* and *angry*. Thus, the verb *to be* is called a *linking verb*. It is almost like an equals sign between ideas, showing their close relationship.

Some other verbs can also function as linking verbs: *act, appear, become, feel, look, remain, seem, smell, sound,* and *taste.* For instance,

> Millie *acts* fearless.
> I *felt* sick.
> Jan *will become* the captain.

Notice that in each of the examples above, you can substitute a form of the verb *to be* for the linking verb:

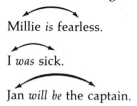

Millie *is* fearless.

I *was* sick.

Jan *will be* the captain.

You have to be careful with this second group of linking verbs, though, because sometimes they are not linking verbs. In the sentence

> I *felt* a hand on my shoulder.

felt is not a linking verb. *Hand* is not the same as *I.* Also, you cannot substitute any form of the verb *to be* for *felt* in this sentence. The sentence

I *was* a hand on my shoulder.

doesn't make any sense.

EXERCISE V

Write ten sentences in which you use linking verbs. At least five of these should use verbs other than *to be*. Circle the linking verb in each sentence. Can you tell the tense of each verb?

Progressive Verbs

Another use of the verb *to be* is as a helping verb. *To be* can be used, for example, with an *-ing* form of another verb. Do you notice any difference in meaning between these two sentences?

She *calls* the restaurant for a reservation.
She *is calling* the restaurant for a reservation.

In both sentences, the action is taking place in the present, but the second sentence, with the verb *is calling,* gives more of a sense of the action being in progress at the present moment. This form is called the *progressive* form.

The progressive form can be used with any tense of the verb *to be.*

PRESENT:	They [*are*] *walking* to the store.
PAST:	Shelly [*was*] *taking* notes.
FUTURE:	I [*will be*] *sending* you a catalog.
PRESENT PERFECT:	Dad [*has been*] *suffering* from these headaches for years.
PAST PERFECT:	We [*had been*] *planning* to close the account anyway.
FUTURE PERFECT:	You [*will have been*] *receiving* the magazine for six months before you will have to pay for it.

Notice that in each case the helping verb establishes the tense of the verb. The *-ing* form does not have a tense.

The progressive form of the verb can be used whenever you want to emphasize the sense that an action is being performed at a certain moment.

EXERCISE W

Write out the forms of the verbs indicated below.

dance   (present)   (present progressive)

I
you
he, she, it

we
you
they

bring   (past)   (past progressive)

I
you
he, she, it
we
you
they

send   (future)   (future progressive)

I
you
he, she, it
we
you
they

claim   (present perfect)   (present perfect progressive)

I
you
he, she, it
we
you
they

invite   (past perfect)   (past perfect progressive)

I
you
he, she, it
we
you
they

select   (future perfect)   (future perfect progressive)

I
you
he, she, it
we
you
they

EXERCISE X

For each of the following sentences, supply an appropriate form of the verb indicated. In the blank, give the regular verb form. Then rewrite the sentence using the progressive form. Be prepared to explain if one form seems more effective than the other.

EXAMPLE: (send)

Yesterday, I *sent* you the report.

Yesterday, I *was sending* you the report.

(dress)   1.   I _____. I will be ready in a minute.

_____

_____

(talk)   2.   They _____ so loudly that no one could hear the music.

_____

_____

(sing)   3.   Gene _____ now; after him comes the magic act.

_____

_____

(shop)   4.   You _____ here for years. Why do you want to go to a different store?

_____

_____

(plan)   5.   Dad _____ this surprise for six months before their anniversary.

_____

_____

(write)   6.   Last year, Phillip _____ in his journal every day.

_____

_____

(teach)   7.   Next month, she _____ for 30 years.

_____

_____

(try)

8. Operator, I _____ this number for half an hour.

_____

_____

(watch)

9. While we _____ that show, I'll set your hair for you.

_____

_____

(make)

10. As soon as Maripat _____ enough money, she moved into her own apartment.

_____

_____

Passive Verbs

The verb *to be* can also be used as a helping verb with the past participle. Notice the difference between these sentences:

Barry *selects* a representative.
A representative *is selected* by Barry.

The first sentence uses the present tense verb. In this sentence the subject, Barry, is performing the action of selecting. In the second sentence, Barry is still doing the selecting, but he is not placed as the subject of the sentence. In a sentence where the subject is not the doer of the action, the verb *to be* is used as a helping verb with the past participle. When the subject is not the doer of the action, the verb is said to be *passive.*

The passive can be used in any verb tense. Here are some other examples of the use of the passive.

ACTIVE: Mike *made* some spaghetti.
PASSIVE: Some spaghetti *was made* by Mike.
ACTIVE: Someone *built* this monument in 1853.
PASSIVE: This monument *was built* in 1853.
ACTIVE: The teacher *will distribute* the grades.
PASSIVE: The grades *will be distributed* by the teacher.
ACTIVE: Greed *has ruined* many lives.
PASSIVE: Many lives *have been ruined* by greed.
ACTIVE: The Board of Trustees *prohibits* smoking.
PASSIVE: Smoking *is prohibited.*

EXERCISE Y

Write out the active and passive forms of each verb below.

fill (present tense)

Active	Passive
I _____	_____
you _____	_____
he, she, it _____	_____
we _____	_____
you _____	_____
they _____	_____

place (past tense)

Active	Passive
I _____	_____
you _____	_____
he, she, it _____	_____
we _____	_____
you _____	_____
they _____	_____

guide (future tense)

Active	Passive
I _____	_____
you _____	_____
he, she, it _____	_____
we _____	_____
you _____	_____
they _____	_____

shoot (present perfect tense)

	Active	Passive
I	_____	_____
you	_____	_____
he, she, it	_____	_____
we	_____	_____
you	_____	_____
they	_____	_____

EXERCISE Z

Rewrite each of the following sentences, changing active verbs to passive and passive verbs to active. In some sentences, you may need to add a "doer" for the action. Does one version of the sentence seem better to you than the other?

1. The committee rejected the mayor's recommendation.

   _____

   _____

2. The firefighters saved all the residents of the nursing home.

   _____

   _____

3. The first kilometer has been completed by the swimmers.

   _____

   _____

4. By children, *spaghetti* is often pronounced *pasketti.*

   _____

   _____

5. The manufacturer has promised a refund within 48 hours.

   _____

   _____

6. The fruit was delivered on Monday.

   _____

   _____

7. Someone started the ecology movement in the 1960s.

    _____

    _____

8. The teams will end the soccer season in two weeks.

    _____

    _____

9. Sharon had arranged the flowers with special care.

    _____

    _____

10. For twenty years, we have sought peace.

    _____

    _____

Index

Index